The Female Hero in English Renaissance Tragedy

The Female Hero in English Renaissance Tragedy

Lisa Hopkins
Reader in English
Sheffield Hallam University

First published 2002 by
PALGRAVE MACMILLAN
Houndmills, Basingstoke, Hampshire RG21 6XS and
175 Fifth Avenue, New York, N.Y. 10010
Companies and representatives throughout the world

PALGRAVE MACMILLAN is the global academic imprint of the Palgrave Macmillan division of St. Martin's Press, LLC and of Palgrave Macmillan Ltd. Macmillan® is a registered trademark in the United States, United Kingdom and other countries. Palgrave is a registered trademark in the European Union and other countries.

ISBN 0–333–98791–8

A catalogue record for this book is available from the British Library.

Library of Congress Cataloging-in-Publication Data
Hopkins, Lisa, 1962–
    The female hero in English Renaissance tragedy / Lisa Hopkins.
      p. cm.
    Includes bibliographical references (p.) and index.
    ISBN 0-333-98791-8
    1. English drama--Early modern and Elizabethan, 1500–1600--History and criticism. 2. Women in literature. 3. English drama--17th century--History and criticism. 4. English drama (Tragedy)--History and criticism. 5. Heroines in literature. I. Title.

PR658.W6 H66 2002
822'.051209352042--dc21   2002072344

10   9   8   7   6   5   4   3   2   1
11   10   09   08   07   06   05   04   03   02

Printed and bound in Great Britain by
Antony Rowe Ltd, Chippenham and Eastbourne

Contents

Acknowledgements

Working on Renaissance literature continues to be a pleasure because of the collegiality and generosity of my colleagues at Sheffield Hallam University, above all Ian Baker and Matt Steggle. I would also like to thank Michael Worboys for medical help and loan of books; the inter-library loan staff of the Mary Badland Library at Sheffield Hallam University; the two anonymous readers of the typescript; Mariangela Tempera and Pilar Hidalgo for organising the panel on female heroism at the fourth ESSE Conference in Helsinki and inviting me to partici-pate; and, as always, my husband Chris and my son Sam.

Earlier versions of some of the chapters appeared in the following publications, whose editors I would like to thank: part of chapter 1 as '"A place licensed to do men wrong": The Anxious Masculinity of *The Maid's Tragedy*', in *The Image of Manhood in Early Modern Literature*, edited by Andrew Williams (Greenwood Press, 1999); part of chapter 2 as 'Ladies' Trials: Women and the Law in Three Plays of John Ford', *Cahiers Elisabéthains* 56 (October 1999), 49–64; parts of chapter 3 as 'Beguiling the Master of the Mystery: Form and Power in *The Changeling*', *Medieval and Renaissance Drama in England* 9 (1997), 149–61, and as 'The Mothering Principle in Middleton's *Women Beware Women*', *Journal of Gender Studies* 7.1 (March 1998), 63–72; part of chapter 4 as 'Knowing their Loves: Knowledge, Ignorance and Blindness in *'Tis Pity She's a Whore*', *Renaissance Forum* 3:1 (Spring 1998); and part of chapter 5 as 'Play Houses: Drama at Bolsover and Welbeck', *Early Theatre* 2 (1999), 25–44.

Introduction

This book focuses on the representation of the female hero in English Renaissance tragedy. The earliest play I consider is probably Beaumont and Fletcher's *The Maid's Tragedy* (c. 1610); the latest is *The Concealed Fancies*, written during the English Civil War by Lady Jane Cavendish and Lady Elizabeth Brackley – and not in fact a tragedy, but included here because it offers a number of highly interesting reflections on the reception and effect of the developing figure of the female tragic hero on the English Renaissance stage in the thirty or so years preceding the outbreak of the Civil War. What all these plays have in common is that a woman is the central tragic figure, and, in virtually every case, gives her name to the play.

There had been earlier isolated instances of a focus on a female tragic protagonist in English drama, notably Marlowe's *Dido, Queen of Carthage* (1586?) and Heywood's *A Woman Killed with Kindness* (1603), and indeed Arthur Little has recently argued that 'Woman seems to be the natural subject of early modern tragedy ... almost all translations of Greek tragedy ... printed before 1560 focus on female sacrifice'.[1] Lady Jane Lumley's translation of Euripides' *Iphigenia at Aulis* certainly fits this pattern, and Shakespeare too had allowed Juliet and Cleopatra shared billing with Romeo and Antony respectively, and in each case the woman dies after the man, so that her death rather than his becomes the climax of the play. Little is right, above all, to point to the centrality of sacrifice in the representation of tragic heroines in this earlier period. With the notable exception of Cleopatra, these women are victims. Marlowe's Dido, compelled by Venus to fall in love with Aeneas, has to watch helplessly as he deserts her, and can do nothing but kill herself. Heywood's Anne Frankford drifts weakly into a love affair with the insipid and untrustworthy Wendoll, and she too

1

effectively commits suicide when she refuses to eat. Even the much feistier Juliet stabs herself with Romeo's dagger, and Cleopatra puts the asp to her bosom.

In sharp contrast to this passivity and victimhood, the majority of the female characters in the plays I shall be looking at in this book neither seek nor welcome death. Both Webster's female heroes, the Duchess of Malfi and Vittoria Corombona, do eventually accept death, but only on their own terms and only because this is clearly a more dignified attitude than continuing to resist, as the Duchess's attendant Cariola does. It is true that in *The Broken Heart* both Penthea and Calantha will their own deaths, but Annabella in *'Tis Pity She's a Whore* seems to hope that hers can be avoided even when it is obvious to the audience that it cannot. Mariam in *The Tragedy of Mariam* and Mother Sawyer in *The Witch of Edmonton* are both put to death against their will, and I shall argue that in both cases their death does much to challenge the system which condemned them. Evadne in *The Maid's Tragedy*, Bianca in *Women Beware Women*, Beatrice-Joanna in *The Changeling* and the Lady in *The Lady's Tragedy* all accept or engineer their death only when some goal of their own has already been fulfilled or to ensure that it shall be so. The great majority of these women are neither passive nor victims, but active agents in their own fate.

The rise of the strong female hero, who may be in some respects a victim but is also an initiator, emerges as a widespread phenomenon in the period from about 1610, when we find a rush of female tragic protagonists on the English stage, including Webster's Duchess of Malfi and Vittoria Corombona, Middleton's Bianca and Beatrice-Joanna, and Ford's Annabella and Calantha, all of whom are the eponymous heroes of their plays. The rise of the female protagonist is not incidental, but can be linked to a specific historical moment and to particular and highly contested debates within early modern culture and drama in England, including changing ideas about the relationship between bodies and souls and between men's bodies and women's, marriage and mothering, the law, religion and the nature of theatrical representation itself. Moreover, the stunning theatrical success of *The Maid's Tragedy* meant that Beaumont and Fletcher's innovations in this as in other areas caught on, so the phenomenon is to a considerable extent a self-perpetuating one. And as these dramatic representations of women enter the literary and cultural field they themselves work cumulatively to effect a collective transformation of understanding of the female condition, so that there are, in turn, new ideas about women to stage and examine. Ironic though it may seem, the staging of a constant stream of bad or fallible women worked not to reinforce misogyny, but to prise it open, revealing the grounds on which it was constructed, as both *The Broken Heart* and *The Tragedy of Mariam* make clear.

I use the term hero rather than heroine for these characters for two reasons. First, the OED shows that the word heroine was not used in its modern sense until 1662, and then only with reference to Elizabeth I; when Margaret Cavendish wanted to depict what we would now call heroines in her play *Bell in Campo*, she had to coin the term 'Heroickesses'.[2] Second, the vast majority of these characters are not in fact what we would now call heroines at all, but come closer, if anything, to being villainesses. Indeed, it was an essential part of the contemporary conception of what was possible for women that this should be so, since action, even heroic action, was seen as unsuitable for women and indeed as unsexing them.[3] Though there were rare exceptions to this general rule, they were invariably either biblical or classical, and the vast majority of the plays I discuss here are pointedly set in the present or the recent past, as if to highlight the extent to which they are examining the experiences not just of their titular, fictional female heroes but, through them, those of the contemporary women of the audience and the world beyond. (The exceptions are *The Tragedy of Mariam* and *The Broken Heart*, and, I shall argue, their unusually recuperative view of the cultural power of representations of women is partly to do with their insistence on the antiquity of their settings.) I have, therefore, chosen the term 'female hero' as a compromise between how such women may have appeared to their own age and how they may perhaps appear to ours.

The book has five chapters: 'Women's Bodies: *The Changeling* and *Women Beware Women*'; 'Woman as Emblem: *The Maid's Tragedy* and *The Lady's Tragedy*'; 'Women and the Law: *The White Devil* and *The Witch of Edmonton*'; 'Women's Souls: *The Duchess of Malfi* and *'Tis Pity She's a Whore*'; and 'Women and History: *The Tragedy of Mariam*, *The Broken Heart* and *The Concealed Fancies*'. I also consider in passing two other tragedies with a female hero, *Sophonisba* and *The Insatiate Countess*. Though I think that the cultural power of these plays is cumulative, and that part of the impact of each individual play therefore depends on which others were already in existence, I have not attempted to deal with them in strict chronological order. This is partly because questions of composition cannot always be satisfactorily settled – we do not, for instance, know when Elizabeth Cary wrote

The Tragedy of Mariam, which may even have preceded *The Maid's Tragedy*, we do not know when Middleton wrote *The Lady's Tragedy* (or even that he did); and *'Tis Pity She's a Whore* has been dated as early as 1614 and as late as 1632. I have also chosen to group the plays thematically rather than chronologically because it seemed to me more important to draw attention to the ways in which dramatic representations of women all through the period are conditioned and overarched by a number of broad cultural categories and modes of understanding, which I have here categorised (of necessity crudely) as the medical, emblematic, the legal, the spiritual and the literary. Nevertheless, there is an element of chronological progression in that after a discussion of the most basic of all ways of imagining women, the purely physical, we move from what I have categorised as a retreating, perhaps even residual, mode of understanding women, the emblematic, to a definitely emergent one, the literary, which would not have been possible without the works considered in the preceding chapters.

In chapter 1, 'Women's Bodies: *The Changeling* and *Women Beware Women*', I consider the most basic and also the most disabling of all ways of categorising women, which is simply in terms of their bodies. This insists on absolute equivalence between sex and gender, rather than on the distinction between the two which modern feminist thought prefers to draw,[4] and ideas about the innate instability of the womb and the residual theory of humoral psychology made it all too easy to pathologise women. This chapter situates Middleton's plays within contemporary medical theory and argues that the many references to medicine and to physicalised perspectives keep women firmly confined within a framework in which they are identified with nature and men with culture.

In chapter 2, 'Woman as Emblem: *The Maid's Tragedy* and *The Lady's Tragedy*', I look at one of the oldest and indeed to some extent the reflex mode of imagining the feminine in the Renaissance. In both cases, the authors of these plays draw on some of the wide cultural stock of emblematic and allegorical representations which were gendered feminine – a process assisted by the gendered nature of the classical languages from which many such images were derived. The female characters of *The Lady's Tragedy* in particular inhabit a world in which overtly feminised abstractions such as honour, place and virtue are mentioned so much as to become almost characters in their own right. Ultimately, the ways in which women are spoken to and thought of are shown to be ingrained and largely unaffected by anything that any actual woman *does*. However, the allegorical was essentially an antiquising mode, and during our period it can be seen steadily giving way to others, as plainer language takes the place of imagery on the stage.

Other taxonomic mechanisms therefore come into play. Particularly potent discourses were those of the law, examined in chapter 3, 'Women and the Law: *The White Devil* and *The Witch of Edmonton*', and of religion, examined in chapter 4, 'Women's Souls: *The Duchess of Malfi* and *'Tis Pity She's a Whore*'. Of these, the law had perhaps the most obvious and direct control over people's lives, but surprisingly it seems in these plays to be a less coercive and shaping force than other elements of the collective cultural heritage, particularly literature. The Church, too, is experienced as a perhaps unexpectedly beneficent force at least by Ford's Annabella, which may remind us of the extent to which women were often particularly devoted adherents of religion, especially of Catholicism. (Indeed the mother of the Earl of Peterborough, to whom Ford dedicated *'Tis Pity She's a Whore*, was at the time sheltering the head of the Jesuit mission to England, at great personal risk.)

Chapter 1 suggested that the one overarching discourse which offered little scope or freedom to women was that of medicine, which was increasingly concerned to draw rigid distinctions between men and women. However, medical thought itself was under pressure, as too were some religious concepts, for though the power of the Church remained strong throughout the period, the discourses of bodies and the discourse of souls were becoming increasingly co-opted into one of the psyche, which laid less emphasis on the importance of gender and more on that of the human in general. Thus chapter 5, 'Women and History: *The Tragedy of Mariam*, *The Broken Heart* and *The Concealed Fancies*', traces these twinned cultural forces, created as new written texts offering new ways of understanding the human condition, and finds that ultimately they prove enabling for women, since the very plethora of available representative modes now allows for choice. Morever, while literary stereotypes weigh heavily on a character like The Witch of Edmonton, by the time of *The Concealed Fancies* we see that the very writing of such narratives has allowed that process in itself to become transparent. As I shall argue, the witch of Edmonton might have suffered, but *The Witch of Edmonton*, by showing and explaining why the events which it stages have occurred, reduced the chances of such suffering being repeated in the future. The book as a whole thus traces a movement from coercion by images to co-option of images, and argues that these plays not only reflected their historical moment, but helped make it, and, most centrally, that such images, however stark and inflexible in themselves, are liberating in their effect. Indeed, it is a striking paradox that the two plays which seem to offer the most crudely negative imagings and descriptions of women, *The White Devil* and *The Witch of Edmonton*, actually prove to mark the turning point in my argument, since they allow us to see women contesting the images offered of them rather than being merely constrained by them.

This book discusses eleven plays. Each takes its title from a leading female character (or in two cases, characters), but each finds a different way of describing its female hero or heroes – changeling, women, maid, lady, devil, witch, duchess, whore, Mariam, broken heart and concealed fancies. This list is a suggestive, indeed startling one, and to each title rich, deep ironies accrue. In both *The Changeling* and *Women Beware Women*, the two plays which I discuss in the opening chapter, the titles tease rather than guide. Not until the end of *The Changeling* are we really likely to see that it might be Beatrice-Joanna who is meant by the title, and even then the identification is by no means a certainty. In *Women Beware Women* identifications are even more riddled, since we have to try to prise apart the difference between the group of women who should *do* the fearing and the group of women who *cause* the fear – if, that is, there is indeed a difference. In fact, such distinctions hardly matter: here, anatomy is destiny. Moreover, within each play couplings and pairings (the double name of Beatrice-Joanna, the kinship groupings which put Bianca and the Mother on one side and Livia and Isabella on the other) stress the extent to which women are conceived of not as complex beings, but in terms of simple binary oppositions. Even those women who are virtuous, like Isabella in *The Changeling*, cannot be happy; she survives, but remains trapped in an unhappy marriage.

A system of binary oppositions is also clearly implied by the title of Beaumont and Fletcher's *The Maid's Tragedy*, which suggests a radical distinction between women who are virgins and women who are sexually experienced. The play's title also allows us to see the difficulty of maintaining this distinction, though, because it is not clear who the maid is. It used to be generally accepted that the title referred to Aspatia, but it has also been suggested that the term might apply just as well to Amintor. Of course, neither of these is in fact the character most likely to attract the attention of readers or audiences; that will undoubtedly be Evadne, as her spectacular combination of transgressive sexuality and violence abundantly ensures. Indeed modern readers, not attuned to the overwhelming importance placed in the Renaissance on female chastity, often assume that it *is* Evadne who is meant by the title. It is important, though, to register that not only is it *not* Evadne who is identified as the tragic hero, but that it might even be a deliberate part of Beaumont and Fletcher's implication that she *could not* be so. The formula of calling a play someone's tragedy was well established in Renaissance drama – there had already been *The Revenger's Tragedy* and *The Atheist's Tragedy* – and in both these cases it seems implicit that the fate which befalls the hero is likely to lie in store not only for this particular individual, but for everyone else who falls into the same category – that is *all* revengers and *all* atheists. Generic expectation would lead us to look for the same principle to be at work in *The Maid's Tragedy* too. Maids, though, are a rather different class of people from atheists and revengers. One may choose whether or not to take revenge, and in Renaissance thought, one similarly had to take a willed decision to be an atheist; but the state of being a maid is rather different. It is true that Evadne has chosen to lose her virginity, but Aspatia is quite unable to make the same choice; she has to remain a maid whether she wants to or not, and Beaumont and Fletcher were writing not in a Catholic society which valued virginity, but in one which jested that those who died virgins would spend the afterlife leading apes in hell. Aspatia is, therefore, doubly trapped, within her own virginity and within a culture which classifies women so remorselessly according to their sexual status. Evadne too is caught within this wider trap, for though she has succeeded in losing her virginity, to do so has, it seems, also precluded her from attaining the dignity of tragic status. At the same time, though, readers and audiences can rarely help feeling that Evadne *is* the tragic centre. The title of this play thus simultaneously exposes the rigidities of the society it portrays and the difficulties which visibly beset the attempt to maintain those rigidities.

The censor's original decision to give the name *The Second Maiden's Tragedy* to the play which I am here calling *The Lady's Tragedy* suggests that the same kind of thing might be going on there. In fact, though, the play's habitual word for its female hero is not 'maiden' but 'Lady', a classificatory term which works very differently from 'maid'. Here it is not sexual status which is at issue (and indeed there is, as I shall discuss, some ambiguity about the Lady's sexual status), but a woman's place in the hierarchy so clearly laid out by the play's division of its characters into Lady, Woman and Wife. Initially, status might seem to be a less constricting and reductive category than simply dividing women into virgins and non-virgins – it does, after all, allow for at least a three-part schema (lady, woman, wife) rather than a simple binary one – but in fact it too proves restrictive in the same way as 'maid' did because, again, it is not a matter of choice. In the world of the play, one either does have the status of Lady or one does not, and indeed when one woman does occupy that position, all other women are precluded from doing so. For the revenger, for the atheist, tragedy is about what they choose to do; for these women, it is simply a matter of what they already are.

Matters may well seem to be much simpler in the cases of the two plays in chapter 3, *The White Devil* and *The Witch of Edmonton*. 'Witch' is self-explanatory, and since 'white devil' means a hypocrite, both look like straightforward terms of abuse – a typical demonisation of women which allows male sinners like Bracciano and Sir Arthur to walk away unpunished while the law does its utmost against Vittoria and Mother Sawyer. Both plays, however, prove to be rather more complicated than this. The very nature of a 'white devil' reminds us that things may not be what they seem and that we should not therefore take them at face value. Similarly the title of *The Witch of Edmonton* implicitly invites us to consider whether geographical location has anything to do with the detection and treatment of witches – and early modern audiences, as I shall show, would have been abundantly aware that it had. In effect, therefore, both titles take words that initially seem to gesture at transhistorical and transcultural essences situated in a spiritual realm and in fact locate them very firmly within specific material contexts. This, moreover, is a process which is continued in the plays themselves, where we are constantly reminded of the extent to which things are relative rather than absolute. In these two plays, then, we can still feel the weight of the kind of overarching cultural definitions which pressed so heavily on women in *The Maid's Tragedy* and *The Lady's Tragedy*, but we can also begin to see ways in which those images can be contested or subverted. We still see their power, but we do not have to agree with them, any more than we are likely to agree entirely or maybe even partly with the verdicts of the two law courts in these plays which so clearly represent the coercive power of society.

In *The Duchess of Malfi* and *'Tis Pity She's a Whore*, the subjects of chapter 4, Webster and Ford develop the strategies of *The White Devil* and *The Witch of Edmonton* still further. This time they take on a body with even greater powers of repression and coercion than the law – the Church. Both these plays feature a Cardinal whose power over the lives of those around him reaches frightening proportions, with each Prince of the Church readily perverting the course of justice to serve his private ends. Each play, though, also clearly registers the point that though its Cardinal may be the most visible symbol of the Church, he does not represent its spiritual essence. Indeed, both the Duchess and Annabella, despite the hostility or indifference of their respective Cardinals, die calmly and with a full confidence that they are on their way to a better world, and though to our materially minded age this may seem small compensation for their earthly sufferings, it is important to remember that many – probably most – members of a Renaissance audience would not have concurred and would have valued spiritual welfare more than material. Moreover, the plays' clear instantiation of a separation between the Church and its living symbol also works to suggest that symbols and emblems in general need not have binding and overdetermining force, but can be challenged and subverted.

This approach is taken even further in *The Broken Heart* and *The Concealed Fancies*, two of the three texts treated in chapter 5. *The Tragedy of Mariam*, which I also look at here, is a rather different case, because not only was it written much earlier, but it was also never publicly acted and so did not enter into the dramatic tradition in the same way as the other plays I have considered. Nevertheless it commands attention. It is the first original English tragedy written by a woman, and, even more importantly, it represents the extreme case of a female hero trapped inside images imposed on her by those around her, by history and even by language, and yet nevertheless managing to fight back, so that by the end of the play even Herod, who, like everyone else, has so far considered Mariam purely in terms of her beauty, is finally able to apprehend her as a moral and intellectual being. In the cases of *The Broken Heart* and *The Concealed Fancies*, the power of categorising structures is even further undermined. It is true that *The Broken Heart* is a profoundly emblematic play and that the characters find themselves trapped inside names which would normally represent transient emotional states, but here seem to have become frozen into permanent modes of being (such as Penthea, meaning 'sorrow', or Orgilus, meaning 'angry'). However, the whole point of these states is that they are ones which the characters have forged for themselves rather than ones belonging to some external schema which has been imposed upon them; indeed no external force proves able to contend with the will of the characters or alter their chosen modes of being, because the emotional truth of the self is all-powerful and all-encompassing. The female hero's fate remains a tragic one, but the core of her selfhood proves utterly untouchable. For the female heroes of *The Concealed Fancies*, moreover, even tragedy is averted, as the comic conventions of disguise and inventiveness presaged by the concealment and the fancies of the title prove triumphant even in the most unpromising of circumstances. Here, it is unquestionably the women themselves who have *imposed* the 'fancies' rather than being passively constructed *by* them. Moreover, their numerous references to earlier plays leave us in no doubt that it is in fact the plethora of pre-existing dramatic images of women which have allowed them their free choice and enabled their versatility and ultimate success. We thus see that, however flawed they might be in themselves, the female heroes produced by the imaginings of these successive playwrights did, in the end, make female heroism possible.

1

Women's Bodies: *The Changeling* and *Women Beware Women*

Although neither of the plays considered here actually stages the trial of a woman, they do both focus on women whose conduct is examined and judged by those around them, and is, in each case, found totally or partly wanting. Where these plays differ from those considered in both chapters 2 and 3, however, is in their ascription of blame. Whereas other plays may show us women who are conditioned by the societies in which they live, here it is people's innate, overriding and fundamentally gendered nature which is seen as paramount. Indeed, the central female characters of *The Changeling* and *Women Beware Women* are all able to set their societies at defiance, bending all the rules, accomplishing astonishing social rises or descents, overturning the most long-established and deeply cherished of customs and taboos, and pursuing and obtaining their sexual desires. They all, however, pay for it with their death and leave behind them a cultural legacy of even further entrenchment of the practice of defining and describing women's nature as reified and physiologically conditioned.

This is because although these characters are not constrained by their society, they are nevertheless seen as guided less by their conscious wills than by the irresistible impulses of their nature(s). A great deal was written in the sixteenth and seventeenth centuries about the nature of women, and very little of it was complimentary. The Middleton of *The Changeling* and *Women Beware Women* would certainly seem to share that general scepticism, and indeed I shall argue that what *Women Beware Women* seems to suggest is that even the apparently better part of female nature is ultimately pernicious. In both *Women Beware Women* and *The Changeling*, however, female nature is pitted against, and ultimately proves weaker than, male-controlled art. In both plays, women's bodies, and especially their procreative powers, take centre stage, and women's bodies, with their ability to change shape and hide secrets, represent a threatening nature which the taxonomies and structures of patriarchally-conceived culture must at all costs control.

This emphasis on female nature and female bodies is partly to be ascribed to changes in medical ideas about women, which led to a much stronger emphasis on their biological distinctiveness from men. In earlier scientific thought, there are clear signs of at least some degree of belief in the one-sex model inherited from Galen, which suggested that male and female sexual organs were essentially the same basic structure differentially developed (and alarmingly prone to continuations of that development, which could even lead to sponta-neous changes of gender). Although Thomas Laqueur famously claimed that the one-sex model remained prevalent for another 200 years after Middleton and Rowley were writing, he also concedes that as early as the sixteenth century 'a new and self-consciously revi-sionist science was aggressively exploring the body'.[1] Indeed Katharine Park and Robert A. Nye claimed in their review of Laqueur's book that 'a more complete reading of the sources shows that there never was a one-sex model in Laqueur's sense – not in Aristotle, not in Galen, not in Paré';[2] for them the picture was always more complex, with a choice available of models and of modes of belief in them, ranging from the literal to the abstract and metaphysical. Certainly, however, whatever belief in the one-sex model there may ever have been was radically challenged, and conceivably even effectively destroyed, by Fallopius' discovery of the fallopian tubes in 1562 and his incipient, though hesi-tant, recognition of significant differences rather than similarities between men and women.[3] (Fallopius also claimed that he, rather than Renaldus Columbus who claimed in 1559 to have been the first to identify it, had discovered the clitoris.)[4] Thereafter, medical writing increasingly presented woman, especially in her procreative capacity, as not the inverse of man, but his physical and temperamental oppo-site pole, and women's bodies thus increasingly become a favoured arena for medical investigation – Jonathan Sawday observes that '[t]he womb or uterus was an object sought after with an almost ferocious intensity in Renaissance anatomy theatres'[5] – and provide the domi-nant discourse for describing their mental as well as their physical processes.

Increasingly, then, bodies, and in particular motherhood, or at least the biological ability to be a mother, become perceived as both the defining characteristic of women and as the means of their pathologisation and indeed criminalisation, as evidenced by the 1624 infanticide statute, which presumed the guilt of any woman who had concealed a pregnancy and whose child subsequently died. At the same time, ironically, women themselves are marginalised from the representation of their own biological processes: Elaine Hobby points out that '[t]he management of childbirth in early-modern Britain was almost entirely in the hands of women; midwifery manuals, by contrast, were almost all written by men'.[6] Despite an increasingly experimental bias in the philosophy and practice of science, female experience of one's own or others' birthing processes remained the one kind of wisdom not valued, as is indicated by the meteoric rise of a physician like Sir Theodore Mayerne, increasingly consulted for the confinements of aristocratic women where previously a midwife would have been, and also often applied to for advice on their other ailments as if all bodily functions of women were implicitly connected to that root cause. (In the case of Margaret Cavendish, whose husband, the Earl of Newcastle, consulted Mayerne about her failure to conceive, the advice received was that her depression at her brother's death was inhibiting the proper function of her womb.) For women, physical and mental operations are never far apart, and are indeed conceived of as intriniscally linked.

Beguiling the master of the mystery: form and power in *The Changeling*

Alicante, the town in which Middleton and Rowley's *The Changeling* is set, is dominated by a rock which looks like a human head.[7] This image of an overarching natural feature forms a fitting backdrop for a play which pits a feminised world of dark, secret spaces, redolent with images of closets, wombs and dungeons,[8] against a 'masculine' one of swords, fingers and books. We have moved a long way in this play from the ideological territory of *The Maid's Tragedy* and *The Lady's Tragedy*, for here there is no sense even of the participation of women in the realm of the abstract. Instead, they seem to be considered almost as personifications of the concrete, with their physicality repeatedly underlined by the play's many references to medicine. When, as Caroline di Miceli puts it, '[a]t the end of the play we see [Beatrice-Joanna's] father agreeing to replace their blood relationship by a surrogate relationship with his son-in-law Alsemero',[9] Vermandero seems symbolically to mark her as belonging to a realm of the body which rational man can transcend. In the same way, Beatrice-Joanna's nature seems to be fundamentally altered by the sexual act, since she becomes 'the deed's creature' (III.iv.137), in a way that De Flores is not.[10] He acts in the same way afterwards as he did before, but although only a few moments of stage time elapse between Beatrice-Joanna exiting with De Flores and entering deflowered, her entire personality seems to have been radically changed. Previously, she was reliant on De Flores for the performance of villainy; now, she seems to have acquired a new resolution and independence, as she single-handedly raids her husband's closet and suborns Diaphanta for the bed-trick. It is also, I think, suggestive that Middleton and Rowley omit a detail which they would have found in their source, John Reynolds' *The Triumph of Gods Revenge, against the Crying, and Execrable Sinne of Murther* (1621), where 'the souring marriage of Alsemero and Beatrice-Joanna prompts him to praise '*England*, *France* and *Germany*, where generally the women vse (but not abuse) their libertie and freedome, granted them by their husbands, with much ciuility, affection, and respect'.[11] Such a comment might, as we have seen, have found a home in *The White Devil*, but this is a play not about cultural differences but about innate, gendered ones.

Women thus seem to embody the personal rather than the communal or civic – Isabella is entirely confined to the house and Beatrice-Joanna has no public role. Moreover, although her name has been read in symbolic terms, as a combination of Beatrice, 'the blessed one', and Joanna, connoting Gehenna or hell,[12] this seems strained. The name's unusual and obtrusive particularity seems more calculated to stress her individuality than an iconic role.) Women's world, therefore, seems to be definitively established as different from men's. At first the female world threatens to swallow up the male one (one of the play's most striking images is of the thrusting of a man's fingers into a woman's glove, which functions as a sign that he will subordinate her will and moral sense to his);[13] but ultimately the male world wreaks a spectacular vengeance on the female one, and it does so in a way which is specifically marked as characterised by the 'masculine' qualities of artfulness, learning and orderliness, rather the 'feminine' ones of naturalness and instinctiveness. For if in *The Witch of Edmonton* literature and learning seem to be incidentally destructive to women, in *The Changeling* they are deliberately targeted at them, as Middleton in particular uses his self-conscious and metatheatrical artistry to assert his own control over his plot and to crush his uppity heroine.

When Beatrice-Joanna opens the closet of her new husband

Alsemero, she is appalled to discover that it contains a pregnancy test. She immediately plans her strategy for outwitting him:

> None of that water comes into my belly:
> I'll know you from a hundred. I could break you now,
> Or turn you into milk, and so beguile
> The master of the mystery, but I'll look to you.[14]

These lines perform a swift and probing exposure of the dynamics of gender and power relations in *The Changeling*. Alsemero presumably imagines that his scientific experiments will offer him full access to the hidden secrets of women's bodies. In terms of Renaissance fears about female sexuality, this would surely represent a powerfully attractive fantasy to the male members of the audience of the play,[15] and a lively source of fear and *frisson* to the female ones. All the men in this play seek, as Cristina Malcolmson among others has shown,[16] to exercise a highly repressive control over the actions of women; but while men like Alibius (whose name really *is* symbolic of the way in which he is always elsewhere) must suffer in a constant state of uncertainty about their wives' chastity, Alsemero believes himself to have to hand the infallible means of prying into the last secret of women and, consequently, exercising over them a control that is utterly unchallengeable. Ironically, he secretes the mechanism of this ostensible tool of control in his 'closet', traditionally, as evidenced by the titles of such cookery books as *A Closet for Ladies and Gentlewomen* and *The Good Huswifes Closet*, a space as likely to be demarcated for the exclusive use of women as for that of men, and one, moreover, associated with the domestic skill of food preparation, to which Alsemero's own 'concoctions' are thus paralleled, his invasion of the often feminised space of the closet and his parody of the female-dominated process of cooking tellingly imaging his intended probing of the elusive internal secrets of the female body.[17]

Beatrice's pre-emptive discovery of the closet, however, strikes a fundamental blow at the position of superiority into which Alsemero is confident that he has manoeuvred himself. It is one of the scene's most telling structural ironies that before her discovery of the actual *means* of Alsemero's bid for omniscience, Beatrice was already firmly convinced that he *was* omniscient:

> Never was bride so fearfully distressed.
> The more I think upon th'ensuing night,

And whom I am to cope with in embraces –
One who's ennobled both in blood and mind,
So clear in understanding (that's my plague now),
Before whose judgement will my fault appear
Like malefactors' crimes before tribunals
(There is no hiding on't) – the more I dive
Into my own distress.

(IV.i.2–10)

Beatrice's faith in Alsemero's 'understanding' and 'judgement' is absolute, leading her to subscribe to the myth that a man can detect the presence or absence of a hymen. But it is not in these physical terms that she envisages the processes of her detection: her language instead clusters round the metaphorical, the non-specific and the abstract – 'ennobled', 'clear in understanding', 'judgement', 'fault', 'malefactors' crimes'. Mechanics and specifics have no place here; within the transparency of the soliloquy, where Beatrice-Joanna's mental processes are revealed to us, she herself imagines a transparent world, where a phenomenology of 'clarity' and 'appearance' lays bare all crime to a detached surveillance. There is no personal dynamic encoded within her talk of 'whom', 'one who's ennobled' and 'tribunals'; she figures instead an impersonal authority manifested in an appraising eye. She offers no theory of the mechanism of disclosure; although a daughter of the citadel, within which are 'secrets' (I.i.164), it seems that she cannot, here, conceive of any process by which secrecy may be maintained, but rather thinks of herself as fully constituted as a subject of transparent, impersonal and infallible processes of law.

All this changes when she herself performs precisely the act of laying bare which she imaginatively attributes to others, and when, in so doing, she becomes aware of the particular structures conditioning the epistemological power-relations which have been previously mystified for her. The rifling of Alsemero's closet becomes a means whereby she can read, pre-emptively, his own reading of her when she learns that rather than relying on the innate and impersonal 'judgement' with which she had so Foucauldianly credited him, Alsemero's superior knowledge and power need in fact to be maintained by the most artificial of helps. Moreover, the tools of his mastery are not exclusive to him. Much is made in this play of exclusivity of possession, particularly in Alibius' obsessive attitude to Isabella; what we see here is precisely that, as in the case of Alonzo de Piracquo's ringed finger, demarcators perceived as essential to the maintenance of male identity can with the greatest of ease be transferred to others, whom they empower. Once she has understood this, Beatrice-Joanna can indeed proceed to 'beguile / The master of the mystery' (IV.i.37–8).

The means by which she does so are telling, for she has learned her lesson well. Her words chart a complete transformation from the abstractions which had earlier characterised her figuring of the processes of knowledge acquisition; she begins instead to pay precise attention to detail, having now understood that it is the medium of information transfer which conditions the message. The pregnancy test consists of 'two spoonfuls of the white water in glass C'. To forestall it, Beatrice-Joanna decides that she has essentially two options: 'I could break you now, / Or turn you into milk' (IV.i.36–7). The idea of turning the water into milk is presumably suggested to her by the fact that the water is white, but it is, in the context, in its turn suggestive of other aspects of the situation, and in particular the fundamental association of milk with pregnancy. The presence of milk in the breasts is at once often one of the early signs of pregnancy and also provided a standard test to which a woman suspected of having recently given birth could be subjected. Beatrice-Joanna's mention of milk in this connection, then, represents a deliberate subversion of the processes of gynaecological inspection designed to ensure male control of female sexuality. She will deprive the master of the mystery by a mystery of her own, the inscrutable processes of pregnancy and lactation, and the female body will successfully mystify the scrutiny of the male eye. Interestingly, Cristina Malcolmson's account of the play links its fear of Spanish infiltration in general with a particular fear of a particular woman, the Spanish Infanta, as a mother, or at least as the mother of the future king of England. Relating the play to the Puritan opposition to the proposed marriage of Prince Charles to the Infanta, she points out that 'the marriage negotiations largely focused on the number of Catholics that would be associated with the nursery, and the number of years that the prince would be under his mother's influence'.[18] Beatrice-Joanna's proposal to suborn the processes of lactatation to deceive her husband must have seemed doubly resonant in this context.

Ironically, of course, this particular plan of evasion is never put into action, for Beatrice-Joanna herself does not yet know whether she is pregnant or not, and so whether or not this is necessary; moreover, the rapidity of the play's narrative momentum means that even at the time of her death the state of her womb will remain a mystery to herself and the audience alike. But what she discovers next makes the pregnancy test redundant:

> Ha! That which is next is ten times worse:
> 'How to know whether a woman be a maid or not.'
> If that should be applied, what would become of me?
>
>   (IV.i.39–41)

Here at least Beatrice-Joanna is sure of the truth, and she knows that Alsemero must not know it. This test, unlike the pregnancy one, comes equipped with a full scientific pedigree – 'the author / Antonius Mizaldus' (IV.i.44–5)[19] – but, as Middleton surely knew and as Shakespeare certainly indicated in Hamlet's warnings to the players, the intentions of the *author* are always vulnerable to those of the *actor*. Beatrice-Joanna can frustrate Alsemero's processes of inquisition here too, but this time it will be through performance.

The notion of performance is one which often figures prominently in Middleton's tragic dramaturgy. *The Revenger's Tragedy* and *Women Beware Women* both culminate in elaborately ironic masques of death which, in the latter case at least, are pointedly at odds with the representational aesthetics prevalent in the bulk of the play: the 'realist' setting of the widow's house forms an unlikely preparation for the spectacular court finale with its mesh of tightly interlocking plot and counter-plot, while in *The Revenger's Tragedy* the theatricalisation of the closing scene stylises and attenuates the force of the moral point. In *The Changeling*, performance becomes openly equated with the immoral mendacity castigated by Puritan opposition to theatre when Beatrice-Joanna first vicariously rehearses and then personally enacts a staging of virginity – in itself, ironically, a state guaranteed precisely by an *absence* of performance – which completely deceives her audience, Alsemero.

The performance of virginity here would, to a Jacobean audience, undoubtedly have been strongly reminiscent of the allegedly similar method employed in the divorce case of Frances Howard, daughter of the Earl of Suffolk, and her first husband, Robert Devereux, 2nd Earl of Essex (son of Queen Elizabeth's favourite). Middleton's reworking of the story of Frances Howard both here and in his play *The Witch* has often been remarked.[20] I want to focus particularly, though, on his use not only of specific motifs and actions but in the processes of dramatisation which he both employs and represents in relation to the Howard divorce case. (As the later trial of Frances and her second

husband had revealed, the events surrounding the divorce had themselves been conceived of by those involved as highly theatrical in
character, with correspondence using code names for the principal
participants and the Lieutenant of the Tower referring to Frances' lover
as 'so great an actor in this sta[g]e').[21] Frances Howard's campaign to
have her marriage annulled had in itself involved careful presenting
and indeed staging of the evidence. Her initial petition was very
anxious to represent her as frustrated by the impotence of her husband
only because she wished to 'be made a mother',[22] rather than because
of any specifically sexual desires; when it came to establishing her
virginity, she set up an elaborate scene in which a heavily veiled
woman who was widely believed to be a substitute was examined, as
Diaphanta fears to be, by a female jury. Performing the self continued
to feature strongly in Frances Howard's behaviour when, two years
after the granting of her annulment and by now married to Robert
Carr, Earl of Somerset, she was tried for the murder of Carr's friend, Sir
Thomas Overbury. Decoratively dressed and weeping prettily, she
succeeded in winning hearts at her trial in the most unpromising of
circumstances. Lady Anne Clifford, no soft touch, commented in her
diary that 'my Lady Somerset was arraigned & condemned at
Westminster hall where she confessed her fault and asked the King's
Mercy, & was much pitied by all beholders'.[23] The king spared her life
and indeed released her from the Tower shortly before Middleton and
Rowley wrote their play.

That Diaphanta's reference to a female jury and the staging of the
virginity test clearly allude to the Frances Howard story has often been
remarked. There are, however, two other references to the history of
Frances Howard in the play which both relate closely to the performative element of Beatrice-Joanna's response to the discovery of the
virginity test which have not, as far as I know, been commented on by
previous critics. The first time that we see Beatrice-Joanna and De
Flores together, she drops a glove, which De Flores retrieves for her.
She rejects the returned glove angrily:

> Mischief on your officious forwardness!
> Who bade you stoop? They touch my hand no more:
> There, for t'other's sake I part with this –
> > [*Takes off and throws down the other glove*]
> Take 'em and draw off thine own skin with 'em.
> > (I.i.225–8)

The episode, apparently Middleton's invention,[24] seems to rework an occasion when Frances Howard, who may well have been angling to catch the attention of Prince Henry, is said to have dropped a glove which the Prince declined to take up on the crudely pointed grounds that it had been 'stretcht by another'.[25] The Prince's use of sexual symbolism here is certainly similar to De Flores' suggestive delight at the thought that he 'should thrust my fingers / Into her sockets here' (I.i.231–2); moreover, there is, arguably, a possible parallel with the celebrated episode of the Countess of Salisbury's garter, and a telling contrast between the lubricity of the Jacobean interpretations and the pure-mindedness of Edward III's famous dictum 'Honi soit qui mal y pense'. In Middleton's retelling, though, the roles of the participants are dramatically reversed to make the Frances Howard figure not the recipient but the inflicter of the insult. If we see this episode as encoding an allusion to Prince Henry, in short, we must recognise that Beatrice-Joanna has here too beguiled the master of the mystery by using his own weapons against him.

The other occasion in which the past of the real Frances Howard becomes reworked in that of the fictional Beatrice-Joanna is even more pointedly, and literally, dramatic. Immediately before his defloration of Beatrice-Joanna, De Flores comments:

> 'Las, how the turtle pants! Thou'lt love anon
> What thou so fear'st and faint'st to venture on.
>   (III.iv.169–70)

Here he echoes very closely the Epithalamion of *Hymenaei*, the masque written by Ben Jonson for Frances Howard's first marriage to the Earl of Essex:

> Shrink not, soft virgin, you will love
> Anon what you so fear to prove.[26]

Middleton is very likely to have been aware of Jonson's wedding poetry for Frances Howard, because he himself had been the author of the now lost *Masque of Cupid*, performed as part of the celebrations of Frances Howard's marriage to the Earl of Somerset. Jonson too was involved once more: his *A Challenge at Tilt* and *The Irish Masque* formed part of the entertainment. Since *A Challenge at Tilt* was spoken by two Cupids, there may well have been enough thematic overlap between this and Middleton's Cupid-based masque to necessitate at

least some degree of cooperation in ensuring programmatic continuity. Moreover, the passage in *Hymenaei* in which Truth and Opinion
debate the relative merits of marriage and virginity may be seen as
ironically paralleled in the exchange between the wife and supposed
virgin, Beatrice-Joanna, and the maid, Diaphanta, who is so anxious to
be rid of her virginity.

David Lindley has recently speculated at some length on the poets'
feelings at discovering that they had, in effect, been inveigled into
composing epithalamia for a wedding based on a web of deceit and
murder. In Jonson's case, his situation may well have been particularly
uncomfortable, since he had provided offerings for both the
Countess's marriages; he would therefore surely have been struck even
at the time of the second wedding by some element at least of incon-
gruity in this second fêting of a ritual which had proved so ill-fated the
first time round. Nevertheless, Lindley has argued strongly that the
writers of praise poems for the second marriage need not necessarily
have had to grit their teeth quite so much as we, with the benefit of
hindsight, might imagine:

> a lack of scrupulousness about the precise awareness that poets like
> Donne might be supposed to have had can fatally colour everything
> that follows. Since almost all critics also assume that an adulterous
> relationship between the couple was public knowledge in 1613,
> they are compelled to the position that the poets must have chosen
> to shut their ears and avert their moral gaze in order to praise
> Frances Howard. Since most critics have an investment in the
> defence of their authors' integrity they then search for the criticism
> that must, somehow, be present in the texts.[27]

He argues that the wedding was arranged in such haste that practical
considerations would probably have been more pressing than ideological ones, particularly in the case of Middleton himself, 'if
Chamberlain's assertion that they only had "fowre dayes warning" be
credited. It must have been an "off-the-peg" piece, and can scarcely
have had much verbal material – one reason perhaps, why it has not
survived.'[28] Nevertheless, when the poets later came to hear all the
sordid details of the Overbury murder, and to see that the Countess's
demeanour in the witness stand apparently excused her from the penal-
ties applied to her subordinates and assistants, they may well have felt
that their services had been procured under false pretences and that
Frances Howard had, indeed, beguiled the masters of their mystery.

Middleton's rewriting of Frances Howard's story in *The Changeling* certainly seems to take a revenge on her, and, moreover, a peculiarly literary one. Beatrice may speak of her own 'art',[29] but Middleton cerainly displays his. When Alsemero finally perceives Beatrice's false-hood, he offers, at the same time, an ironic recognition of the cleverness with which she has deceived him: 'You read me well enough. I am not well' (V.iii.16). Beatrice at first attempts to face it out, and discovering that Alsemero suspects that Diaphanta was impli-cated, demands 'Is your witness dead then?' (V.iii.57). (Interestingly, the Countess of Somerset's sorcerer, Simon Forman, had died before her case came to trial, but his name was nevertheless much used in the evidence against her, after searches of his house and interrogations of his widow.) Finally, Beatrice attempts to clear herself by admitting what she clearly sees as the less damaging part of the truth: she confesses to the murder of Piracquo, but continues to deny adultery, revealing the extent to which she has internalised her society's ideo-logical fetishisation of female chastity at the apparent expense of all else. In reply, Alsemero imprisons her, fittingly enough, in the very closet which she has violated; by the time she emerges from it she is mortally wounded, and makes, finally, a full and free confession.

In this, she differs strikingly from the attitudes of many other Jacobean stage villains. Iago refuses explanation to the last:

> Demand me nothing; what you know, you know:
> From this time forth I never will speak word.[30]

Hieronimo in *The Spanish Tragedy*, despite previously having been quite forthcoming, goes to the lengths of biting out his own tongue rather than provide further information, though what else remains for him to tell is unclear; Vittoria in *The White Devil* offers splendid defi-ance to the tribunal of her accusers. Beatrice-Joanna, however, adopts a position of unmitigated repentance and self-abnegation, and, in what was presumably a pointed contrast with the behaviour of the Countess of Somerset, regards herself as unworthy of any mercy. Just as the outset of her closet scene soliloquy saw her fully interpellated into a position of ideological subjugation in which her image of herself was as a helpless and transparent prey of a culture of ceaseless surveil-lance, so she has now come again to internalise her husband's, father's and even her lover's assumptions about her status as a whore and villainess. The brief moment of freedom in which Beatrice-Joanna's pre-emptive reading of Alsemero had rendered her opaque has been lost; she has resumed her designated position as the objectified other of demonisation. Middleton, in short, has, by his staging of Beatrice-Joanna, returned the mystery to the master, reversing the perceived injustice of the Countess of Somerset's pardon by insisting on the full exaction of the processes of the law on her dramatic representative. Beatrice-Joanna and Frances Howard may each have been able to produce a substitute to beguile the master of the mystery of their own virginity tests, but Middleton regains the upper hand by his own dramatic substitution of the publicly chastised Beatrice-Joanna for the recently released Countess.

In doing so, the weapons he deploys against the figure of Frances Howard are derived precisely from the same species of theatricality as animated her own performances of herself (whether vicarious or personal) as virgin and as penitent. Had his *Masque of Cupid* survived, it would be fascinating to see whether he drew on its motifs, but the close parallel with the Jonson Epithalamion certainly suggests a reappropriation of dramatic material which had been previously 'misused' in the service of the Howard/Somerset wedding. In many ways, *The Changeling* is in fact careful to present itself as a reworking of other plays. Cristina Malcolmson has remarked on its many affiliations with *Twelfth Night* (itself perhaps staged as a part of the celebration of a wedding),[31] and Joost Daalder points to Vermandero's echoing of *Doctor Faustus* when he says of Hell, 'We are all there; it circumscribes [us] here'.[32] Even more pointedly, *The Changeling* recasts many motifs and moments found in Middleton's own *Hengist, King of Kent*, written two or three years earlier.[33] Indeed, the parallels are so insistent that it seems as though Middleton is deliberately boosting the metatheatricality of *The Changeling* by inviting the audience to read one play in terms of the other. Both plays are lavish in the use of dumb-show; both revolve round a licentious woman (Beatrice-Joanna, Roxena) believed to be virtuous, and a chaste one (Isabella, Castiza) mistreated by an unworthy husband; and the role taken by Horsus, the secret lover of Roxena, in planning villainies is not dissimilar to that of De Flores. Moreover, *Hengist* has an overriding concern with chastity, and Grace Ioppolo has recently argued that it, too, is engaged in meditation on the Frances Howard scandal.[34] The play opens in the reign of a king, Constantius, who has (most unusually for a male character in Jacobean drama) vowed perpetual chastity because of his strongly Catholic religious beliefs, and who persuades Castiza, the woman he is forced to marry, to take a similar resolve. Much is made of the religious angle – Constantius wishes to fast because it is the eve of Saint Agatha (I.ii.216–20), and

Vortiger resists the incoming Saxons on the grounds that 'y'are strangers in religion Cheifly' (II.iii.34). At one point, chastity is associated with both Catholicism and with the image of the closet:

> *Hers.*   ... Faire is shee and most fortunate may shee bee
> But in maide lost for ever, my desire
> Hath beene ye Close Confusion of that name
> A treasure tis, able to make more theeues
> Then Cabinetts set open to entice ...
> ...
> *Heng.*   Mary pray help my memory if I should
>
> (II.iii.160–8)

To prevent the detection of this loss of her chastity, Roxena spontaneously offers herself for an on-stage virginity test. When Horsus falls down with grief at hearing that Vortiger desires her, she declares:

> Oh tis his Epilepsie, I know it well,
> I holp him once in Germany, Comst agen?
> A virgins right hand stroakt upon his heart
> Giues him ease streight But tmust be a pure virgin
> Or ells it brings no Comforth
>
> (II.iii.249–53)

At first Horsus threatens to shame her by refusing to cooperate; eventually, however, she persuades him that she has a plan, and he is duly 'cured'. Throughout this scene, it is Roxena who takes the lead, as is emphasised in the parodic visual image of the man, instead of the woman, 'falling backwards'. (There is also further ironic play on this motif when Castiza, who has been raped by her husband in disguise, refuses to swear on stage that she is chaste.) When Middleton reworks this scene in *The Changeling*, the comparison with *Hengist* works to ensure that although Beatrice too may seem, as Roxena was, in control, our awareness of the metatheatrical ancestry of the episode serves to stress that, however much greater her knowledge may be than that of Alsemero, she is merely a puppet of the omniscient author.

Another play which can be seen as being revisited by *The Changeling* is *The Insatiate Countess*, which seems to have been written up by William Barksted and Lewis Machin from a draft left unfinished by John Marston. Published in 1613, the same year as *The Duchess of Malfi*, *The Insatiate Countess* is almost an inversion of Webster's play, with Isabella too retaining her title after her marriage and finding herself similarly surrounded by a medicalised culture. (One character is actually called Mizaldus, the Latin version of Mizauld, the physician whose prescriptions are cited in *The Changeling*, which gives a brilliantly ironic edge to his wife's remark, 'belike you know I am with child'). When Claridiana, who mistakenly believes himself a cuckold, faces death, he tells his wife, 'I had rather Chirurgeons' Hall should beg my dead body for an anatomy than thou beg my life'.[35] Moreover, after wishing all sorts of physical tortures on his wife, Claridiana tops his list with 'may the opinion of philsophers prove true, that women have no souls' (V.ii.34–6); assured that she is in fact chaste, he says, 'Had she been an hermaphrodite, I would scarce have given credit to you' (V.ii.145). Earlier, his wife Abigail and her friend Thais have discussed men's and women's 'stomachs' for sex (III.iii.15–20), and Thais, the wife of Mizaldus, then observes,

> Faith, if we were disposed, we might sin as safe as if we had the broad seal to warrant it; but that night's work will stick by me these forty weeks. Come, shall we go visit the discontented Lady Lentulus, whom, the Lord Mendosa has confessed to his chirurgeon, he would have robbed?
>
> (III.iii.27–30)

Mendosa confesses not to his priest but to his surgeon; Thais anticipates Beatrice-Joanna by pre-empting the male medical gaze by her own empirical knowledge of the state of her womb. Equally medicalised is Sago's lament over the corpse of the murdered Rogero:

> By this fresh blood that from thy manly breast
> I cowardly sluiced out, I would in hell,
> From this sad minute till the day of doom,
> To reinspire vain Aesculapius,
> And fill these crimson conduits, feel the fire
> Due to the damnèd and this horrid fact.
>
> (V.i.16–21)

Here, a rather abstract mention of hell makes much less impact than an understanding of humanity informed by awareness of its physical constitution and an invocation of the legendary doctor Aesculapius. Similarly Medina, passing final judgement on Isabella, says of Rogero's body, 'Here is a glass wherein to view her soul' (V.i.61).

The Insatiate Countess is also, however, an acutely literary play, with a particular interest in the ways in which women are represented in a literary culture. Abigail notes that in his captivity her husband has 'compiled an ungodly volume of satires against women, and calls his book *The Snarl*' (III.iii.34–5); Roberto imagines songs about Isabella being 'More common than the looser songs of Petrarch' (V.i.173). But although to be talked about is for most of the characters a source of shame rather than of pride – Claridiana fears being the subject of a ballad (V.ii.54–6) – Isabella has no fear of poetry. She says at her execution,

> I have lived too long in darkness, my friend,
> And yet mine eyes with their majestic light
> Have got new Muses in a poet's sprite.
>   (V.i.205–7)

There is a strongly marked contrast here between Isabella's earlier declaration that she is troubled by the rumours about her (IV.ii.1–5) and her pride in her role as an inspirer of poetry. The explanation seems to be that Isabella feels that poetry, unlike rumour, is a form inherently sympathetic to women.

Isabella herself does not write poetry, but she does usurp men's traditional privileges of speech – Anna comments, 'My lady's in her pulpit, now she'll preach' (III.iv.131) – and of deployment of classical mythology.[36] With an unholy mix of classical and Christian, she offers to 'lead the way to Venus' paradise / Where thou shalt taste that fruit that made man wise' (III.iv.76–7), and she says in soliloquy:

> Fair women play: she's chaste whom none will have.
> Here is a man of a most mild aspect,
> Temperate, effeminate, and worthy love,
> One that with burning ardour hath pursued me.
> A donative he hath of every god:
> Apollo gave him locks, Jove his high front,
> The god of eloquence his flowing speech.
> The feminine deities strewed all their bounties
> And beauty on his face: that eye was Juno's,
> Those lips were hers that won the golden ball,
> That virgin blush Diana's: here they meet,
> As in a sacred synod.
>   (I.i.55–66)

Seizing for herself a man's role of wooer and co-opting male poets' traditional discourse of the blazon, she not only metaphorically unmans the men around her, but rejoices in the deed. It is little wonder that a woman so brazen is prepared to assure Roberto,

> Sir, though women do not woo, yet for your sake
> I am content to leave that civil custom
> And pray you kiss me
>
> (II.iii.87–9)

Indeed, the surprise of the play is not Isabella's behaviour, amply prepared for by both the title and her opening soliloquy, but the slowness of the men around her to react to or register it. Roberto, despite the unusual and scandalous start to their relationship, can casually observe,

> When I was absent, then her gallèd eyes
> Would have shed April showers and out-wept
> The clouds in that same o'er-passionate mood
> When they drowned all the world
>
> (II.iii.137–40)

He cannot, by definition, possibly know what Isabella did when he was absent, but so confident is he of the categories within which her behaviour can be read that he feels free to assume it anyway. This brings us indeed to the crux of the play, which is that while we would now term Isabella's behaviour nymphomania, the characters of the play have no word for it other than the 'insatiate' of the title, and this, surely, is why they are so slow to assimilate and respond to it. In this play full of doctors and medical discourse, woman remains a monster which defies classification; further enquiry into her nature is, it seems, urgently needed, but Isabella has so pre-empted speech and seized the initiative that she has effectively disabled the offering of it. Just as Thais and Abigail have run rings round their husbands, she too has deprived the master of the mystery by her bafflement of his classificatory gaze.

In making *The Changeling* so pointedly and consistently a re-presentation of events and speeches already alternatively presented, then, Middleton is doubly able to offer a re-formation of homosocial bonding after disruption by threatening women, not only in the father–son and brother–brother relationship sealed between Alsemero and Vermandero and Alsemero and Tomazo over the dead body of Beatrice-Joanna, but also in the links that bind Middleton and Rowley themselves with Marlowe, Shakespeare, Jonson, Marston, Barksted and Machin in a controlled demonstration of mastery over the mysteries of performance which women's attempts at fallacious self-staging had attempted to beguile.[37] Metatheatricality is thus made the crucial tool for the undermining of Beatrice-Joanna's own too potent theatricality.

For the Puritan in Middleton, the idea of performance securing and enacting its own punishment must have been an appealingly ironic one. His characteristic tragic strategy is indeed to involve his characters in fantastically complex self-staging situations in which their deaths are ironically brought about in ways that frustrate their performance intentions, as with the double masque of revengers at the end of *The Revenger's Tragedy* or the plotting and counter-plotting of the closing scene of *Women Beware Women*. In each of these instances those who attempt to wrest control of the script are brutally punished by the workings of a deeper plot of whose existence they have no inkling: the revenger's tragedy is in one sense at least precisely the revenge of the dramatist, and of metatheatrical conventions and extradiegetic allusions invisible to the intra-diegetic character. The falsity which in Puritan ideology inheres in all acting is aptly countered by an aesthetic which punishes precisely the performative nature of the theatrical self, while at the same time ironically heightening the theatrical pleasure of the *audience* by its sophisticated self-referentiality. *The Changeling*, with its extravagantly theatrical deployment of a Webster-like anti-masque of madmen and of the consciously archaic form of the dumbshow, partakes here of the same aesthetic of self-reflexivity as characterises Middleton's habitual use of tragic form,[38] and makes his reinscription of Beatrice-Joanna into the cultural norms she has challenged so much the more overt an act of deployment of the most privileged forms of that culture.[39] Ultimately, then, it is the master who retains the mystery, by means of his co-option of the language of art, and woman who remains penalised by that master's inherently self-conscious deployment of the binary opposition which relegates her to the realm of nature, the othered of culture.

Women Beware Women and the mothering principle

The title of *Women Beware Women* does not, as is often the case in Renaissance drama, offer merely a convenient description of the play's principal characters or concerns; while 'women beware women' could be a simple indicative statement, the equally probable option of reading it as an imperative also marks it as prescriptive. As such, it is unusual not only in its form, but also in its overt assumption (or recognition) of a female audience: centuries before the invention of the 'woman's film' or 'women's novels', we appear to be confronted with a perhaps unexpected acknowledgement of women's importance as consumers of fiction. Moreover, the title's explicit exclusion of men might well be seen as inviting a considerable degree of intimacy, indeed collusion, between the dramatist and these favoured addressees.

What the beginning of the title apparently holds out, however, the end abruptly cancels. The seemingly benevolent warning signalled by the first two words, 'Women beware', is abruptly turned back on itself as the object of the verb is paradoxically revealed as a duplicate of the subject: women must beware *themselves*, suggesting the necessity not only of avoiding other members of one's sex but also of a psychological splitting equivalent to the fragmented sense of self which marks the collapse of a character like Shakespeare's Richard III. Intimacy and benevolence are both revoked, to be replaced, as so often in Renaissance ideologies of the female, with the *impasse* of a double-bind.

Such a glossing of the text as a piece of thinly veiled misogyny might appear to be supported by the later lines 'Upon the tragedy of My Familiar Acquaintance Tho. Middleton', by Nathaniel Richards, which are printed at the beginning of the play:

> Women beware Women: 'tis a true text
> Never to be forgot. Drabs of state vexed
> Have plots, poisons, mischiefs that seldom miss
> To murther virtue with a venom kiss –
> Witness this worthy tragedy, expressed
> By him that well deserved amongst the best
> Of poets in his time. He knew the rage,
> Madness of women crossed; and for the stage
> Fitted their humours, hell-bred malice, strife
> Acted in state, presented to the life.
> I that have seen't can say, having just cause,
> Never came tragedy off with more applause.[40]

Richards' poem post-dates Middleton's death, as indicated by its use of the past tense, but it is nevertheless evidence from someone who both knew Middleton and saw the play in performance. His doggerel verse paints a depressing picture, and one rather at odds with the notion of a play primed to please a female audience. After quoting Middleton's title, he immediately reverts to a much cruder term for the female sex: 'drabs', meaning 'whores'. And the play, he implies, was received as being hostile to women, was thought to be justly so and was much applauded for it.

Indeed even a modern audience might well be tempted initially to concur with such a reading, for the play provides us from an early stage of the proceedings with a representation of a woman so spectacularly manipulative that it would be mere common sense to beware of her. Livia not only outrages the proprieties of seventeenth-century womanhood by taking a toyboy and planning a murder; she is also a direct danger to her own sex, as she singlehandedly betrays Bianca to the duke, and abuses the confidence of her niece Isabella to trap her into unwitting incest with her uncle. One might well feel, however, that her career of lust and violence is so egregious as to make her hardly representative of her sex in general; on this reading, *Women Beware Woman* might perhaps have been a better title, and such a reading strategy could possibly serve to make the play seem marginally less obnoxious to a feminist reader. I would like, however, to propose a rather different, less recuperative reading, and to suggest that this most woman-oriented of plays is in fact one of the most reactionary, since it is equally possible to see Livia as being presented to us not as an aberration, but as absolutely typical of woman in one of the most basic of all her aspects – as a mother, or, more properly in the case of Livia, as a substitute mother.[41]

In *Women Beware Women* as a whole, as Inga-Stina Ewbank points out, family relationships are crucial: 'the ordinary appellations of kinship are used with more than ordinary care and point'.[42] In particular, images of motherhood abound throughout the play. Its opening lines are spoken by a woman identified throughout the text only as Mother (the source narrative provided Leantio with a father as well, but Middleton has removed him), and her words draw explicit attention to her role:

> Thy sight was never yet more precious to me;
> Welcome, with all the affection of a mother,
> That comfort can express from natural love:
> Since thy birth-joy – a mother's chiefest gladness
> After sh'as undergone her curse of sorrows –

Thou wast not more dear to me, than this hour
Presents thee to my heart.

(I.i.1–7)

This may well read as a celebration of motherhood, with its emphasis
on the unique event of childbirth which sets a mother's experiences
apart, but it also contains an ominous warning about the nature of the
link which both enables and bedevils mother–child relationships:
when the Mother looks at her adult son, she still sees her baby. The
very bond which gives her her importance to him may, in short,
prevent her from apprehending him realistically in his later life.

After this striking opening, the idea of motherhood is invoked
repeatedly in the play. The Ward is complained of by a protective
mother whose child he has hurt (I.ii.94–7); Fabritio reminisces at
length about Isabella's mother getting ready for parties (II.ii.65–70);
Bianca describes the Mother's house as paying her the duty of a child
(III.i.42–6), and the Duke, in his seduction of Bianca, invokes the idea
of her mother (II.ii.373–4). Indeed, the sexual initiations of both
Bianca and Isabella are almost immediately followed by a general
presumption that they themselves will shortly be mothers, in ways
that seem insistent even given a general Renaissance tendency to
suppose that sexual activity is inevitably followed by pregnancy. In
Bianca's case, the expressions of this assumption range from Leantio's
promise to his mother at the beginning that he will 'make you a grandmother in forty weeks' (I.i.109), to Guardiano's 'Much good may't do
her – forty weeks hence, i'faith' (II.ii.462), and to Bianca's own 'Here's
a house / For a young gentlewoman to be got with child in!'
(III.i.29–30). Bianca also says, 'If you call't mischief, / It is a thing I fear
I am conceived with' (III.i.234–5), and vouchsafes her thoughts on
how she would bring up a daughter (IV.i.34–40).

Isabella even before she is married is the subject of similar comment:

> *Fabritio.*   How like you her breast now, my lord?
> *Bianca.*   Her breast!
> He talks as if his daughter had given suck
> Before she were married, as her betters have;
> The next he praises sure will be her nipple.
>
> (III.ii.159–62)

Isabella herself takes up the theme in her song, 'She that would be /
Mother of fools, let her compound with me' (III.ii.153–4), and towards

the end of the play she pointedly comments, 'Well, I had a mother, / I can dissemble too' (IV.ii.180–1). Perhaps most oddly of all, Leantio figures the adulterous relationship between his wife and the Duke as one of mother and child: 'There's no harm in your devil, he's a suckling; / But he will breed teeth shortly, will he not?' (IV.i.78–9).

Amongst this matrix of references to motherhood, it is Livia who can be read as the arch-mother. On a literal level she is, of course, childless; nevertheless, there are many aspects of Middleton's portrayal of her that bring motherhood forcefully to mind. Her name, for one thing, is resonant of one of the most famous of all politically-minded wives and mothers, the consort of the Emperor Augustus, who according to the historian Suetonius schemed throughout her marriage for the sole purpose of ensuring that her son by her first marriage, Tiberius, should be included in the succession. She was eventually successful, with Tiberius following his stepfather in the Purple. Livia's appearance in the masque as Juno serves explicitly to link her further with ancient Rome, and her intrigues are certainly reminiscent of the kinds of plot described by Suetonius, so that an informed audience might well be rendered particularly receptive to the possibility of a reference. Juno, moreover, was in mythology the wife of Jove and the mother of several of his children, so that Livia's choice of this particular persona for the masque would also serve to underline such associations, while adding the ironic resonance that Livia, the destroyer of both the marriages in the play, should be playing the part of the goddess of marriage. Certainly such an association between the two Livias seems to have been suggested to Una Ellis-Fermor when she remarks of Middleton's character that '[w]e might have met her in Augustan Rome or modern London'.[43]

More obviously than this, however, Livia presents herself as a motherly figure. At her first appearance, she describes herself, unusually enough, as advanced in years:

> *Fabritio.*   Th'art a sweet lady, sister, and a witty.
> *Livia.*   A witty! Oh, the bud of commendation,
> Fit for a girl of sixteen! I am blown, man!
> I should be wise by this time – and, for instance,
> I have buried my two husbands in good fashion,
> And never mean more to marry.
>
> (I.ii.47–52)

Livia here proposes to exercise a restraint very rare amongst the middle-aged women of Renaissance drama. Unlike Webster's ageing flirts and Shakespeare's amorous Gertrude, she seems ready to renounce her sexuality and take her place as one of the older genera- tion rather than among the still marriageable. She does this to the extent of readily aligning herself with the Widow, who is, as Leantio informs us, 'threescore' (I.i.117) to Livia's own, freely confessed, 'nine and thirty' (II.ii.157); and her initial attraction to Leantio is expressed in the suggestive question, 'Is that your son, widow?' (III.ii.62).

Even more strikingly, though, it is directly through mothers and images of mothers that Livia attacks her victims. She lures Bianca to her house in the apparently safe company of her mother-in-law, and it as the supposed confidante of her niece Isabella's mother that she is able to trick the younger woman into incest:

> *Livia.* No, 'twas a secret I have took special care of,
> Delivered by your mother on her deathbed –
> That's nine years now –
>
> (II.i.102–4)

> You are no more allied to any of us,
> Save what the courtesy of opinion casts
> Upon your mother's memory and your name,
> Than the mer'st stranger is, or one begot
> At Naples when the husband lies at Rome
>
> (II.i.135–9)

> Your mother was so wary to her end;
> None knew it but her conscience, and her friend,
> Till penitent confession made it mine,
> And now my pity, yours
>
> (II.i.152–5)

The repeated invocation of the dead mother here guarantees Livia's psychological ascendancy over her niece and ensures that Isabella is thoroughly duped into the affair that will eventually cause both her bitter self-disgust and her death. As Bruce Thomas Boehrer notes, 'Livia is at her best and safest when she acknowledges no special ties of kinship whatever';[44] when she speaks the language of motherhood, she is dangerous.

In this way, Livia, while not a mother herself, repeatedly offers herself as an effective surrogate to entrap younger women. Her troubled relationships with Bianca and Isabella can thus be seen in the light of the first and potentially either most rewarding or most fraught of all connections between woman and woman, the mother–daughter relationship. Livia's literal childlessness and metaphorical surrogacy enable her to ring the changes on the roles of both wicked stepmother and good real mother. Her initial presentation of herself as a motherly figure seems motivated primarily by a desire to be associated with the apparent asexuality of the good mother, but her involvement with Leantio also leads her to take on the threatening sexuality of the bad stepmother of fairy tales who traditionally usurps the affections of the virtuous, unmarried heroine's father.

While fairy tales frequently deal in such psychologies of motherhood, however, tragedy rarely does so. Though mother–son relationships – Hamlet and Gertrude, Oedipus and Jocasta – may on occasion figure prominently, convention and the small number of boys available to take women's parts mean that there are so few women in Renaissance tragedies as a whole that by the time the dramatist has written the parts of hero's mother and hero's love-interest there is hardly likely to be room, either actantially or in terms of plot, for the heroine's mother to come along too. Gratiana in *The Revenger's Tragedy* and Lady Capulet in *Romeo and Juliet* prove rare exceptions to this general rule, and the former of these actually features primarily in the more usual capacity of hero's mother. In general, therefore, close relationships between younger and older sets of women go largely unexplored in Renaissance drama.

Women Beware Women, then, offers an unaccustomed emphasis both in the number of its older women and in the degree of their interaction with younger women. One of the more obvious effects of this is sharply to alert us to the relative paucity of alternative authority figures in the play. There is only one metaphorical reference to fatherhood,[45] in contrast to the many to motherhood, and it is wholly negative, as Leantio muses,

> But all the fears, shames, jealousies, costs and troubles,
> And still renewed cares of a marriage bed
> Live in the issue when the wife is dead.
>
> (III.ii.293–5)

This seems to suggest that fatherhood is nothing but a burden (and one, moreover, imposed on men by women), and it is clearly the case that of the literal father figures, neither the Duke in the secular sphere, nor the Cardinal in the religious, offers effective leadership. Fabritio's influence over his daughter is clearly negligible compared with Livia's. Hippolito is too emotionally involved with the younger generation of his family to provide a role model for it, Guardiano is a venal pandar and Leantio's father is dead. This failure of patriarchal authority is strikingly underlined by the fact that this play, like so many of the later generation of revenge intrigues, has no ghost come from the grave to warn the living, incarnate the authority of the father and provide clear proof of the existence of a spiritual dimension to human destiny. Pointedly, Livia even usurps the traditional force of the *nom-du-père* by inventing and naming an alternative father for Isabella, whose imaginary authority will utterly displace the incest prohibition instituted by her real one. Moreover, Livia's figuring of the deathbed scene in which 'penitent confession' (II.i.154) supposedly led Isabella's mother to tell her the secret effectively casts Livia herself into the fatherly role of confessor. And in the absence of the discipline and control exerted by the father, the mother runs rife, with disastrous consequences for both herself and her offspring.

One of the most striking aspects of Livia's character and actions is that her 'crimes' are neither for her own profit nor, in one sense, obviously intended to harm her victims. If the old test of *cui bono* (to whose benefit do the events work) were to be applied, it would prove impossible to pinpoint Livia as the source of the mischief: what has she to gain from the affairs either of Isabella and Hippolito or Bianca and the Duke? Her own relationship with Leantio is clearly presented as an unforeseen spin-off, after the fact. In a bizarre way, indeed, Livia's actions could almost be presented as altruistic, for she puts herself to a fair amount of trouble and effort simply to give other people what they want (or perhaps, in the case of Bianca, what she thinks they ought to want); Ann Christensen sees her as 'conspir[ing] with domestic openings to grant other women a certain mobility'.[46] The Duke wants Bianca? The Duke shall have her. Isabella and Hippolito want each other? It can be arranged. Both families want the union of Isabella and the Ward? That, too, is feasible. As for Leantio, Livia positively outdoes herself in supplying him with clothes and money. It is interesting, in view of Isabella's remark that 'Well, I had a mother, / I can dissemble too' (IV.ii.180–1) and her comments about 'She that would be / Mother of fools' (III.ii.153–4), that the first thing that we hear about Livia should be that she is witty (I.ii.47); in the persistent games-playing atmosphere of the play, Livia, effectively trying, like her Roman namesake, to jockey for the best possible positions for her surrogate children, can indeed be seen as a 'mother-wit', rather than, as she herself says she should be, 'wise by now' (I.ii.48).

Like some fairy godmother run mad, Livia in fact represents impulses not so much of uncontrolled evil as of uncontrolled gratification, and, in particular, the archetypal desire of all self-sacrificing mothers, the wish to gratify others. This is, indeed, precisely how she sees herself: as a toiling mother. She says to Hippolito,

> I can bring forth
> As pleasant fruits as sensuality wishes
> In all her teeming longings. This I can do.
>
> (II.i.30–2)

Here, 'bring forth', 'teeming' and 'fruits' all point directly to images of gestation; but the positive force of 'this I can do' may well be seen as less traditionally maternal and as indicative of the potential for disruptions of the norm posed by one who takes on the role of mother without any of the usual social, psychological or – most tellingly in this play – economic handicaps customarily associated with the practicalities of motherhood.

A little while later, in soliloquy, Livia herself stresses the lack of *personal* gratification produced by her efforts, as she apostrophises the absent Hieronimo:

> Beshrew you, would I loved you not so well!
> I'll go to bed, and leave this deed undone;
> I am the fondest where I once affect,
> The carefull'st of their healths, and of their ease, forsooth,
> That I look still but slenderly to mine own.
>
> (II.i.63–7)

Livia's lack of literal children of her own body also serves to underline the striking absence of the personal in her motivations.

But her plans to make everyone happy go horribly wrong, and they do so primarily because she never thinks of the consequences. The mother who indiscriminately indulges is abruptly reined in by reality, and by a restoration of masculine power: as Leantio puts it, 'love that is respective of increase / Is like a good king, that keeps all in peace' (I.iii.46–7). In one way, this kind of control is what the Cardinal supplies, when he invokes a restored order in the name of the most powerful of all Fathers:

Sin, what thou art, these ruins show too piteously!
Two kings on one throne cannot sit together
But one must needs down, for his title's wrong:
So where lust reigns, that prince cannot reign long.
(V.ii.220–3)

The stern morality of this pat summing-up elides the truth, however: the contest has not been between two kings, but between men and women, and, even more, between women and women. Kings, with their decisive legislation, have in fact been noticeably absent in this city governed only by a venial and self-serving duke.

The other primary reason for Livia's failure is something of which she herself has no understanding; her position as would-be surrogate mother blinds her to it just as the Mother's memories of Leantio's infancy interfere with her apprehension of the man he has become. Livia sees herself as the provider of all needs; but in the economy of desire, the object desired must constantly shift, and certainly does not for long remain identical with the mother. Attempting to present herself to her would-be children as the reincarnation of the mother who has been for so long missing from their lives, Livia, like the Mother, seems to have no inkling that, for them, time has not stood still, and that their goals have moved on. Leantio's 'I desire no more / Than I see yonder' (I.iii.16–17) and Bianca's 'Kind mother, there is nothing can be wanting / To her that does enjoy all her desires' (I.i.125–6) will both inevitably give place to a newer, more restless quest, which the mother cannot assuage.

Ultimately, then, this tragedy, which begins when a son trusts his mother with the care of his wife, demonstrates the dire effects of an untrammelled motherhood. Livia's fatal desire to gratify everyone's wishes, to allow free access to all bodies and to abolish such traditionally male-guarded institutions as naming, property rights and ownership in marriage, serves as a crushing indictment of empowered mothers and seems starkly to underwrite the necessity of the many contemporary ideologies which sought to impose control on women. And also, and more profoundly, it probes the tragedy of a woman who learns through bitter experience that the trajectory of desire is always to carry it away from what the mother can supply, leaving her redundant and despised. What women most need to beware of, it seems, is this fundamental aspect of their own womanhood, seen as so deeply rooted in the feminine psyche that it manifests itself as a mothering instinct even in the literally childless. Once again, biology for women is seen as destiny; but even more troublingly, biology has also been so thoroughly internalised that even when not literally fulfilled it still configures and overdetermines woman's entire psychology.

Once again, too, the equation of women with nature has, as in *The Changeling*, been further hammered home by a stress on the association between men and culture. It has often been observed that during the course of its length *Women Beware Women* appears to undergo something of a genre shift. It begins very much in the vein of a domestic tragedy, with a tight-knit, bourgeois family group discussing their concerns about money, work and the suitability or otherwise of a recently contracted marriage alliance – Inga-Stina Ewbank comments that 'the themes of the play are the favourite domestic and social ones of love, money and class'.[47] By the end, though, the play has been transformed almost beyond recognition: the two most obviously middle-class of the characters, Leantio and his mother, have both disappeared from the story – one of them dead, the other simply forgotten – and the domestic setting has given place to a courtly one, where the most elaborate of élite entertainments, complete with complex special effects and arcane mythological and allegorical resonances, rounds off the play with a finale as spectacularly artificial as its opening scene belonged to the naturalism which has seen Middleton termed a seventeenth-century Ibsen.[48] Nicholas Brooke observes that the play 'opens with apparent naturalism in a carefully designed humble factor's home, and develops by deliberate stages towards the extreme stylization of the court masque in act V',[49] and on much the same lines Stephen Wigler remarks, 'the opening acts present the characters realistically ... but the final act subjects them to caricature as Middleton's dramaturgy takes a sudden turn into allegory and farce'.[50] Dorothy M. Farr argues that 'in the fifth Act, where it should reach its resolution, the action stops short or seeps away into "staginess"',[51] while one of its editors comments that 'the play gallops to an unashamedly theatrical conclusion',[52] but thinks that this is because 'deprived of the convention of the masque, Middleton would have had to leave them alive, without salvation in an infinity of soulless intrigue'.[53]

Surely, though, this cannot be the case. Although the masque is undoubtedly a convenient way of ensuring the death of so many characters at once, there are – as Jacobean dramatists showed themselves so abundantly aware – other means of disposing of people. Illness, accident, duel, execution or even less synchronised forms of individual revenge could all have served the playwright's purpose, so that it seems logical to conclude that there are thematic as well as functional reasons for the decision to move so decisively towards the overtly performative quality of the masque. Moreover, art and artifice do not inhabit the play only in this most obvious example of this presence, but increasingly pervade its later stages.[54] In its consciously shifting generic allegiances, *Women Beware Women* becomes not only a public staging of the effects of art, but also, increasingly, a sustained reflection upon art, and especially upon art in its relationship to its complementary pole of nature.[55]

The turning point in this process is undoubtedly Bianca's visit to an actual art gallery, the private collection of paintings and statues in which her seduction (or perhaps one should more properly term it a rape) takes place.[56] When the supposed 'monument' (II.ii.277) turns out to be a living duke, the arranging, shaping qualities of art find themselves unceremoniously usurped by an erratic, 'natural' lust which, as in *The Changeling*, will transform not only the life but also the character of Bianca, changing her from a loving and tolerant woman into an aggressive and impatient one. It is ironic that Sir Philip Sidney's comments on the epiphanic potential of the imagination should be so grotesquely fulfilled in the unrecognisability of the Bianca who emerges from this most ostensibly 'natural' of encounters. What we have here may well be seen as a (surely conscious) virtual rewriting of the celebrated statue scene of *The Winter's Tale*, where an apparent monument to death comes similarly to life, but this time to quench lust (in the shape of Leontes' potentially inappropriately sexual interest in his own disguised daughter) and to exercise an influence which we regard as benign and indeed quasi-miraculous on the lives of those around her. It is hard to believe that the deliberate debate on art and nature which lies so near the surface of *The Winter's Tale* is not being drawn on here too, but with a quality of vicious reversal which tips the balance of power very firmly back in the direction of art; it certainly seems to be on some such quality of the play that Inga-Stina Ewbank picks up when she refers to its scenes as 'genre-paintings'.[57]

Until her visit to the art gallery, it might well be possible to see Bianca very much as a child of nature, her values ones of simple affections and homely desires and appetites. Nevertheless, she is explicitly presented from the outset as a child of Venice, daughter of that most sophisticated of societies which, in Shakespeare's *Othello*, coped so ill with containing a Moor in its midst; and her love for her husband has made her a citizen of Florence. The Florence/Venice pairing is one already familiar to English Renaissance audiences from *Othello*, where it seems to account for part of the animus felt by the Venetian Iago against the Florentine Cassio. It also provides a familiar opposition in Renaissance art theory, since the two cities espoused opposing aesthetics of colour, line and definition: 'although they did not eschew the so-called Florentine qualities of draftsmanship and linear perspective … [t]he objectives of … Venetian painters thus tend to be characterized in terms of their concern with colour and light at the expense of space and form'.[58] (Interestingly, Jonathan Sawday reminds us that both aesthetics and indeed art of the Italian Renaissance in general was predicated on an assumption that 'without knowledge of the interior configuration of the body, representation of its exterior was impossible', so that painting too is radically medicalised to the extent that it is dependent on the idea that its figuring of its subjects must be conditioned by its knowledge or perceptions of their anatomies.)[59] It would be rash to suppose that Middleton had much purchase on these aesthetic differences, but he may well have been aware of tensions between the political and religious as well as the artistic agendas of the Venetian Republic and the Florence which, as we are so forcibly reminded in the play, had shed its own republican past and was now ruled by dukes. Indeed J. B. Batchelor has suggested that we should 'see the play as a diptych, a double perspective in which a Venetian and then a Florentine present contrasting versions of the same picture', and points out that the only names mentioned in the first scene are the two place-names of Venice and Florence,[60] while a similar argument, based on the contrasting reputations of the two cities, is very tellingly applied to the play by J.R. Mulryne.[61] Would it be too fanciful to suggest that Bianca, coming from Venice, which, because of the prevailingly damp conditions, had, unlike Florence, virtually no fresco tradition,[62] is unaware of the effect she creates when her framing within the window encloses her in effect within the visual traditions of fresco?[63] (She is, as Verna Ann Foster points out, 'quite content to believe her mother-in-law's rejoinder that the Duke probably did not see her at all'.)[64] Or that, as a Venetian born, her isolation from the Florentine cultural tradition of *intermedii*[65] is strikingly figured by the fact that she, alone of those who die at the masque, does not interact with anyone else even to the extent of being killed by them, and has in fact to commit suicide?

At any rate, although Bianca is only too willing to renounce her cultured, patrician background, it nevertheless informs her in ways of which she herself is unaware. Moreover, however she may try to align herself with the sexual/affective orientations of the family into which she has married, the first time we see her after her initial appearance she is presented to us very much within the framework of culture rather than nature, and indeed explicitly as a work of art. Framed in the window, she is seen by the duke as being as much a market commodity as the wares in a shopfront; framed as a painting is, she is an object for the eye; framed as Juliet was on her balcony in Verona, she becomes an *aide-mémoire* for the skills of the audience to compare her appearance with that of characters in other Renaissance plays. Straddling the liminal space between the privacy of the domestic interior and the public forum of the street (and straddling, too, the gap between the 'reality' of the tiring house and the fantasy world of the stage) the window encloses Bianca and interpellates her firmly within its own multivalent frames of meaning. It is particularly ironic that balcony appearances should be so frequently associated, then as now, with the public appearances attendant on the celebration of royal weddings – the Goldenes Dachl at Innsbruck, for instance, was specifically constructed for the wedding of Maximilian I to another Bianca, Bianca Maria Sforza – since one of the meanings the framing balcony inscribes on Bianca Cappello is precisely that of future ducal bride. Her present husband Leantio, however, has no desire to display her thus; when they eloped, he 'took her out … of [a] window' (IV.i.44–5) and, he has, as Michael McCanles points out, an 'obsession with keeping Bianca hidden away',[66] subscribing in effect to an aesthetic of privacy rather than of display, and treating Bianca like an *objet* to be hidden in a curio cabinet (at one point he tries to conceal her in a secret room) rather than a public work of art. It is Bianca's own instinct to display herself, but it is her tragedy that her lack of awareness of the protocols of art ensures that by doing so she unwittingly inserts herself into frames which, however unaware she herself seems to be of them, will nevertheless frame her meaning for others. Once again, it is the master who controls the mystery, and the woman who is relegated to the realm of the body and appearance.

In both *The White Devil* and *The Witch of Edmonton*, learning can certainly be used as a weapon against women, but at the same time it is not particularly an asset to men, being more likely to backfire on them than assist them. By moving the contest to the metatheatrical level, Middleton has ensured that he not only chooses the weapons, but retains control of the overall fight. At the same time, he draws attention to the ways in which he is doing so, since the plays to which he alludes are ones which his audience is likely to know. Not until very late in the development of the genre, in Lady Jane Cavendish and Lady Elizabeth Brackley's *The Concealed Fancies,* will female authors seize this allusion-loaded pen and write back.

2
Women as Emblem: *The Maid's Tragedy* and *The Lady's Tragedy*

It is sometimes suggested that the court of Elizabeth I was unfriendly to women, with the queen herself functioning more as an honorary man than as a source of support and encouragement to other women.[1] Nevertheless, the customs of the age demanded that the queen surround herself with those of her own sex, and the forty-five years of existence of her totally female Privy Chamber provided ample opportunities for women of three generations to support themselves independently almost in the way that nunneries had. (The extent of the analogy is suggested by the fact that although many of the women who served Elizabeth married, others, like Blanche Parry, her Keeper of the Jewels, chose not to.) The court of Elizabeth thus provided a space which was of necessity open to a wide variety of women and which accommodated as much of a range of lifestyles and choices as was possible within the constraints and ideologies of the time.

With the accession of James I, however, many of these possibilities were abruptly closed down. The king had little time for his wife or even for Elizabeth, his clever, lively daughter; now the door to the Privy Chamber was open only to attractive young men, and a woman like Lady Anne Clifford, struggling for her estates against the patriarchal imperatives of her husband and uncle, found no support from the king. The dominant celebratory images of women produced in this period were all of dead women – the tombs in Westminster Abbey of Elizabeth I, of James's mother Mary, and of his two infant daughters Anne and Sophia – and while masques continued to glorify (in an arguably qualified way) the queen, Anne of Denmark, the characteristic image of women at court in Jacobean drama is of beleaguered creatures, judged only in terms of their appearance and sexuality, and beset by temptations on all sides. Very often, they succumb, but we are

rarely invited simply to condemn them for this, since we are continually reminded of the social processes which have conditioned their
fall, in ways which encourage us to interrogate the norms of the societies depicted rather than to endorse them. Even a woman who resists
temptation, like the Lady of *The Lady's Tragedy*, proves the catalyst for
the exposing of a strong strand of misogyny which chequers the court
and remains essentially unchallenged and unchanged by her own
example of heroineism, because at every turn we are reminded of how
deeply misogynist phrases, metaphors and assumptions are embedded
in the language of the court.

In this chapter I shall look at one heroine who succumbs to the
temptations offered by the court, Evadne in Beaumont and Fletcher's
The Maid's Tragedy, and at one who rises above them, the Lady in
Middleton's (?) *The Lady's Tragedy* (also sometimes called *The Second
Maiden's Tragedy*). In my discussions of these two plays, I concentrate
on the relationship between language and gender. In recent years our
understanding of this has been radically transformed: for a theorist
like Kristeva, woman is always radically alienated from language.
Jacobean dramatists could have had no access to such a concept, but
they do nevertheless, with varying degrees of intensity, sympathy and
insight, map a world in which words belong primarily to men, and in
which expressions, metaphors and the use of abstractions all insist on
the inferiority of women. At the same time, however, these dramatists
show themselves acutely aware of how femininity had traditionally
been co-opted for iconographical and emblematic purposes in ways
which often divorced actual from symbolic genders.

Although she does not discuss either of them in her text, Laura
Levine's book *Men in Women's Clothing: Antitheatricality and
Effeminization 1579–1642* bears on its front and back covers two very
striking illustrations.[2] The first, *François I en Travesti* (*c.* 1545), shows
François I of France dressed as Minerva, wearing the head of the
Gorgon (with which Perseus had presented the goddess) and carrying
a sword and a caduceus. The second, *Portrait Monstrueux et Allégorique
d'Henri III* (*c.* 1589), shows François' grandson Henri III as a large-
breasted harpy, carrying a rosary and an image of a (conventionally
dressed) king surmounted by a cross. In both cases, the representation
of the allegorical meaning of a painting of a man seems to require, or
at least be facilitated by, a reliance on a radically feminised vocabulary
of abstraction and emblematisation. This had nothing to do with
either the gender or the sexuality of the actual subject – although there
was considerable speculation about the sexuality of Henri III, leading

to many accusations of effeminacy, François was rampantly hetero-sexual. The reason that these two kings are shown wearing women's clothing is not that the gender of either is being questioned but that the allegorical traits which these portraits are meant to illustrate are so firmly identified as feminine.

Some of this imagery, and certainly some of these techniques, recur in portraits of Elizabeth I, but unlike the feminised allegorical person-ifications, the real woman, ironically, does not carry a sword. There is one close to her in the portrait issued to commemorate her death, but she is obviously not going to use it: it lies beside her left hand rather than her right, and both hands are in any case already fully occupied in holding the orb and sceptre. Only well after her death, in the fully-blown allegory *Truth Presents the Queen with a Lance* (1625), is Elizabeth represented carrying a weapon.[3] However firmly a sword may be asso-ciated with allegorical females such as Victory and Bellona, the Roman goddess of war, the artists who painted the queen seem to have been uncomfortable about showing a sword in too close proximity to a real woman.

Both Evadne in *The Maid's Tragedy* and the Lady in *The Lady's Tragedy* do use swords, and the ambivalence which surrounds their doing so neatly encapsulates the tension between allegorised and actual femininity. Evadne kills a wicked king, and in doing so seems to some extent to redeem her own dishonour; but no such compensatory benefit accrues to Aspatia, who also wields a sword, and both she and Evadne seem to produce the spin-off effect of compromising the already embattled masculinity of the men of the Rhodian court. The Lady of *The Lady's Tragedy* is far less morally suspect than Evadne, and her depersonalised nomenclature (a marked feature of the female char-acters of this play) clearly stresses her affiliation with the realm of the emblematic, but nevertheless her action too is counterpointed by the suggestive image of Govianus having swooned away, suggesting that abstract feminised virtues are not quite so comfortably accommodated when actually personified. That, then, is what I want to look at in this chapter: what have these 'real' women, Evadne, Aspatia and the Lady, to do with the gendered language of abstraction which conditions the moral and ethical codes within which they operate, and can that which is gendered feminine continue to be accommodated within a world in which 'real' women are marginalised and demonised? Since *The Maid's Tragedy* is the earlier of the two plays, and was also clearly perceived by the censor who gave Middleton's play its first name as being a crucial influence on *The Lady's Tragedy*, I shall begin there.

The Maid's Tragedy: the language of gendering

Beaumont and Fletcher's *The Maid's Tragedy*, one of the very few tragedies to feature a cross-dressed heroine, plots an image of masculinity uneasily positioned at the interstices of machismo, homo-eroticism and the fear of effeminisation. Anxieties here are heightened even beyond those which, Mark Breitenberg has argued, always attend early modern masculinity.[4] Men in the play aspire to success in both love and war; they find the latter easy to achieve, but the bedroom proves a far more problematic arena for them.[5] Ironically, the cause of this proves to lie in the King, who nominally presents his society's most stable and reassuring example of empowered masculinity, but whose sexual predatoriness has reduced the number of women available for other men, not only limiting their opportunities for sexual pleasure but also, and more seriously, foreclosing the possibility for strengthening male–male bonds through the exchange of women. The chaos thus produced spreads outwards to compromise male valour, making the soldier Melantius notably and pointedly unable or unwilling to use his sword, and effectively lays bare the fact that the all-male networks in this society are actually structured and underpinned by the possessing and othering of women. I propose to examine the play's representations of manhood by considering the terms used to describe the two sexes, the language of the body rather than of the tongue to which some characters resort instead as an attempt to impose essentialist meanings, and the use of brother/sister pairings to delineate the boundaries between the genders. Ultimately, I shall argue, the play shows a world in which men feel secure only when they are able to put distance between themselves and women, but in which attempts to separate masculinity from feminity are radically compromised at every turn.

The male characters of the play have little or no insight into the ways in which these processes work, but Beaumont and Fletcher clearly do, and it is perhaps worth pausing for a moment to stress this. Beaumont and Fletcher are often maligned as unreflective and unintelligent writers, interested only in sensationalism and in unthinking and slavish support of the politics of the court. Unusually among the dramatists of their time who are still read today, they have very few passionate admirers. There has been no monograph on them since Philip J. Finkelpearl's *Court and Country Politics in the Plays of Beaumont and Fletcher* was published in 1990, and those relatively few critics who do turn their attention to them tend to do so almost apologetically, or concentrate mainly on the riddle of why their contemporaries, and the two or three generations that followed, should have considered them to be the equals if not the superiors of Shakespeare and of Jonson. It is as though one needs only to solve the enigma of how these plays which are not in fact serious works of art ever managed to masquerade as such, and then Beaumont and Fletcher can finally, and not before time, be forgotten, the only admiration we need accord them being based solely on their skill in being theatrical without being dramatic, and in ever having acquired a reputation as good playwrights without being so indeed. Perhaps the fact that they operated as a team did not help; since there clearly was not a *single* controlling intelligence behind the plays, maybe critics have found it harder to believe that there is a controlling intelligence at all.

It is certainly an accusation of meaninglessness which is most often found at the heart of traditional criticism of Beaumont and Fletcher. Lawrence B. Wallis declared that they 'had no other significant aim than entertainment. They had no serious philosophy of life to offer; no profound interpretation of human nature to give; no deep political, social or poetic insight to reveal.'[6] Robert Ornstein has spoken of the 'ethical frivolity of Fletcher's drama' and also maintains that 'Fletcher guided Jacobean drama from Shakespearean heights to a valley of mediocrity',[7] while Philip Edwards has said of the plays that 'their comment on contemporary society is trifling'.[8] M.C. Bradbrook found that 'there is no serious morality in these plays at all' and sees them as 'simply ... exploiting the feelings and combining the pathetic and the pornographic',[9] and Una Ellis-Fermor regards them as representing 'the withdrawal from the pursuit of reality'.[10] Occasionally, a less harsh note is sounded: John Danby attempts to intercede on behalf of Beaumont at least by calling the younger dramatist 'a part of his contemporary situation in a pejorative sense',[11] and Arthur Mizener attempts some excuse for both authors by declaring: 'I cannot believe that the attitude towards life implied by Beaumont and Fletcher's plays is not a reflection of the ... society for which they wrote and of which they were part, rather than the result of any special immorality in them.'[12] However, there have been notably few attempts to argue for moral seriousness in the plays.

What is even more conspicuous by its absence is any attempt to argue that an overtly morally serious and tragic view of life, such as one which would perhaps have damned Arbaces for being sinful in thought though not in fact in deed, would not have 'improved' the plays of Beaumont and Fletcher but would, rather, have run the risk of draining from them such meaning and significance as they may be thought to carry. There has, of course, been no shortage of critics acute enough to realise that since Beaumont and Fletcher are not trying to be Marlowe, Shakespeare or Webster it is not fruitful to judge them as though they were;[13] nevertheless, the underlying assumption, time after time, is that these plays are seriously, perhaps indeed almost tragically flawed by their decadence and by their lack of any tragic view of the world in which a man is ultimately responsible for his own actions and must accept a just punishment for his misdeeds. It is, however, possible to take one step further Philip Edwards' inspired observation that Fletcher at least displays an interest in the difficulties inherent in the nature of his own dramatic art,[14] and to argue that these very problems are foregrounded to such an extent that they become in fact one of the primary concerns of the plays. The concentration on form in itself may be taken to indicate an enforced dislocation of meaning from the content; these plays are not so much flawed by their own limitations, as in themselves a sustained discussion and exploration of those limitations.

It would be impossible not to notice that each of Beaumont and Fletcher's most famous plays – *Philaster, A King and No King* and *The Maid's Tragedy* – contains as a prominent member of its *dramatis personae* a king, whose authority is invariably believed by himself and by at least one other character to be unquestionable and absolute, and who in each case seriously abuses that authority, thereby placing either the hero or the heroine, or both, as well as other more minor characters, in danger. It is also an obvious characteristic of all three plays that this authority which the king himself takes to be unquestionable is always called into question by one or more of the other characters, and is, indeed, shown in both *Philaster* and *A King and No King* to be radically spurious, the king in the first play being an usurper and the king in the second a changeling and a commoner. It is interesting to note that it is only when the king's authority cannot be successfully challenged on legal but only on moral grounds, as in *The Maid's Tragedy*, that tragedy results, while both the tragicomedies depend for their happy endings on the successful shaking off of the much-resented power of the monarch – and indeed of monarchy itself, for it is notable that the government which by general consent is finally established at the end of each play is to be conducted by not one but two rulers. It takes a marriage between Philaster and Arethusa in the one case, and between Arbaces and Panthea in the other, to produce legitimate and acceptable rule, and it would not have taken exceptional acumen on the part of the audience to read into these interesting facts a possible implication that it would require a union between James I of England and his Parliament to bring about rule that would be acceptable to the general populace, especially since the general populace had been pointedly shown, in *Philaster*, as having effectively brought about the downfall of the tyrannous King of Calabria. Monarchs in all these plays are invariably shown as both dangerous and foolish, and also demonstrate a persistent desire to arrogate to themselves powers which are not rightfully theirs.

Perhaps most tellingly of all, they are throughout displayed as being manipulators, corruptors and, where possible, total silencers of language. The characteristic utterances of a Beaumont and Fletcher king are either an attempt to deny free speech altogether to one of the other characters, or an injunction to speak only such words as are pleasing to the ears of the king. This is a world where innocence is all too likely to find the normal channels of self-expression and of self-revelation either resolutely closed to it or else liable to be disconcertingly corrupted, so that those characters who have nothing to hide and who would be advantaged by a state of affairs in which things were what they seemed are increasingly driven to search for channels of communication which can never be silenced or meddled with. Given this pervasive insistence on the constraints conditioning speech, it would be futile to expect any open condemnation of the events described in a Beaumont and Fletcher play. That does not mean, however, that a distinctively shaped perspective on events is not more subtly and quietly articulated.

In fact, Beaumont and Fletcher's carefully crafted plays always allow us to see the possibility of an oppositional as well as an official reading, and *A Maid's Tragedy* is no exception. Amintor and Menelaus may blame Evadne and the King for what happens to them, but we – and surely Beaumont and Fletcher's original audiences also – can see that the tragedy which overtakes the Rhodian court is ultimately a result of the ways in which fears about the permeability of the borderline between masculinity and femininity have led to a tragic overcompensation. With all forms of behaviour so policed and hedged round by fears and concerns, both natural and reasoned responses to events have become impossible, and with gender boundaries so hysterically enforced, neither men nor women can find a meaningful role for themselves.

The frontispiece to the 1619 edition of *The Maid's Tragedy* shows an unusual and rather disturbing image. Two figures are shown in poses which clearly indicate that they have just been duelling with swords; indeed one has wounded the other, who has blood gushing from the breast. Both are wearing doublet and hose, and thus appear to be men, though only one has a moustache. However, one is labelled 'Amintor' and the other 'Aspatia'. The image thus hints at an interchangeability between men and women, a difficulty of distinguishing the boundaries between the sexes, which resurfaces at numerous points in the text. Melantius demands of his sister, 'Do you raise mirth out of my easiness? / Forsake me then, all weaknesses of nature / That make men women!'[15] Melantius has earlier said of Aspatia,

> She has a brother under my command
> Like her, a face as womanish as hers,
> But with a spirit that hath much outgrown
> The number of his years.
>
> (I.i.108–11)

This idea of the indistinguishability of the two recurs in Aspatia's successful impersonation of her brother: in a prelude to the moment illustrated in the frontispiece, she tells Amintor, 'till the chance of war marked this smooth face / With these few blemishes, people would call me / My sister's picture, and her mine' (V.iii.37–9), and Amintor is unable to penetrate her disguise.[16]

Moreover, Aspatia and her brother are only one of the play's significant brother–sister pairings. Early in the play comes an exchange between Melantius and Evadne:

> *Melantius.*   Sister, I joy to see you and your choice.
> You looked with my eyes when you took that man;
> Be happy in him.
>
> > > > *Recorders* [*play*].
> *Evadne.*   O my dearest brother,
> Your presence is more joyful than this day
> Can be unto me.
>
> (I.ii.113–17)

Beneath the officially licensed affective ties celebrated by the marriage, others, for which there can be no recognised ritual expression, also make their presence felt: Melantius' strong friendship with Amintor, and Evadne's apparent love for her brother, which may well sound ominously in view of the so nearly incestuous relationship between

Arbaces and Penthea in the other Beaumont and Fletcher play very close to this in date, *A King and No King*.

Ominousness is certainly and brilliantly made the keynote of the masque, which Sarah P. Sutherland calls 'a spectacular anomaly among masques in Renaissance tragedy'.[17] Its unusual position in Act I means that it will obviously not be available later as an emblem and seal of harmony, while its content offers both a suggestive guide to the gender contestations to come and a telling reminder of the importance and protocols of allegorical means of expression. The masque, too, involves a brother–sister pairing, that between Cynthia, the moon (and a favourite persona of Elizabeth I), and her brother, the sun. Like Aspatia's likeness to her brother, this linking, too, symbolically unsettles gender norms. Night invokes Cynthia with the words, 'Appear; no longer thy pale visage shroud, / But strike thy silver horns quite through a cloud' (I.ii.122–3). Cynthia's possession of horns, albeit a standard part of her iconography, links her not to any of the women in the play but to the cuckolded Amintor, whose obviously pastoral antecedents further align him with the world of classical deities.[18] Cynthia goes against gender convention again when she claims sovereign authority even over a male god:

> Rise, rise, I say,
> Thou power of deeps, thy surges laid away,
> Neptune, great king of waters, and by me
> Be proud to be commanded.
>
> (I.ii.170–3)

She is also notably insubordinate to her brother:

> whilst our reign lasts, let us stretch our power
> To give our servants one contented hour,
> With such unwonted solemn grace and state
> As may for ever after force them hate
> Our brother's glorious beams, and wish the Night,
> Crowned with a thousand stars and our cold light
>
> (I.ii.146–51)

Though Cynthia must eventually retire, acknowledging 'I must down / And give my brother place' (I.ii.270–1), and does resemble Evadne in her ambition (though that in itself is defined and demonised as unwomanly), overall, the brief impression she creates means that amongst the other traditions and conventions it upsets, the masque also strikes a blow at the notion of secure and separate gender identity.

As well as brother–sister pairings, the text also offers two pairs of brothers, Diphilus and Melantius and Lysippus and the King. Ostensibly, brother–brother relationships operate much more to endorse the status quo than to threaten it, especially in the case of Lysippus and the King, since the existence of a younger royal brother means that the succession is secured and that at the end of the play, despite the removal of one monarch, the system itself survives intact. The brother–brother relationships may also initially appear to suggest a paradigm of contrasting pairings of good / bad types of masculinity: Melantius is active, Diphilus is passive; the King is vicious, Lysippus is restrained and reasonable. It is disturbing, however, that while in one pair, the 'good' brother, Lysippus, prospers, in the other, the 'weak' brother, Diphilus, fares better than the 'strong'. An early exchange between Melantius and Diphilus reveals much about how brotherhood works within the world of the play:

> *Melantius.*   I thank thee, Diphilus; but thou art faulty:
> I sent for thee to exercise thine arms
> With me at Patria; thou cam'st not, Diphilus;
> 'Twas ill.
> *Diphilus.*   My noble brother, my excuse
> Is my king's strict command, which you, my lord,
> Can witness with me.
>
> (I.i.28–33)

Melantius speaks here with the full privilege of an elder brother's authority over a younger in a system based on male primogeniture: he feels no hesitation about sweeping away the social niceties of greeting and publicly reprimanding Diphilus for a perceived failure in valour – a failure manifested, suggestively enough, at a location named 'Patria', a variant of the more normal 'Patras' which directly translates as 'fatherland' and thus neatly encodes an invocation of patriarchal authority. Diphilus, who throughout the play is unquestioningly loyal to his brother, shows no resentment at this treatment, but despite this apparent submissiveness his reply actually wreaks considerable ideological damage: to 'Patria' he opposes the 'king', and he thus, however inadvertently, prises open a disjunction between the theory and the embodiment of patriarchal authority which will eventually tear Rhodes apart. Since, as Robert Y. Turner points out, 'the only speaking character without a name is the King',[19] we are even more aware that it is issues and abstracts which are at stake here, rather than simply personalities.

The clear protocol governing the relationships of brothers in a system governed by primogeniture means that the potential tensions between Melantius and Diphilus on the one hand, and the King and Lysippus on the other, rarely break the surface. It is when men are not brothers that their interaction may more overtly threaten subversion of social and political strucures, since the strong emotions generated, not contained within any named or formalised relationship, may so easily tremble on the brink of homoeroticism. This is most particularly the case with Melantius and Amintor, whose affection is expressed in terms so extravagant as to border on the comic:

> *Melantius.* Melantius calls his friend Amintor. [*Embracing him*]
> O, Thy arms are kinder to me than thy tongue.
> Speak, speak!
> *Amintor.* What?
> *Melantius.* That little word was worth all the sounds
> That ever I shall hear again.
> (V.iii.256–61)

Melantius' rapturous response to the word 'What' may well be thought excessive here, and we may also take note of some of the vocabulary used in Melantius' earlier description of their friendship:

> When he was a boy,
> As oft as I returned (as, without boast,
> I brought home conquest) he would gaze upon me
> And view me round, to find in what one limb
> The virtue lay to do those things he heard;
> Then would he wish to see my sword, and feel
> The quickness of the edge, and in his hand
> Weigh it; he oft would make me smile at this.
> (I.i.49–56)

Amintor's gazing and viewing are sufficiently suggestive in themselves, but the notable and unusual reduction of Melantius' bodily force to the achievements of 'one limb' irresistibly evokes the phallus even before the mention of how Amintor would make Melantius smile by feeling his sword. The sword will become a keynote in the two men's relationship, as they take it in turns to draw, flourish and sheath their weapons, and the language which surrounds such encounters leaves us in no doubt of their erotic subtext: Melantius orders his sister, 'Speak, you whore, speak truth. / Or, by the dear soul of thy sleeping father, / This sword shall be thy lover' (IV.i.95–7). Later, it is Amintor's turn to associate Evadne with their sword-brandishing:

> [*Sheathing his sword*] O, my soft temper!
> So many sweet words from thy sister's mouth,
> I am afraid, would make me take her,
> To embrace and pardon her.
>
> (III.ii.237–40)

However, bringing women into the equation not only emphasises the inherent sexuality of the situation; it also provides a safety-valve for it. Indeed, triangulation of such strongly affective male relationships around women proves to be society's preferred way of defusing their potentially dangerous energies.[20]

No sooner has Melantius exhibited the strength of his affection for Amintor than, seemingly almost in a deliberate counter-move, he mentions his heterosexual interests:

> But I have a mistress
> To bring to your delights, rough though I am;
> I have a mistress and she has a heart,
> She says, but, trust me, it is stone, no better;
> There is no place that I can challenge in't.
>
> (I.i.148–52)

Despite the extreme exiguousness of her role in the plot, Melantius' mistress bulks large in his thoughts. He is furious when Calianax casts aspersions on her status:

Calianax.   It may be so. [*To Diagoras*] Who placed the lady there
So near the presence of the King?
Melantius.   I did.
Calianax.   My lord, she must not sit there.
Melantius.   Why?
Calianax.   The place is kept for women of more worth.
Melantius.   More worth than she! It misbecomes your age
And place to be thus womanish. Forbear!

What you have spoke I am content to think
The palsy shook your tongue to.
Calianax.   Why, 'tis well
If I stand here to place men's wenches.
Melantius.   I shall quite forget
This place, thy age, my safety, and through all
Cut that poor sickly week thou hast to live
Away from thee.
Calianax.   Nay, I know you can fight for your whore.
Melantius. Bate me the King, and be he flesh and blood
'A lies that says it! Thy mother at fifteen
Was black and sinful to her.

> (I.ii.59–73)

Melantius' mistress is repeatedly redefined during this exchange, in increasingly pejorative terms: she goes from 'lady' to 'woman', 'wench' and 'whore'. Melantius can retaliate only by equating her with Calianax's mother; more direct redress is denied him by the fact that Calianax himself is not fully manly, being unwilling to fight and so aged that his own status as man is open to question. In this way, then, this episode not only reveals tensions at court about social status, but uneasiness about gender too.

This is all the more damaging because the extent to which male camaraderie is structured around a strict cultural notion of the feminine is repeatedly revealed in the play. It is there in the ribald jesting underpinned by an agreement to traffic in women:

Diphilus. What odds he has not my sister's maidenhead tonight?
Strato. None: it's odds against any bridegroom living, he ne'er gets it while he lives.
Diphilus. Y'are merry with my sister: you'll please to allow me the same freedom with your mother.
Strato. She's at your service.
Diphilus. Then she's merry enough of herself, she needs no tickling.

> (III.i.5–11)

It is there, too, in Amintor's desire for fellowship in cuckoldry – 'Gentlemen, / Would you had all such wives, and all the world, / That I might be no wonder!' (III.i.101–3), and later:

> *Amintor.*   [*Aside*] Men's eyes are not so subtle to perceive
> My inward misery: I bear my grief
> Hid from the world. How art thou wretched then?
> For aught I know, all husbands are like me,
> And every one I talk with of his wife
> Is but a well dissembler of his woes,
> As I am; would I knew it, for the rareness
> Afflicts me now.
> *Melantius.*   Amintor, we have not enjoyed our friendship of late,
> For we were wont to change our souls in talk.
> *Amintor.*   Melantius, I can tell thee a good jest
> Of Strato and a lady the last day.
>
> (III.ii.46–57)

For Amintor, the only recourse in his desperate misery is to continue to share in the male community; making jokes about women may mask the fact that he doesn't know what is happening in other men's lives at all, and whether their bravado may be only a cover for the fact that all are cuckolds.

Finally, the attempt to bolster male bonding by sharing assumptions about a common superiority to women can also be seen in the gendering of the language of conquest. This is a trope of considerable importance in English Renaissance culture, and one which is much recurred to. In almost all Elizabethan and Jacobean writing on Ireland, for instance, images of monstrous femininity figured very prominently. Ireland itself was often represented as a woman,[21] in line with the common Renaissance trope which analogises land to be conquered to women to be married (by the virtuous English) or raped (by the villainous Spanish). As Lynda Boose comments,

> although the equation between land and the female body which makes rape and imperialism homologous is a metaphor of masculine ownership that is neither peculiarly English nor new to England's enclosure period, the collocation of the two discursive fields clearly acquired new energy at precisely this historical moment of heightened land anxieties.[22]

In *The Maid's Tragedy*, however, it has a slightly unsuual valency. It is not, as is usually the case, the land that is to be conquered that is gendered feminine, but the act of conquest itself, by virtue of the feminine gender of the abstract nouns *victoria* and *nike* in Latin and Greek

and the subsequent tradition of representing Victory as a female
figure.

> *Melantius.*   I might run fiercely, not more hastily
> Upon my foe. [*Embracing him*] I love thee well, Amintor;
> My mouth is much too narrow for my heart.
> I joy to look upon those eyes of thine;
> Thou art my friend, – but my disordered speech
> Cuts off my love.
> *Amintor.*   Thou art Melantius:
> All love is spoke in that. A sacrifice
> To thank the gods Melantius is returned
> In safety! Victory sits on his sword
> As she was wont: may she build there and dwell,
> And may thy armour be, as it hath been,
> Only thy valour and thine innocence!
> What endless treasures would our enemies give
> That I might hold thee still thus!
>
> (I.i.112–25)

When Melantius' speech becomes disordered, Amintor is able to
restore shape and style to it by overwriting his friend's language of
love and the heart with a more publicly acceptable allegory of a feminised Victory, in the context of which their embrace can jokily be read
as only a temporary interruption of Melantius' martial identity. At the
same time, though, Amintor's words imperil the very gender boundaries they seek to confirm, since he runs contrary to the normal
polarities of the gendered language of conquest by equating that
which he genders feminine with agency rather than with weakness.

All the rhetorical strategies attempted by these speakers depend
primarily on a sense of rigid separation between masculine and feminine spheres, and many characters in the play try to enforce this
distinction. Amintor tries to reason Evadne out of her perversity by
appealing to what he sees as essential truths about gender:

> O, we vain men,
> That trust all our reputation
> To rest upon the weak and yielding hand
> Of feeble woman! But thou art not stone;
> Thy flesh is soft, and in thine eyes does dwell
> The spirit of love; thy heart cannot be hard.
>
> (II.i.262–7)

Working along similar lines, Melantius, after his initial gaffe about the wedding, laments that he may have appeared deliberately to target Aspatia:

> I am sad
> My speech bears so infortunate a sound
> To beautiful Aspatia. There is rage
> Hid in her father's breast, Calianax,
> Bent long against me, and 'a should not think,
> If I could call it back, that I would take
> So base revenges as to scorn the state
> Of his neglected daughter.
>
> (I.i.81–8)

Melantius is anxious to make it clear that he does not consider women legitimate targets, as again when Calianax says, 'O, Melantius, / My daughter will die', and Melantius replies, 'Trust me, I am sorry; / Would thou hadst ta'en her room' (III.ii.2–4).

Melantius is also eager to keep defining the parameters of manhood: when Calianax terms Amintor 'such another / False-hearted lord as you', Melantius replies, 'You do me wrong, / A most unmanly one, and I am slow / In taking vengeance, but be well advised' (I.ii.61–4). Unfortunately for Melantius' project, though, the word 'manly' cuts with a double edge here, for if a man can do an unmanly wrong, then in the very act of demarcating what constitutes manhood Melantius has implicitly conceded that it is not innate in men. Similar difficulties bedevil his other attempts to categorise manliness. He says to Amintor,

> Dry up thy watery eyes,
> And cast a manly look upon my face,
> For nothing is so wild as I thy friend
> Till I have freed thee
>
> (III.ii.195–8)

Again, though, the connotations that accrue to manliness here are potentially negative: ought it not to be a state of reason, rather than of wildness? Equally troubling is Amintor's similar warning to Evadne:

> Do not mock me:
> Though I am tame and bred up with my wrongs,
> Which are my foster-brothers, I may leap
> Like a hand-wolf into my natural wildness,
> And do an outrage. Prithee, do not mock me.
>
> (IV.i.193–7)

For Amintor, the only alternative to an infantilised state of domestication and tameness is a 'natural wildness' which is prone to do 'outrage[s]'. The implied definition of manhood here is constructed purely in terms of what it is not; there is no positive image.

Melantius, less ready-tongued than Amintor, systematically attempts to circumvent such difficulties with language and with the full expression of his meaning and emotion. Instead of the slippery world of words, he prefers an essentialist and unitary language of the body, saying, for instance:

> My lord, my thanks, but these scratched limbs of mine
> Have spoke my love and truth unto my friends
> More than my tongue e'er could.
>
> (I.i.20–2)

He reverts to the language of the body when trying to force a confession from his sister:

> *Evadne.*   My faults, sir? I would have you know I care not
> If they were written here, here in my forehead.
> *Melantius.*   Thy body is too little for the story,
> The lusts of which would fill another woman,
> Though she had twins within her.
>
> (IV.i.28–32)

Here, he is able neatly to co-opt the capacity of the female body to increase during pregnancy as an index of its greater capacity for evil.

The women, however, resist such attempts to define them as essentially separate. Evadne from the outset is ruthlessly phallic when, as the 'Eve' concealed in her name suggests, she associates herself with serpents:

> I sooner will find out the beds of snakes,
> And with my youthful blood warm their cold flesh,
> Letting them curl themselves about my limbs,
> Than sleep one night with thee. This is not feigned,
> Nor sounds it like the coyness of a bride.
>
> (II.1.209–13)

Even the submissive Aspatia not only criticises men, but duplicates Evadne's language of snakes, with its suggestions of auto-eroticism and phallic femininity:

> Then, my good girls, be more than women, wise;
> At least be more than I was, and be sure
> You credit anything the light gives life to
> Before a man. Rather believe the sea
> Weeps for the ruined merchant when he roars;
> Rather the wind but courts the pregnant sails,
> When the strong cordage cracks; rather the sun
> Comes but to kiss the fruit in wealthy autumn,
> When all falls blasted. If you needs must love,
> Forced by ill fate, take to your maiden bosoms
> Two dead-cold aspics, and of them make lovers;
> They cannot flatter nor forswear: one kiss
> Makes a long peace for all. But man –
> O, that beast, man!
>
> (II.ii.14–27)

With her clear echoes of the gender-bending Cleopatra here, Aspatia inverts the usual norms by figuring procreation as decay, men as beasts, and women as capable of transcending and improving their natures.

Perhaps even more unsettling, however, is that even when it is not under threat from mannish women, the category of manhood can never be entirely stable, because it is challenged from within by two anomalous men – Calianax, and the King.[23] The age and cowardice of Calianax repeatedly militate against counting him as a man, especially when we are invited to read his challenge of Melantius as being just as futile as Aspatia's challenge to Amintor. Moreover, he is unable to take full part in the male community because he cannot join in the traffic in women: since there is no one willing to marry his daughter, he has, as it were, no goods to trade in, and our awareness of this structural problem in his situation highlights our sense of the extent to which male identity is informed and underpinned by women. That manhood is a state that must be attained to is plain in Melantius' remark that 'When I was a boy / I thrust myself into my country's cause / And did a deed that plucked five years from time / And styled me man then' (IV.ii.161–4); Calianax makes it clear that it also has an expiry date, and the disempowerment which he experiences as a result of his daughter's disgrace does further damage, since it not only implicates him but also lays bare the extent to which men's position is dependent on women.

The masculinity of Calianax is, then, so compromised that if Aspatia is not a worthy opponent for Melantius, no more, in fact, is her father, for Melantius exclaims:

> Some god pluck threescore years from that fond man,
> That I may kill him and not stain mine honour!
> It is the curse of soldiers, that in peace
> They shall be braved by such ignoble men
> As, if the land were troubled, would with tears
> And knees beg succour from 'em. Would that blood,
> That sea of blood, that I have lost in fight,
> Were running in thy veins, that it might make thee
> Apt to say less, or able to maintain,
> Shouldst thou say more! – This Rhodes, I see, is nought,
> But a place privileged to do men wrong.
>
> (I.ii.80–90)

Melantius' last line makes it clear that, for him, men are the victims in Rhodes – which has a sort of ironic appropriateness given that Rhodes is famous primarily as the location of the Colossus, a gigantic, celebratory image of manhood, which was toppled soon after its erection – no pun intended, but the word lay in wait for me – by an earthquake. If men in Rhodes are victims, though, it is notable that, in this instance as elsewhere in the play, it is also a man who is their oppressor; even if Calianax is implicitly defined as 'not-man' here, that is hardly more reassuring, since it suggests that the entire nature of manhood and the extent to which it coincides with biological maleness are open to question. Even when Melantius later explicitly defines Calianax as a man, saying to him, 'Good my lord, / Forget your spleen to me: I never wronged you, / But would have peace with every man' (III.ii.290–2), the ascription to him of 'spleen' emphasises his advanced years and crotchetiness – and by the time of Pope, at least, would definitively feminise him. As Calianax himself bitterly observes, in this society 'Old men are good for nothing' (V.ii.18) and are indeed always in danger of being seen as enemies of masculinity in others: when Calianax asks the King, 'Why, am not I enough / To hang a thousand rogues?', the latter replies, 'But so you may / Hang honest men too, if you please' (IV.ii.25–7), as if Calianax were a threat from whom men need to be protected.

As for the King himself, his position with regard to other men is even more worrying than that of Calianax.[24] Theoretically, he should be the exemplar and arbiter of empowered masculinity, but there is a worrying disjunction between his public position and his private behaviour which reminds us that patriarchy, with its insistence on heredity and male primogeniture, has the unfortunate side-effect of not always producing the most appropriate individual patriarch. In fact, the King's main effect is to emasculate the men around him and to render the women mannish; though the masque may represent Boreas as wild, untameable, masculine sexual desire,[25] the men of the actual play are tame, and Michael Neill also comments that the masque discloses hidden truths about the King's rule in other ways, since it reveals 'Night as the presiding deity of the Rhodian court, Queen of its shadows'.[26] Just as Day in the masque has been upstaged by his sister the Moon, so the King too appears little more than a puppet, presiding over a court which is actually governed by forces entirely beyond his control and to which he is himself subject.

Indeed the agency and autonomy of all the men in the play is seriously imperilled. At an early stage of the play, Amintor muses on Aspatia:

> I did that lady wrong. Methinks I feel
> Her grief shoot suddenly through all my veins;
> Mine eyes run; this is strange at such a time.
> It was the King first moved me to't, but he
> Has not my will in keeping.
>
> (II.i.127–31)

The first five words offer a sentence of great clarity and simplicity which, even despite its status as an admission of injustice, is, in many ways, reassuring: Amintor's 'I' claims agency, grasps and pithily articulates the situation, and differentiates itself securely from 'that lady'. After this assured opening, however, all such certainties rapidly break down. 'Methinks I feel' speaks of an 'I' much less sure of events and of its own relation to them; this is a feminised language of emotion, rather than a 'masculine' one of action, and it leads the way to Amintor's state of empathy with Aspatia – indeed the parallels between them are so great that it has even been suggested that he, as much as she, is the 'maid' of the title,[27] which would lead to an emphasis on male virginity both unprecedented on the English Renaissance stage and quasi-revolutionary in its implications that men as well as women can be categorised by their sexual status. It also leads to his tears, invariably demonised as feminine in the values of Renaissance drama. There is a brief resurgence of agency at the end: the King may have 'moved' Amintor, but the latter can still assert some independence of 'will', with all its phallic connotations – but this new sense of control will not last long.

As the plot develops, the pernicious consequences of the King's action multiply, and more and more givens are called into question. Amintor threatens that if women prove rebellious,

> we will adopt us sons;
> Then virtue shall inherit, and not blood.
> If we do lust, we'll take the next we meet,
> Serving ourselves as other creatures do,
> And never take note of the female more,
> Nor of her issue.
>
> (II.1.223–8)

In his personal misery, what he contemplates is no less than the abolition of the entire system of primogeniture and descent – the very system which, indeed, has produced the King's power.[28] Suggestively, Evadne too strikes a blow at the whole principle of differentiation which has privileged the King:

> *King.*   This subtle woman's ignorance
> Will not excuse you; thou hast taken oaths
> So great that methought they did misbecome
> A woman's mouth, that thou wouldst ne'er enjoy
> A man but me.
> *Evadne.*   I never did swear so:
> You do me wrong.
> *King.*   Day and night have heard it.
> *Evadne.* I swore indeed that I would never love

> A man of lower place, but if your fortune
> Should throw you from this height, I bade you trust
> I would forsake you and would bend to him
> That won your throne.
>
> (III.i.164–74)

The King's invocation of day and night may well recall the Moon's attempt to upstage her brother Day in the masque, which is recapitulated in Evadne's flat contradiction of him and her lordly use of 'I bade you'. The King's argument is premised on essentialist gender assumptions – Evadne is displaying a generic 'subtle woman's ignorance', and only certain oaths are suitable for women – but his little phrase 'A man but me' is fraught with a question with wider and more dangerous implications: if the King himself is a man comparable with others, what makes him special?

The question of to what extent the King is a man is repeatedly addressed, even by the First Gentleman, who comments when Evadne leaves the King's room, 'How quickly he had done with her! I see kings can do no more that way than other mortal people' (V.i.118–19). When she and the King are quarrelling over whether or not she has slept with Amintor, Evadne tells him, 'I am no man, / To answer with a blow, or, if I were, / You are the King' (III.i.189–91). The King is sure she cannot have confessed the truth to Amintor: 'He could not bear it thus: he is as we, / Or any other wronged man' (III.i.200–1). Amintor himself draws on the same set of assumptions when he finally confirms that Evadne has indeed confessed:

> I will not loose a word
> To this vile woman, but to you, my king,
> The anguish of my soul thrusts out this truth:
> Y'are a tyrant, and not so much to wrong
> An honest man thus, as to take a pride
> In talking with him of it.
> *Evadne.*   Now, sir, see how loud this fellow lied.
> *Amintor.*   You that can know to wrong, should know how men
> Must right themselves. What punishment is due
> From me to him that shall abuse my bed?
> Is it not death?
>
> (III.i.219–29)

Here, words for males cluster tellingly: 'my king', 'a tyrant', 'an honest man', 'men', 'this fellow' and 'him', all counterpointed with 'this vile woman'. There is a wide degree of social difference plotted between the two poles of 'my king' and 'this fellow', with its connotations of lower-class status, but Amintor also asserts an inherent equality of masculinity which ought to prevent any man from holding this conversation with another.

Perhaps the most disturbing consequence of the King's actions in terms of contemporary ideologies, however, is the extent to which they not only make men effeminate, but make women masculine. This is most obvious in the surprising development of Evadne's character from whore to king-killer: the men may be unable to exercise their phallic power or wield their swords, but Evadne experiences no such difficulties, making the men appear even more ineffectual and feminised by comparison. The precise reasons why it has to be Evadne, rather than Melantius or Amintor, who kills the King are repeatedly mystified. It is first mooted by Melantius:

> *Evadne.*   No, I feel
> Too many sad confusions here to let in
> Any loose flame hereafter.
> *Melantius.*   Dost thou not feel, amongst all those, one brave anger
> That breaks out nobly and directs thine arm
> To kill this base King?
> *Evadne.*   All the gods forbid it!
> *Melantius.* No, all the gods require it:
> They are dishonoured in him.
> *Evadne.*   'Tis too fearful.
> *Melantius.*   Y'are valiant in his bed, and bold enough
> To be a stale whore, and have your madam's name
> Discourse for grooms and pages; and hereafter,
> When his cool majesty hath laid you by,
> To be at pension with some needy sir
> For meat and coarser clothes:
> Thus far you knew no fear. Come, you shall kill him.
>
> (IV.i.139–53)

At the outset of this exchange, Evadne seems for the first time in the play to have been chastened into a proper femininity. Melantius, however, instantly undercuts this apparent reversion to a norm: the words 'brave', 'nobly', 'valiant', 'bold' and 'knew no fear' all work to make Evadne occupy a subject position described previously and elsewhere in the play as an exclusively masculine one. Melantius apparently assumes, whether disingenuously or not, that Evadne will *want* to kill the King; when she demurs, he tells her simply that 'all the gods require it'. This is the nearest we ever come to a reason, and indeed in succeeding discussions Melantius' logic becomes, if anything, even less clear, as when he tells his sister,

> This must be known to none
> But you and I, Evadne, not to your lord,
> Though he be wise and noble, and a fellow
> Dare step as far into a worthy action
> As the most daring, ay, as far as justice.
> Ask me not why. Farewell.
>
> (IV.i.171–6)

It is possible that the use of the term 'fellow' here for Amintor is significant: previously, this has been used only as denigratory. Apart from that, though, there is no clue. 'Ask me not why' applies, it seems, as much to the audience itself as to Evadne, and, as William Shullenberger notes, '[t]he possible motives are manifold, yet each in itself seems insufficient'.[29] Nor is an explanation vouchsafed to Amintor, in an exchange where the emasculation of the latter effected by the King becomes increasingly obvious:

> *Melantius.   [Aside]*   He'll overthrow
> My whole design with madness. [*To him*] Amintor,
> Think what thou dost. I dare as much as valour,
> But 'tis the King, the King, the King, Amintor,
> With whom thou fightest. [*Aside*] I know he's honest,
> And this will work with him.
> *Amintor.   [Letting fall his sword*] I cannot tell
> What thou hast said, but thou hast charmed my sword
> Out of my hand, and left me shaking here
> Defenceless.
>
> (IV.ii.308–16)

We can only guess that the reasons lie in Beaumont and Fletcher's extra-diegetic desire to extract the maximum possible *frisson* from events by having a woman perform the murder, or that their choice of Evadne is perhaps the logical consequence of the earlier feminisation of victory and conquest.

Whatever the motivations for Melantius' decision to make Evadne his tool, however, it seems to have remarkably beneficial effects on her. Evadne embarks on a positive orgy of self-abnegation, lamenting, 'sure, I am monstrous, / For I have done those follies, those mad mischiefs, / Would dare a woman' (IV.i.182–4). Her rehabilitation, though, is by no means easy. Amintor is incredulous in the face of her protestations:

> Can I believe
> There's any seed of virtue in that woman
> Left to shoot up, that dares go on in sin
> Known, and so known as thine is? O, Evadne,
> Would there were any safety in thy sex,
> That I might put a thousand sorrows off
> And credit thy repentance; but I must not
>   (IV.i.206–12)

His desire to trust and to seek 'safety' in her quails before his residual belief in Evadne's transgressive masculinity: he credits her with 'seed' which he images as 'shoot[ing] up'. Appropriately, therefore, Evadne's renewed assurances of transformation continue to draw very strongly on the language of more traditional gender stereotyping:

> I do not fall here
> To shadow my dissembling with my tears
> (As all say women can) or to make less
> What my hot will hath done, which heaven and you
> Knows to be tougher than the hand of time
> Can cut from man's remembrance; no, I do not.
>   (IV.i.220–5)

She falls, she weeps, she accepts the truth of general misogynist discourse, she suggests a binary opposition between men and women, and she implicitly aligns Amintor with the perspective of heaven. She follows this with even more extravagant gender-based self-reproach:

> All the creatures
> Made for heaven's honours have their ends, and good ones,
> All but the cozening crocodiles, false women.
> They reign here like those plagues, those killing sores

> Men pray against; and when they die, like tales
> Ill told and unbelieved they pass away
> And go to dust forgotten. But, my lord,
> Those short days I shall number to my rest
> (As many shall not see me) shall, though too late,
> Though in my evening, yet perceive I will,
> Since I can do no good because a woman,
> Reach constantly at something that is near it.
>
> (IV.i.245–56)

In these devastating lines (later so resonantly appropriated by George Eliot for the epigraph to the first chapter of *Middlemarch*) Aspatia's earlier alignment of men with beasts has been completely inverted; now it is women who are no better than animals.

This imagery, though, is rapidly destabilised. In keeping with his earlier talk of hand-wolves, Amintor exclaims:

> What a wild beast is uncollected man!
> The thing that we call honour bears us all
> Headlong unto sin, and yet itself is nothing.
>
> (IV.ii.317–19)

Evadne, too, sees men, or at least the King, as animalistic:

> 'A sleeps: O God,
> Why give you peace to this untemperate beast
> That hath so long transgressed you? I must kill him,
> And I will do't bravely: the mere joy
> Tells me I merit in it. Yet I must not
> Thus tamely do it as he sleeps: that were
> To rock him to another world
>
> (V.i.24–30)

Other things are also going on in this speech. Especially notable is Evadne's invocation of the ultimate patriarchal authority, God. Originally, Melantius had spoken of 'the gods', as was indeed made necessary by the prohibition on mentioning the Deity's name on stage; the prohibition is here violated, a fact underlined by the King's reference to pagan rather than Christian gods – 'I'll be thy Mars; to bed, my Queen of Love' (V.i.50) – so that we are fully aware of the extent to which Evadne conceives of her actions as identical with patriarchal imperatives. Moreover, her image of 'rock[ing]' the King may sound maternal and hence feminine, but her reluctance to kill the King while he is asleep not only clearly recalls *Hamlet* (already an obvious influence on the characterisation of Aspatia, though she, in pointed contrast, is identified not with Hamlet himself but with Ophelia), but also serves to align her specifically with the hesitating Prince, and thus to masculinise her once more. Indeed she explicitly disclaims a female identity:

> *King.*   How's this, Evadne?
> *Evadne.*   I am not she, nor bear I in this breast
> So much cold spirit to be called a woman:
> I am a tiger; I am any thing
> That knows not pity.
>
> > (V.i.64–8)

And the extent to which she has violated the codes of feminine behaviour is further emphasised by the First Gentleman's instinctive reaction to the murder scene: 'This will be laid on us: who can believe / A woman could do this?' (V.i.128–9). Shakespearean echoes are of course at work here too, and again reinforce the sense of Evadne's transgressiveness. The Gentlemen's fear that they will be blamed surely reminded the original audiences that this was in fact exactly what had happened to the attendants of Duncan in *Macbeth*. There, moreover, Lady Macbeth really had been unable to commit the murder. Evadne has thus gone one step further than the most violent, transgressive and immoral female character previously seen on the English Renaissance stage.

Moreover, it is not only Evadne who is challenging the boundaries of masculinity. Aspatia, too, has a date with destiny. Initially, she presents her behaviour as a normal function of her femininity:

> This is my fatal hour. Heaven may forgive
> My rash attempt, that causelessly hath laid
> Griefs on me that will never let me rest,
> And put a woman's heart into my breast.
>
> > (V.iii.1–4)

And she continues to subscribe to a theory of radical gender difference, although one that privileges women over men:

> How stubbornly this fellow answered me!
> There is a vile dishonest trick in man,
> More than in women. All the men I meet
> Appear thus to me, are harsh and rude,
> And have a subtlety in everything,
> Which love could never know; but we fond women
> Harbour the easiest and the smoothest thoughts,
> And think all shall go so. It is unjust
> That men and women should be matched together.
>
> (V.iii.21–9)

She goads Amintor into fighting her by appealing, successfully, to similarly traditional notions of male honour:

> *Aspatia.*   Thou art some prating fellow,
> One that has studied out a trick to talk
> And move soft-hearted people; to be kicked, *She kicks him.*
> Thus to be kicked! (*Aside*) Why should he be so slow
> In giving me my death?
> *Amintor.*   A man can bear
> No more and keep his flesh.
>
> (V.iii.91–6)

Nevertheless, despite all the lip-service Aspatia pays to gender distinctions, the inherent transgressiveness of her male attire cannot simply be talked away, and the implicit challenge posed to masculinity by her ability to ape it is underlined when Amintor finds himself confronted by not one but two armed women: '*Enter EVADNE, her hands bloody, with a knife*' (V.iii.105 s.d.).

The male characters' response to the women's violence is both unexpected and unanimous. Initially, Amintor makes some attempt to reassert gender norms: he says to Evadne, 'I dare not stay; / There is no end of woman's reasoning' (V.iii.165–6). But when he sees her stab herself, he discards gender roles altogether and says, 'I have a little human nature yet / That's left for thee, that bids me stay thy hand'(V.iii.170–1), and gender identity is also considerably downplayed as he contemplates his own death and says, 'There's man enough in me to meet the fears / That death can bring, and yet would it were done!' (V.iii.183–4). Even more suggestive of collapsed distinctions, though, is Melantius' death. Initially, Melantius' heroic identity appears to remain comfortably intact, as he exclaims, 'I never did /

Repent the greatness of my heart till now; / It will not burst at need'
(V.iii.270–2). Almost immediately, however, things start to look different:

> Melantius.   I am a prattler; but no more. [*Offers to stab himself.*]
> Diphilus.   Hold, brother!
> Lysippus.   Stop him!
>   [*Diphilus and Strato hold Melantius.*]
> Diphilus.   Fie, how unmanly was this offer in you!
> Does this become our strain?
>
> (V.iii.276–9)

Unmanly to stab himself? Perhaps only in a play where two women
have usurped the male prerogative of violence to wield their own
weapons could so surprising an association be made. Far more conventionally unmanly is the method Melantius next proposes for his death:

> Is not my hands a weapon sharp enough
> To stop my breath? Or if you tie down those,
> I vow, Amintor, I will never eat,
> Or drink, or sleep, or have to do with that
> That may preserve life: this I swear to keep.
>
> (V.iii.286–90)

There seems something almost luxurious about the quality of
Melantius' death-wish, as he virtually suggests to those around him
that they should tie down his hands and then resolves on self-starva-
tion, a method of suicide which elsewhere in Renaissance tragedy is
the exclusive preserve of female characters such as Penthea in *The
Broken Heart* and Anne Frankford in *A Woman Killed with Kindness*. (It
was also rumoured to have been the cause of death of Elizabeth I, said
to have starved herself in grief over the Earl of Essex.)[30] The inversion
is complete: masculinity, unable to sustain itself in the face of the
female invasion of its traditional territory, has, it seems, decided to
colonise that of femininity instead. When the King is merely a man,
the men hierarchically below him become women, with the revolutionary implication that, in the world of this play, gender is as socially
constructed as class. The old story that Beaumont and Fletcher were
arrested while writing the play, after an innkeeper heard them discuss
which of them should kill the King, misses the point: by writing a play
in which the King is the villain, and in which the early departure of

Cynthia, a figure so reminiscent of Elizabeth I, is followed by the revelation of the chaos he has wreaked, they had already done ideological
damage far more effective than mere physical violence, as indeed their
own representations of the power of language and the difficulty of
wielding swords have shown.

The Lady's Tragedy: narrative and metaphor

The play which I am here calling *The Lady's Tragedy* has had a very
troubled history. For a long time it lacked not only an acknowledged
author, but even a name. The censor, Sir George Buc, noting that it
came to him with no name, registered it as *The Second Maiden's
Tragedy*, apparently because he thought it similar to *The Maid's
Tragedy*. It is certainly true that in both plays a king is killed, and in
both plays one of the central female characters (Aspatia, the Lady) has
a father who is at least initially foolish, but the similarities do not seem
to me to go much further than that, and *The Lady's Tragedy*, with its
overt necrophilia, enters into the realms of true horror, more reminiscent of Webster than of the simpler sensationalism of *The Maid's
Tragedy*. Nevertheless, the title stuck and was retained for the earliest
scholarly edition of the play, produced by Anne Lancashire. In the
forthcoming Oxford complete works of Middleton, though, the play is
called *The Lady's Tragedy*, while in the Oxford World's Classics series,
in a collection entitled *Four Jacobean Sex Tragedies*, it appears under the
name *The Maiden's Tragedy*, on the grounds that this was essentially
what Buc meant when he called it 'This second *Maiden's Tragedy*'[31]
(something which also has the subsidiary effect of switching attention
away from the Lady, since it is not now to be taken as being called after
her but as after another play, making the focus on the female hero
incidental rather than integral). It is from this edition that I quote
here, since it is the most up-to-date and readily accessible, but nevertheless I have preferred to refer to the play as *The Lady's Tragedy*, first
to differentiate it securely from *The Maid's Tragedy*, and second because
the heroine is in fact referred to as 'the Lady' throughout the play (she
has no name), whereas it is not even absolutely clear that she actually
is a maiden, at least by the close of the play, when she is referred to as
Govianus' wife (4.5.24) and crowned as his queen.[32] (The wife of
Govianus' brother also refers to her as 'my noble sister' [5.1.80], and
though in the next line the Wife calls the Lady Govianus' 'mistress',
the Wife herself is shortly afterwards called a 'mistress' by her own
husband [5.1.138], so that the precise force of the term is muddied.)

The Lady is thus virtually unique in Jacobean drama in being a woman whose sexual status is unclear, in startling contrast to Middleton's other tragic heroines, Beatrice-Joanna and Bianca, whose defloration and subsequent sexual adventures can be pinpointed with almost split-second certainty, and this, combined with the insistent stress on her status, does indeed mean that her tragedy can be read as produced in part by the pressures of being a 'lady' in such a world as hers, which is another reason why I favour that title.

Part of the reason for the lack of clarity about the Lady's status originates in the fact that it is not only the play and the author which lack a securely defined name; several of the most important characters do so too. The Lady, the usurper and the wife of Govianus' brother Anselmus are all known simply by their functions, as Lady, Tyrant and Wife. Perhaps this is just a sign of the generally cavalier way in which the play seems to have been treated, having been left untitled, but it may seem that the term 'Wife' operates in some form of contradistinction to 'Lady', suggesting, perhaps, that 'wife' is a term of lesser honour and status than 'lady', particularly in view of the fact that the wife in this play behaves herself so much less well than the Lady. Indeed, this is typical of the play's dominant strategy for representing women. Officially, whichever title is adopted, the narrative centres on the Lady, whose behaviour is beyond reproach, and it therefore might briefly seem on the surface like that rare thing in Renaissance drama, a play which celebrates and glorifies a woman. However, although this may seem to be the message of the central story of the play, other elements of the text tell a rather different tale. In the first place, the Lady's story unfolds in sustained counterpoint to that of the deceitful Wife and her equally lustful woman, Leonella (who is repeatedly referred to as 'woman', as if it were a term beneath even 'wife' in the hierarchy of female nomenclature), a grouping whose tripartite nature aligns it with obviously evaluative, morally weighted structures such as rhetorical and iconographical tactics. And in the second, the entire play is peppered with yet another, quite separate and distinctly misogynist counter-narrative of femininity, inscribed in the speeches of the characters as they debate and discuss not just what is happening but also the causes and emotions which lie behind human actions, most of which are gendered feminine.[33]

In only the second speech of the play, Govianus laments his deposition thus:

> So much
> Can the adulterate friendship of mankind,
> False fortune's sister, bring to pass on kings
> And lay usurpers sunning in their glories
> Like adders in warm beams.
>
> (1.1.6–10)

In this speech, it is a man, the Tyrant, who has committed the wrong against Govianus, by deposing him; but what Govianus actually blames is a feminine force, 'False Fortune's sister'. This mythical female persona governs both the verbs in the passage; she '[c]an ... bring to pass', and she can reduce 'usurpers', including the actual perpetrator of the crime, to complete passivity by 'lay[ing] them'. Govianus thus strikes the note for the play's sustained demonisation of that which is gendered feminine. He continues to talk in similar terms, excoriating femininity even as he deplores the loss of his love:

> The loss of her sits closer to my heart
> Than that of kingdom, or the whorish pomp
> Of this world's title that with flattery swells us
> And makes us die like beasts fat for destruction.
> O she's a woman, and her eye will stand
> Upon advancement, never weary yonder;
> But when she turns her head by chance and sees
> The fortunes that are my companions,
> She'll snatch her eyes off and repent the looking.
>
> (1.1.59–67)

The overt misogyny of this speech is reinforced by Govianus' curt dismissal of pomp as 'whorish', and thus feminised. And he continues to associate disgrace with the sphere of women when he accosts First Nobleman:

> O sir, is it you?
> I knew you one-and-twenty and a lord
> When your discretion sucked; is't come from nurse yet?
> ...
> You're scholar good enough for a lady's son
>
> (1.1.80–2, 88)

Once again, women, for Govianus, are the source of all evil.

His assumptions seem to be comprehensively disproved by the

entrance of the Lady. Her first words, 'I am not to be altered' (1.1.122), demolish all his expectations of her fallibility and corruptibility and strike the keynote for the absolute chastity and constancy which will define her character.

At the same time, however, the words also do some damage, for 'I am not to be altered' approximates to a translation of the motto of Elizabeth I, 'Semper eadem', always the same. Allegorical and emblematic representations of the queen were so numerous and so diverse that to some extent they can always be seen as overarching any subsequent allegorical treatments of women for a long time to come, as I have suggested in the case of Cynthia in *The Maid's Tragedy*. Middleton – if this play is indeed by him – has played before the game of alluding to Elizabeth I: the dead sweetheart of Vindice in *The Revenger's Tragedy*, which is now also attributed to Middleton, is called Gloriana, and thus clearly recalls the dead queen. But as Steven Mullaney has recently pointed out in his essay 'Mourning and Misogyny', allusions such as this are by no means unequivocally complimentary: the queen was not solely beloved, she was also feared and mocked.[34] It is indeed these darker sides of the age of Elizabeth which are openly recalled in the play. Leonella's joke about sieves – 'I have a trick to hold out water still' (2.2.36) – refers to the ability to carry water in a sieve as being a legendary test of virginity; sieves were therefore used in the iconography of the queen, who was painted with one in her hand, and the fact that Leonella, who is obviously not a virgin, expects to be able to pass the sieve test perhaps plays on the persistent doubts about Elizabeth's own virginity and the rumours that she had borne an illegitimate child or children. (A similarly uneasy note may be struck by Govianus' apostrophising of the dead Lady as 'Eternal maid of honour' [4.5.37], since the queen's maids of honour had an unfortunate tendency to involve themselves in amorous escapades: Elizabeth Throckmorton found herself pregnant by Sir Walter Ralegh, and Lady Catherine Grey was unable to substantiate her claim that the Earl of Hertford had married her and was therefore imprisoned in the Tower.) The more burdensome aspects of the cult of Elizabeth are also recalled by the tyrant:

> Has there so many bodies hewn down,
> Like trees in progress, to cut out a way
> That was ne'er known, for us and our affections,
> And is our game so crossed? There stands the first
> Of all her kind that ever refused greatness.
>
> (1.1.177–82)

The Tyrant's words here perform three distinct but related functions. In the first place, the mention of the queen's habit of going on yearly progresses, and the crippling costs so frequently associated with them, underlines the extent to which the ghost of Elizabeth hovers over this scene much as that of the Lady will preside over later ones. In the second, he capitalises on the evocation of the queen to take a casual sideswipe at women in general, terming them all greedy for power – an accusation which the phantom presence of a woman who had been queen of England can of course only resoundingly confirm. Third, he thus underlines the general spirit of misogyny so embedded in the commonplaces and truisms of this society.

The presence of the feminine in the everyday speech of the play is made still clearer in the second scene. Here, matters of considerably less importance are being discussed, which suggests that the habit of describing the world and its events in feminised terms is virtually reflex. Anselmus, brother of Govianus, says to his friend Votarius,

> He's lost the kingdom, but his mind's restored.
> Which is the larger empire, prithee tell me?
> Dominions have their limits; the whole earth
> Is but a prisoner, nor the sea her jailer
> That with a silver hoop locks in her body;
> They're fellow-prisoners, though the sea look bigger
> Because he is in office, and pride swells him.
>
> (1.2.6–12)

Here the effect is almost like listening to a gendered language such as French, where the presence of feminine nouns is part of the basic fabric of speech. In Anselmus' mind, it seems taken for granted that the earth is female and the sea male, and the earth is clearly the weaker half of the partnership, being a prisoner, smaller in appearance, and less proud than the sea. Indeed Anselmus' whole mental universe is peopled by personalised abstractions: he goes on to say of Govianus,

> My brother's well attended: peace and pleasure
> Are never from his sight. He has his mistress:
> She brought those servants and bestowed them on him;
> But who brings mine?
>
> (1.2.18–21)

Peace and pleasure walk in person here through the landscape of

Anselmus' mind. The fact that they have been led there by the Lady may seem to work towards the exculpation and celebration of women, but Anselmus moves on immediately to lament that his own wife brings him no such attendants, and indeed this entire discussion of the feminised body of the earth proves the prelude to a discussion of his doubts about the literal body of his wife. When he moves on to this, his language becomes openly scornful of literal as well as metaphorical women:

> Nor does it taste of wit to try their strengths
> That are created sickly, nor of manhood.
> We ought not to put blocks in women's ways,
> For some too often fall upon plain ground.
> (1.2.58–61)

Votarius picks up on this strain when he tells Anselmus,

> Nay, hark you, sir,
> I am so jealous of your weaknesses
> That rather than you should lie prostituted
> Before a stranger's triumph, I would venture
> A whole hour's shaming for you.
> (1.2.65–9)

To Votarius, it comes naturally to use the word 'prostituted', habitually associated with a fate that befalls only women, to express the worst kind of disgrace he can envisage for his friend, just as later he will express his dislike and distrust of Bellarius by applying to him not one but two denigratory and feminising adjectives, 'whorish' and 'barren' (2.2.122).

Notably, when Anselmus' wife enters, she uses almost the same imagery of a feminised earth as her husband, but to significantly different effect:

> I have watched him
> In silver nights when all the earth was dressed
> Up like a virgin in white innocent beams;
> Stood in my window, cold and thinly clad.
> T'observe him through the bounty of the moon
> That liberally bestowed her graces on me;
> And when the morning dew began to fall,

> Then was my time to weep. He's lost his kindness,
> Forgot the way of wedlock, and become
> A stranger to the joys and rites of love;
> He's not so good as a lord ought to be.
>
> (1.2.100–10)

Initially, the wife images the earth as 'like a virgin'; but as the title of the Madonna song reminds us, to be *like* a virgin does not necessarily imply that one *is* so, and indeed the wife's lament turns out to be a distinctly unvirginal one, since she is basically complaining about the current lack of sex in her marriage. We are thus inclined to be sympathetic to Anselmus' refusal to believe in her chastity in the discussion which follows. Suggestively, Votarius prepares to try to convince his friend by saying, 'Now must I dress a strange dish for his humour' (1.2.112). Dressing a dish is a part of food preparation, a sphere of activity traditionally associated with women; since Votarius is planning to deceive his friend, having not actually wooed the wife at all, this strengthens the association which the play is establishing between women and dishonesty, even though it is a man who is actually perpetrating the deception here. Anselmus builds yet further on the idea that women are innately untrustworthy and deceitful when he simultaneously reveals that he is aware of Votarius' deception and refuses to be fobbed off with untested assurances of his wife's fidelity:

> Where lives that mistress of thine, Votarius,
> That taught thee to dissemble? I'd fain learn.
> She makes good scholars.
>
> (1.2.130–2)

It is true that Anselmus does have some good words to say of women:

> How truly constant, charitable, and helpful
> Is woman unto woman in affairs
> That touch affection and the peace of spirit;
> But man to man how crooked and unkind!
>
> (1.2.134–7)

Since the play will shortly afterwards see the first entrance of Leonella, however, and the development of her spiteful and, eventually, mutually destructive rivalry with her mistress, Anselmus' remarks here look less like enlightenment than like further testimony to his gullibility and self-destructive folly.

Typically, when Votarius does, predictably, fall in love with the wife, he blames not himself, but Cupid, whom he here figures as a feminised force, not as fully masculine as himself and fit only to associate with women: 'I will be master once and whip the boy / Home to his mother's lap' (1.2.255–6). His tactic of demonising a feminised abstraction is echoed in the next scene by Helvetius (whose own name suggests a different kind of abstraction on a separate allegorical layer, presumably to do with Swiss Protestantism). He accuses his daughter,

> thy obedience
> Is after custom, as most rich men pray,
> Whose saint is only Fashion and Vainglory.
> So 'tis with thee in thy dissembled duty:
> There is no religion in't, no reverent love,
> Only for fashion and the praise of men.
>
> (2.1.14–19)

Helvetius apparently starts by attacking specifically men, particularly rich men; but not only is the Lady explicitly said to be like them, the crime of these rich men is, furthermore, implicitly feminised, since 'Vainglory' connotes the sin of 'Vanitas', which is both a feminine noun and also traditionally represented by the image of a woman gazing at herself in a looking-glass. Moreover, as Helvetius moves through his denunciation he ceases to target it at men at all; instead the culprit becomes the lady, whose motive is to seek 'the praise of men', making her actions seem to verge on immodesty. Helvetius goes on to make his opinion of his daughter's true morality even clearer when he effectively advises her to sell her favours for the best price she can get:

> having youth, and beauty, and a husband,
> Thou'st all the wish of woman: take thy time, then,
> Make thy best market.
>
> (2.1.98–100)

It is equally notable that when Govianus enters, he may disagree with all of Helvetius' ideas, but he nevertheless virtually duplicates the old man's favoured rhetorical strategy of denigration of the female, telling him, 'list not to the Sirens of the world' (2.1.144). This leads Helvetius to reflect, 'with what fair faces / My sins would look on me!' (2.1.158–9), where wrongdoing is linked with beauty, traditionally (as at 5.2.14–15) associated with women.

However, not everything that is female is bad. When Helvetius reforms, he assures Govianus and the Lady that serving them 'sets my soul in her eternal path' (2.1.164). His soul, the best, the immortal part of himself, is, it seems, gendered feminine, and indeed the play repeatedly suggests that at the heart of every man, but most particularly the virtuous or brave, lies a feminised core. The Tyrant, hearing the reformed Helvetius, muses, 'How comes the moon to change so in this man' (2.3.53), thus imaging Helvetius' determination to behave nobly as something governed, as women's behaviour was supposed to be, by the changes of the moon. The assumption is made even clearer both when the Tyrant goes on, 'I beshrew that virtue / That busied herself with him' (2.3.55–6) and when Helvetius himself says,

> Leave me, thou king,
> As poor as Truth, the mistress I now serve,
> And never will forsake her for her plainness;
> They shall not alter me.
>
> (2.3.87–90)

Here he not only envisages himself as following the dictates of an explicitly feminine power, but also echoes the opening words which defined the character of his daughter, the Lady.[35] Govianus at the tomb of the Lady speaks of a tear which 'Ran swiftly from me to express her duty' (4.5.3), and even the tyrant thinks of his interior self as feminised, as he reveals when he speaks of 'everlasting torment lighted up / To show my soul her beggary' (4.2.32–3), or refers to himself as dominated by an 'affection' explicitly gendered feminine (5.2.2–3).

In the tête-à-tête between Govianus and the Lady which lies virtually at the temporal and certainly at the dramatic heart of the play, there is further significant discussion of feminised abstractions. Told that Sophonirus is approaching and wishes to speak to the Lady, Govianus says,

> Sure, honesty has left man. Has fear forsook him?
> Yes, faith, there is no fear when there's no grace.
>
> (3.1.20–1)

When Sophonirus actually enters, Govianus follows this up by exclaiming, 'O patience, I shall lose a friend of thee!' For Govianus, the mental make-up that is most to be desired seems clearly defined: the best kind of man should be governed by honesty, fear, grace and patience, his mind the mere empty ground for a never-ending, one-sided psychomachia.

But is it a good thing for good men thus to have a feminine soul as their innermost motivation? When the crisis point arrives and Govianus learns that the house is surrounded by soldiers of the Tyrant who are there to carry off the Lady, he becomes strangely passive. It is the Lady who urges him that the only way is to kill her, and when she suddenly stops him so that she may have time to pray, he not only sounds distinctly petulant but completely abnegates any responsibility for his own actions, demanding, 'Lady, what had you made me done now?' (3.1.101). His passivity and his failure to control the situation are even more clearly marked when, instead of killing her, as she has repeatedly requested, to save her from the Tyrant, he faints clean away instead (3.1.150 s.d.). This scarcely heroic moment is, moreover, in sharp contrast to the Lady's own steely resolution, which leads her to seize the sword herself and perform a swift and effective suicide (3.1.164 s.d.). The Lady's act is indeed heroic; but the woman who wields a sword in Renaissance drama is very rarely a good woman, and though Govianus, when he comes to, praises her act, he does so in terms which may, perhaps, give us pause. He apostrophises his dead love,

> And hast thou, valiant woman, overcome
> Thy honour's enemies with thine own white hand,
> Where virgin victory sits, all without help?
> (3.1.176–8)

Govianus certainly extols the Lady, and images her behaviour as governed by an abstract noun, victory, in ways which ought to be well in line with his own creed, but he also, for the first time, calls her 'woman' rather than 'Lady', almost as though her very valiance has demoted her. One might also notice that it is only after the soldiers have broken in that Govianus says, 'Now I praise / Her resolution; 'tis a triumph to me / When I see those about her' (3.1.213–15), with the possible implication that he had not praised it before. Moreover, once again, comparison with the actions of the Wife provides a disturbing counterpoint to those of the Lady, for the Wife too takes up a sword, but she does so in a spirit of lust and deception, and to the ultimate ruination of her entire household; and like the Lady's, too, her act is acclaimed for its uniqueness and lack of precedent, as 'that which never woman tried' (5.1.164); perhaps indeed the play never comes closer to its supposed avatar *The Maid's Tragedy* than in its reiteration of this motif of the two counterpointed, sword-wielding women. A similar effect of demeaning comparison is further present during the soldiers' visit to the Lady's tomb, when one of them is afraid of 'the whorish ghost of a quean I kept once' (4.4.5–6) – using a word that might just echo in our heads when the dead Lady is later crowned a queen.

The death of the Lady is the central turning-point of the play in both dramatic and structural terms, and yet despite all her courage, constancy and chastity, her actions seem initially to have had no effect at all. Indeed, we seem here, as in so many other aspects of *The Lady's Tragedy*, to be reprising the language and motifs of John Marston's *Sophonisba* (1606), the play which first prefigures the soul/body split which is to reach its apotheosis in *The Lady's Tragedy* with Sophonisba's defiant 'Thou mayest enforce my body, but not me' and Syphax's resulting threat,

> Do, strike thy breast. Know, being dead, I'll use
> With highest lust of sense thy senseless flesh,
> And even then thy vexèd soul shall see,
> Without resistance, thy trunk prostitute
> Unto our appetite.[36]

Syphax does eventually relent, declaring 'We dote not on thy body, but love thee' (IV.i.78) and thus apparently subscribing to the idea of an identity for women separate from their bodies, with all the recuperative potential that entails; but Sophonisba,
'Incomprehence in virtue' (V.iv.111) as her husband Massinissa rather alarmingly titles her, not only unmans her would-be rapist but also, more subversively, threatens even the masculinity of the heroic Massinissa himself. Assuring him that she is resolute to die, just as the Lady does Govianus, she instructs him:

> Behold me, Massinissa, like thyself,
> A king and soldier; and I prithee keep
> My last command.
>
> (V.iv.93–5)

After her death, he can say only, 'For piety make haste, whilst yet we are a man' (V.iv.115), and Sukanya Senapati has recently argued that in fact 'Massinissa's eager abandoment of his nuptials to prove himself on the battlefield, his neglect of his heterosexual bond and privileging of homosocial bond, reveal not only the rejection of the female in male identity formation but male sexual anxiety and a deep terror of female sexuality and heterosexual relationships'.[37] Even Sophonisba, virtuous and chaste, can be all too easily assimilated to the paradigm which our own age has come to see as that of the castrating woman; moreover, she too, like the Lady of *The Lady's Tragedy*, is outnumbered by the far less worthy women of the play, like Zanthia, who betrays her, and the witch Erichtho, to whom the odour of Catholicism clings (IV.i.156–62) as well as those of lust and witchcraft. And at the end of the play, when Sophonisba's virtue has triumphed and everything seems set fair for a happy ending after all, the abrupt intervention of Rome means that although Sophonisba may indeed 'die, of female faith the long-lived story' (V.iv.104), the effects of her actions will be confined to the realm of story and will be robbed of all tangible result in the real world.

It is this ultimate ineffectuality as well as the motifs of virtue, Catholicism and necrophilia in which *The Lady's Tragedy* most perniciously copies *Sophonisba*. Not only can the Lady's body be indeed used against her will, as was merely threatened to Sophonisba, but the 'First Fellow' to break in, quite unmoved by what he has just seen, says contemptuously to the body of Sophonirus (whose name looks as though it might indeed have been deliberately intended to recall that of Sophonisba),

> A vengeance of your babbling! These old fellows
> Will hearken after secrets as their wives,
> But keep 'em in e'en as they keep their wives.
> (3.1.229–231)

Despite the example of the Lady, nothing can shake the soldier's facile conviction of women as frail creatures who need to be restrained, and his contempt for men who do not so restrain them; language remains decisively at odds with truth as we have just seen it demonstrated in action. Even the ostensibly very different perspective of Govianus is essentially underpinned by the same set of assumptions. His last words, as he carries out the Lady's body, are 'Help me to mourn, all that love chastity' (3.1.245), and he thus not only praises the Lady but takes us once again into the realm of the feminised abstract virtue which, as the appearance of her ghost will shortly reveal, she, like Sophonisba before her, does indeed now inhabit – something under-lined by the fact that on his first sight of her spirit Govianus invokes abstractions, exclaiming 'Mercy, look to me! Faith, I fly to thee!' (4.5.43), and describes the wrongs done to her body as 'Inhuman injuries without grace or mercy' (4.5.77).

We do not stay in such lofty realms for long, however, for almost immediately the noble actions of the Lady give place to a return to the much less salubrious story of the Wife, who enters angry with Votarius for having, in his jealousy of Bellarius, told Anselmus that she was beginning to veer towards infidelity. To her demand that he account for his actions, Votarius replies,

> A man cannot cozen you of the sin of weakness
> Or borrow it of a woman for one hour,
> But how he's wondered at! Where, search your lives,
> We shall ne'er find it from you. We can suffer you
> To play away your days in idleness
> And hide your imperfections with our loves,
> Or the most part of you would appear strange creatures;
> And now 'tis but our chance to make an offer
> And snatch at folly, running, yet to see
> How earnest you're against us, as if we had robbed you
> Of the best gift your natural mother left you!
>   (4.1.22–32)

The really astonishing thing about this speech is not its wild dislike and fear of women, to which we are surely by now accustomed in this play, but the Wife's reaction to it: ''Tis worth a kiss, i'faith, and thou shalt ha't' (4.1.33). This is internalisation with a vengeance, and it is expressed, neatly enough, in terms of a direct inversion of a more familiar image. The emblematic representation of Opportunity showed it personified as the female figure Occasio, presenting her forelock to be tugged, almost invariably by a man. Here, by contrast, man runs after not Opportunity but Folly, as though women, in Votarius' imag-ination, cannot even be conceived of as offering Opportunity any more.

But though the Wife may be happy to subscribe to such senti-ments, would it be fair to say, ultimately, that the play itself does so? Sometimes we may feel clearly invited to critique some of the misogynist stock-in-trade of daily conversation in this society, such as a reference to 'my wife's tongue ... that drowns a sance bell' (2.3.23), where we are promptly made aware that the speaker, Sophonirus, is a fool. We may also similarly dismiss the Tyrant's refusal to believe in the virtue of any woman other than the Lady, and his fulmination that

> Hadst thou but asked the opinion of most ladies,
> Thou'd'st never come to this! They would have told thee
> How dear a treasure life and youth had been.
> 'Tis that they fear to lose: the very name
> Can make more gaudy tremblers in a minute
> Than heaven or sin or hell; those are last thought on.
>   (4.4.101–6)

Furthermore, the text itself it at some pains to prise apart the literal and the allegorical references to the feminine, as when Votarius tells Anselmus,

> Your friendship, sir,
> Is the sweet mistress that I only serve.
> I prize the roughness of a man's embrace
> Before the soft lips of a hundred ladies.
>   (5.1.4–7)

Here, Anselmus' friendship may be figured as a mistress, but it is sharply contrasted to actual women, who are to be marginalised in comparison. Nevertheless, we cannot help but notice that Anselmus, dying, sums up his his experiences with the final condemnation that 'The serpent's wisdom is in women's lust' (5.1.180). Most strikingly, though, even his brother Govianus, who has so much good reason to know better, still speaks disparagingly of women in general, albeit with the exception of the Lady. He challenges the Tyrant, 'make my end as rare as this thy sin / And full as fearful to the eyes of women' (5.2.134–5), and he greets the Lady with,

> Welcome to mine eyes!
> As is the day-spring from the morning's womb
> Unto that wretch whose nights are tedious
>   (5.2.145–7)

Although the Lady's arrival is welcome, the feminine continues to be demonised, for the state of absence preceding her arrival is compared with the female space of the womb, which is here figured as a prison, withholding what is most desired. And finally, although Govianus, largely through the death of the Lady, is now 'placed / Upon this cheerful mountain where prosperity / Shoots forth her richest beam' (5.2.175–7), he nevertheless ends the play with yet another generalisation about the untrustworthiness of women as a whole: 'I would those ladies that fill honour's rooms / Might all be borne so virtuous to their tombs' (5.2.201–2), as well as declaring his resolution never to take another wife because he will never find another like the one he has lost. The Lady, it seems, can only be a unique exception, whose behaviour we can never expect to be duplicated. Even our admiration for her may occasionally be qualified; while as for women in general, they, the play does not hesitate to assure us, mean nothing but trouble. The play has two major female figures, the Lady and the Wife, of whom one is good and one is bad, and it has two dominant modes of imagining the feminine, through the personification of abstract virtues and through the cultural commonplace of invoking women as emblems of frailty. But just as the subsidiary presence of the unchaste Leonella means that the side of the Wife outweighs the Lady, so the denigratory references to women swamp the invocation of feminised abstractions.

In both *The Maid's Tragedy* and *The Lady's Tragedy*, then, we see a strongly marked tension between, on the one hand, a set of discursive and representational strategies intended to contain and define women, and, on the other, the ways in which these representations have taken on energies and valencies of their own which suggest that women cannot and will not be contained, and that their transgressiveness will indeed be in direct proportion to the energies used in attempting to curb them. In the next chapter, we shall see a less subtle weapon, the law, being deployed to contain women. In this case too, though, the fact of representation of events (which is an inevitable and integral part of the legal process itself as well as of descriptions and imaginings of it) proves to generate an energy of its own, which cuts against official meanings to reveal powerful oppositional ones.

3
Women and the Law: *The White Devil* and *The Witch of Edmonton*

A small but significant number of the Renaissance plays which take women as their main characters focus in particular on the position of women in the eyes of the law. This is partly because the rise of the theatres coincided (perhaps not incidentally) with that of the Inns of Court. Young men from the Inns of Court were well known as regular attenders at the theatres, and a considerable number of those who wrote for the stage, including Beaumont, Fletcher, Marston, Webster and Ford, had had a legal training and were thus particularly well placed to appreciate the considerable dramatic mileage to be had from the antagonistic structures of forensic drama. (Indeed contemporary legal training often required role play.) It was not only the structures of the law that allowed for a number of dramatic possibilities, however; specific laws also offered scope for a pointed exploration of cultural pressure points, particularly in regard to biologically based views of gender.

In one way, it was of course the idea that gender was biologically innate, and that women were thus essentially inferior, which lay at the heart of the law's markedly different attitudes to men and to women. In the eyes of the law, the vast majority of women were *femmes covertes*, with their own identities, for legal purposes, entirely subsumed in those of their husbands or fathers. Effectively, they were considered incapable of independent action and not fully responsible for any actions which they might in fact take. And since every woman was legally considered as either married or marriageable, all were theoretically subject to this disabling classification.

In practical terms, however, one group of women could, and often did, escape from it. The group of early modern women possessed of the greatest personal freedom and economic power was undoubtedly widows. They inherited by law one third of their husbands' estates and were free to dispose of it as they wished, a right of which they often availed themselves: Amy Louise Erickson comments that '[b]ecause married women were precluded from making a will except by special arrangement with their husbands ... the vast majority of women's wills were made by widows (about 80 per cent) and single women (up to 20 per cent)'.[1]

The relative freedom of widows was not in itself enough to destabilise the ideological framework which underlay legal restrictions on women in general. More radically undermining of conventional certainties, though, was the fact that it was clearly visible to Englishmen of the early modern period that the treatment of widows was not universal, but culturally specific. In *A New Way To Pay Old Debts*, we are explicitly told that 'Were I a Spaniard, to marry / A widow might disparage me, but being / A true-born Englishman, I cannot find / How it can taint my honour',[2] and *The Duchess of Malfi* too makes it abundantly clear that attitudes towards the Duchess's remarriage are far more extreme in the Amalfi of the play than they would be in England. There the marriage of widows was a regular and socially approved route to wealth for younger or impoverished sons, as seen in the courtship of Widow Goldenfleece in Middleton's *More Dissemblers Besides Women*, and was frowned upon only if there was a marked discrepancy in age. (Indeed excessive chastity in widows was laughed at, with disbelief in the bare possibility of its existence forming the basis of Chapman's *The Widow's Tears*.) Even the hard-liner Thomas Edgar, in his *The Lawes Resolution of Womens Rights* (1632), descends from the grand absolutes of his title to acknowledgement of the paramountcy of the specific when he writes, 'I have hitherto handled only those gifts [dowries] ... which come from women or their ancestors, as if English men were so dainty and coy that they must be enticed, or our women so unamiable that unless it were by purchase, they could have no husbands'.[3] Even Edgar knows that 'the law' is the law of only one country, and that which pertains in one place does not necessarily pertain in another.

To a certain extent these national differences in attitudes towards women were rooted in the doctrinal and ritual differences between Protestantism and Catholicism. Whereas Protestantism laid primary emphasis on married chastity, Catholicism valued virginity for its own sake. But it is by no means always in these terms that different attitudes are presented on the Renaissance stage; in so far as these are separable, national differences are more likely to be stressed than purely religious ones. It is, therefore, worth particular note that when John Webster presents in *The White Devil* arguably the period's most searching examination of the ways in which a woman's guilt or innocence is constructed in the eyes of the law, he should choose to stress that those present at the trial of Vittoria include not only representatives of the indigenous community but also the ambassadors of a number of other countries, who perform a formal passing over the stage which allows their distinctive national characteristics to be commented on (III.i.65–78). Vittoria makes particular reference to these foreign visitors – 'to the most worthy and respected / Lieger ambassadors, my modesty / And womanhood I tender' (III.iii.131–3), drawing our attention to them still further. Most striking of all is the fact that they all pointedly disagree with each other about the court's treatment of her, with the French Ambassador saying 'She hath lived ill' and the English Ambassador responding 'True, but the cardinal's too bitter' (III.ii.106). Indeed Vittoria herself scathingly lays bare the extent to which justice is a national rather than a universal concept when she requests, 'Let me appeal then from this Christian court / To the uncivil Tartar' (III.iii.128–9), while Flamineo tells the English ambassador, 'You are happy in England, my lord; here they sell justice with those weights they press men to death with' (III.iii.28–30). There are other signs of cultural differences, too. Earlier in the play, the heroine Vittoria's first husband Camillo plays a neat riff on the traditional woman-as-land-to-be-conquered trope when in response to his brother-in-law Flamineo's question 'What travailing to bed to your kind wife?' he replies,

> I assure you brother, no. My voyage lies
> More northerly, in a far colder clime, –
> I do not well remember I protest
> When I last lay with her.
>
> (I.ii.53–6)

The homonym of 'cuntry'/'country' means that this connection is always liable to be made, and to equate women with territories, as Camillo does here, is usually firmly to associate them with nature rather than culture. Webster, though, inverts this perspective by having the representatives of different countries present at crucial points in the play's events to suggest that many aspects of human behaviour and values are cultural rather than natural.

Long before the word was invented, what Webster is here invoking is effectively the possibility of a multicultural perspective, in which standards of normality, morality and legality may be revealed as relative rather than absolute. This is a perspective also found in the work of Thomas Smith, first Regius Professor of Law at Cambridge, who noted that 'Although the wife be … *in manu & potestate mariti*, by our lawe yet they be not kept so streit as in mew and with a garde as they be in Italy and Spaine, but have almost as much libertie as in Fraunce, and they have for the most part all the charge of the house and houshoulde (as it may appear by *Aristotle* and *Plato* the wives of Greece had in their time), which is in deede the naturall occupation, exercise, office and part of a wife'.[4] For Smith there is an interesting tension here between what is natural and what is culturally constructed, and the extent to which the two overlap, and lying behind his comparisons is a clear set of contrasts between Catholic and Protestant on the one hand, and Christian and classical on the other.

For Smith there is ultimately no doubt who is right: what the English do is both natural and also, appropriately, in line with the practice of the greatly revered culture of classical Greece. For Webster, though, things are not so simple. Classical culture underlay Renaissance learning, as his own self-conscious allusions to Greek dramatists and deployment of Latin quotations in the preface to *The White Devil* clearly signals. The two cultures, however, had very different, and indeed fundamentally incompatible, belief systems. Moreover, Christianity itself had been riven in two by schism. In *The White Devil* the terrifying uncertainty on which all Renaissance cultures were built is in turn revealed by Flamineo's devastating question to the ghost of Bracciano,

> In what place art thou? in yon starry gallery,
> Or in the cursed dungeon? No? not speak?
> Pray, sir, resolve me, what religion's best
> For a man to die in?
>
> (V.iv.127–30)

Collective uncertainty about faith is, it seems, so great that Flamineo can be genuinely unsure whether Bracciano, adulterer and double murderer, has gone to hell, because, as Flamineo later says, 'While we look up to heaven we confound / Knowledge with knowledge' (V.vi.259–60) and thus are no longer sure of what is right and what is wrong. Indeed, ultimate uncertainty about the spiritual fates of all the characters is created when at the very end of the play the ambassadors collectively break in on the scene of slaughter, again reminding the audience of the possibility of many divergent viewpoints.

Moreover, the play insistently counterpoints its ostensibly Italian story with a wide array of references to other cultures and countries. Particularly notable is the recurrent strand of allusions to the Irish,[5] but there are also three characters disguised, respectively, as a Moor who has fought for the Venetians in Candy (V.i.4–10) and as two Hungarian noblemen who are Knights of Malta and are proposing to settle in Padua (V.i.13–23). There is also mention of a 'Dansk drummer' charging 'the French foe' (II.i.119 and 122), 'a shav'd Polack' 'ransack[ing] a Turkish fly-boat' (II.i.184 and 188), 'a Spaniard's fart that should have poison'd all Dublin' (II.i.303–4), discussion of Dutch women going to church (III.ii.6) and mention of having to be one's own ostler in France and the forty thousand beggars in Poland (III.iii.4–7). Similarly we hear of 'tribute of wolves paid in England' (IV.i.72), Spanish figs and Italian sallets (IV.ii.61), the 'villainous usage' of Barbary (IV.ii.204–5), the distinctive practices of Italian beggars (IV.iii.82–4), the skill of French riders (IV.iii.96), 'Westphalia bacon' (V.i.181), 'Scotch holy bread' (V.vi.143) and 'the lions i' th' Tower on Candlemas-day' (V.vi.266–7). Isabella, denying that she is jealous, tells Bracciano 'I am to learn what that Italian means' (II.ii.161), casting jealousy as a specifically national rather than a general human trait. Flamineo warns the incensed Bracciano 'I tell you duke, I am not in Russia; / My shins must be kept whole' (IV.iii.55–6), and even when he is dying he asks whether the blade is 'a Toledo, or an English fox' (V.vi.235). It is a truism that Renaissance dramatists set their plays abroad as a way to avoid being suspected of the dangerous act of offering reflections on English politics. Here, though, the apparently safe foreignness of the setting blurs out of focus as England and Spain, traditional enemies, threaten to morph eerily into each other. Events even move dangerously close to home when Bracciano exits from the courtroom with the threat 'Monticelso, / *Nemo me impune lacessit*' (III.ii.178–9), which was in fact the motto of the House of Stuart and thus of James I himself. It can only drive the point still further home that Vittoria is accompanied for much of the play by her black waiting-maid Zanche, like a walking emblem of cultural relativity, and that the behaviour of this Italian widow at her trial seems also clearly to recall that of the Spanish Catherine of Aragon at her own trial in England, which centred on the nature of her status as widow of an English prince – a trial which had in fact been held at the Blackfriars, transformed by the time that Webster was writing into one of the main London theatres.

Issues surrounding widowhood were not the only ones liable to be shown by English Renaissance drama as culturally conditioned. It was well known that marriage itself was also differently regarded and celebrated by the different communions. For Protestants, marriage was an admirable state, but for Catholics it was a poor second to celibacy; thus for Catholics virginity was a quasi-sacred state, while Protestants placed at least as much value, and often more, on chastity in marriage. Even when marriage was contracted, the means by which this was achieved could vary; though there was an increasing preference for public ceremonies, private handfastings such as that contracted by the Duchess of Malfi remained legal. Though relatively little is made of this by Webster, other dramatists saw that there was considerable dramatic capital to be made from this, as Shakespeare shows in *Measure for Measure*, and considerable opportunity also for exploring the relative rather than absolute nature of this apparently most basic of modes of human behaviour. The contracting of marriages, however, tends to be the terrain of comedy rather than tragedy and thus falls outside the scope of my discussion here.

More pertinent to the tragic world is the representation of witchcraft. This was of course a particularly newsworthy and much-debated topic, but again its representation in the drama seems to be marked by a particular slant: when we are introduced to a witch, we are typically told where she is from. In *The Witch of Edmonton*, *Macbeth* and *The Late Lancashire Witches*, the specifics of the locality are vividly evoked, and in both *The Witch of Edmonton* and *The Late Lancashire Witches* much of the point derives from the marked contrast between the provinces and London, with Carter in *The Witch of Edmonton* telling Old Thorney, 'we here about Edmonton hold present payment as sure as an alderman's bond in London, Mr Thorney' and Cuddy scornfully differentiating Edmonton from the nearby Envile Chase, let alone foreign parts such as the Low Countries where 'there are eight days in the week there hard by'.[6] In Marlowe's *Doctor Faustus* too, where, as contemporary audiences would have understood, the doctor is actually a witch and is also repeatedly feminised by the text,[7] geographical details are given much prominence, and even King James' *Daemonologie*, written at a time when he still firmly believed in witchcraft, concedes that succubi and incubi are 'most common in such wild partes of the world, as Lap-land, and Fin-land, or in our North Iles of Orknay and Schet-land', and that although death for witches 'is commonly used by fire ... that is an indifferent thing to be used in every cuntrie, according to the Law or custome thereof'.[8] This presumably represents contemporary awareness of the fact that people were indeed significantly more likely to be tried as witches in some areas than in others – twice as many suffered in Scotland as in England, though the latter had twice the population, and it is an interesting twist that James renounced his own previous belief in witchcraft once safely in England.

James himself attributed the supposed prevalence of incubi and succubi in northern locations to the ignorance pertaining there, leading people to be more readily duped into becoming witches; others might have been at least as ready to ascribe it to greater credulity, leading people to be more readily duped into *believing* in witches, and certainly in Middleton's *The Witch* the credulity of the ignorant becomes a considerable part of the joke. The play is clearly influenced by the notorious divorce of Frances, Countess of Essex, from her first husband and her subsequent remarriage to the King's favourite Robert Carr, Earl of Somerset. The Countess alleged that her husband was impotent and she herself a virgin; this was widely disbelieved, not least because the testimony of a number of women that he was not eventually forced the Countess's legal team to modify the charge to one of *impotentia versus hanc*, impotence in the case of one woman alone. When the Countess, masked and concealed behind a screen, was medically examined and pronounced to be indeed *virgo intacta*, rumours abounded that a substitute had been introduced in her place. These events are obviously reflected in the play, where witchcraft prevents Antonio from consummating his marriage and two separate bed-trick substitutions take place. Presumably in order to deflect attention from these dangerously close parallels with events at court, the play is nominally set in the Italian city of Ravenna, but that this is a mere fiction is soon exposed when Sebastian announces that 'There is a gentleman from the northern parts / Hath brought a letter, as it seems, in haste', and the said gentleman proceeds to respond to an enquiry about Antonio's mother, 'I left her heal varray well sir',[9] in what is clearly intended as a Scottish accent. Once again, then, witchcraft is associated with a highly specific point of causation and origin which is clearly represented as material rather than spiritual in nature. Representations of witchcraft in these plays thus testify less to the universality of wickedness than to the diversity and particularity of human behaviour, and to the different ways in which it may be received. (In one way, of course, all plays with specifically named characters bear witness to particularity rather than to generality, so that theatre can in itself be seen in this sense as a liberal art form, but the process is particularly clearly visible here.)

At first sight witchcraft, marriage and virginity might seem to represent a series of absolutely opposing states, on very different points of the spectrum of female experience. There are, however, structural echoes in these various situations. In Marston's *Sophonisba*, for instance, the wicked witch is Sophonisba's antagonist and opposite, but Sophonisba herself collapses within her own person the two states of virginity and wifehood which would normally be entirely distinct, and ultimately finds her own rhetorical skill an object of far greater suspicion to the Romans than the cruder and more obvious powers of the witch. Many plays in which virginity is a central issue also include a bed-trick, a sanitised form of the shape-shifting associated in the popular mind with the practice of witchcraft: indeed in *The Witch* there are two, as first Florida and then a 'hired strumpet' (V.iii.116) take the place of their social superiors in bed. It is, therefore, notable that Webster counterpoints the story of the Duchess of Malfi's marriage with repeated allusions to the language and objects associated with witchcraft, including a hand of glory, a mandrake, a werewolf and a basilisk, and that in *The Witch of Edmonton*, Dekker, Ford and Rowley too develop their story of witchcraft alongside an equally prominent one of the contraction and dissolution of marriages. Indeed they announce at the outset of *The Witch of Edmonton*, in the Argument of the play, that

> The whole argument is this distich:
> Forc'd marriage, murder; murder, blood requires;
> Reproach, revenge; revenge, Hell's help desires.

Here a perfectly clear chain of causation is set up in which satanic forces can become involved only after manmade marriage practices have wreaked the initial havoc, and the telling parallels between the witchcraft and marriage plots are further reaffirmed when Old Carter tells Warbeck, 'Wedding and hanging are tied up both in a proverb, and destiny is the juggler that unties the knot' (II.ii.4–5) and when the play ends with Winnifride musing on her widowhood (Epilogue). Here again what witchcraft reveals most clearly is how categories bleed into each other rather than how strongly they are opposed, as again when Banks heartlessly but tellingly declares of the deranged Mistress Ratcliffe, 'she's as many wives are, stark mad' (IV.i.197), or as in *The White Devil* when Monticelso confesses to Francesco the existence of his 'black book' of informers, creatures who live within the law yet bring others into its danger, and says 'Well may the title hold: for though it teach not / The art of conjuring, yet in it lurk / The names of many devils' (IV.i.33–5).

The affinity between marriage plots and witchcraft plot is particularly clear in Middleton's *The Witch*, itself unmistakably prompted by a particular story of marriage and divorce, where the plot revolves entirely around issues of precontract, adultery and premarital sex, staged within an overarching framework of a strong sensitivity to issues of cultural difference. The play is only two lines old when Sebastian declares, 'She is my wife by contract before heaven / And all the angels sir' (I.i.3–4), his words roughly prising apart any suggestion that the laws of man and God might be in any way the same. Later he makes the situation even clearer:

> This is no wrong I offer, no abuse
> Either to faith or friendship – for we're registered
> Husband and wife in heaven. Though there wants that
> Which often keeps licentious man in awe
> From starting from their wedlocks, the knot public,
> 'Tis in our souls knit fast – and how more precious
> The soul is than the body, so much judge
> The sacred and celestial tie within us
> More than the outward form, which calls but witness
> Here upon earth to what is done in heaven.
>
> (IV.ii.7–16)

Here the difference between the law of God and the customs of society is imaged as analogous to that between the soul and the body, with the 'outward form' of social observance inferior to the greater truth and good of the soul. Moreover, the play also makes it abundantly clear that what is called witchcraft in this society is closely associated with perfectly normal behaviour – Almachildes visits Hecate in hopes of obtaining 'charms and tricks to make a wench fall backwards and lead a man herself to a country house some mile out of the town, like a fire-drake' (I.i.90–3), just as Cuddy Banks in *The Witch of Edmonton* asks Mother Sawyer for help in enjoying Kate Carter – while 'normal' and socially validated marriages may entail precisely the opposite: the Duke, for whose supposed murder the Duchess will be roundly condemned, regularly has her pledge him in a cup made out of her late father's skull, a habit far more sinister and occult-seeming than

Almachildes' simple desire for sex. Moreover, since the Duke does this because he conquered the Duchess's father in battle, it is clear that the Duke and Duchess are intended to be seen as coming from different and indeed inimical communities, and it is presumably as a result of this that while the Duchess is outraged by the use of her father's skull as a drinking cup, the Duke never once suspects that she will object to it. Since discussion of the use of the cup both inaugurates and closes the events of the play, this reminder of cultural differences frames and shapes our understanding of events.

The fact that the Duke's behaviour is far more eccentric than the witches' in this play may also serve to alert us to the fact that another recurrent and related feature of witchcraft plays is emphasis on folk ritual, and, in particular, the extreme thinness of the line between the culturally acceptable ritualised practice and the culturally demonised one. In the Prologue of *The Witch of Edmonton* we hear the following apology for producing a play about a witch from Edmonton when there has recently been another one about a devil from there:

> But as the year doth with his plenty bring
> As well a latter as a former spring,
> So has this witch enjoy'd the first, and reason
> Presumes she may partake the other season.
> (Prologue, 5–8)

Here the witch is associated with a natural feature which, although abnormal, does not lack precedent, and as the play develops we are offered the suggestive contrast between the vilification heaped on Mother Sawyer and the unquestioning toleration for the equally pagan ritual of the hobby-horse. We also see the even more telling contrast between the normal-seeming sexual behaviour for which the Edmonton locals hold the witch to be responsible and their own far more unusual and superstitious determination to fire her thatch on the grounds that if she is a witch, she will come running back at once (IV.i.1–21).

Moreover, the metaphor of the seasons used in the Prologue points up the extent to which the whole play can be seen as revealing human behaviour as evincing the same pattern of cycles as the seasons themselves. At the beginning of the play Frank Thorney combines contemplation of his imminent fatherhood with continuing awe and fear of his own father. Towards the end, Winnifride declares,

Oh, pardon me, dear heart! I am mad to lose thee, and know not
what I speak; but if thou didst,
I must arraign this father for two sins:
Adultery and murder.

(IV.ii.187–9)

There are a number of puzzling features about this speech. Whatever
can 'if thou didst' mean in this context? Is Winnifride, having just
declared that she herself is not sure of what she is saying, appealing to
a bystander who she thinks might have a clearer grasp of it? Or ought
we mentally to supply an 'it', making her mean something like 'If you
did indeed do what you have been accused of'? Second, the phrase
'this father' seems odd, and indeed leads Old Carter to take immediate
offence:

Arraign me for what thou wilt, all Middlesex knows me better for an
honest man than the middle of a marketplace knows thee for an
honest woman.

(IV.ii.191–2)

It seems quite obvious that Winnifride is not in fact referring to Carter
– the accusation would be quite baseless, and there can be no possible
reason for her to want to offend him – but the momentary confusion
does highlight the extent to which fathers are being replaced in this
play, something still further underlined when Carter himself, instead
of Frank's own father Old Thorney, takes the presumably visibly pregnant Winnifride under his wing after Frank's death. In this context,
the phrase 'this father' presents the characters of the play to us not as
creatures who are fixed and static but who might at any moment slip
uncannily into each other's places, just as Mother Sawyer and Cuddy
inhabit similar situations when both play with Tom, and Mother
Sawyer and Winnifride are both faced with the possibility of repentance after a young man (Cuddy, Frank) shows faith in them – a
structural similarity which further works to parallel witchcraft with
sexual behaviour, as again when Cuddy speaks of Kate Carter's charms
as having 'bewitch'd' him (II.i.215).

Once more, then, it seems that we are being specifically invited to see
witchcraft as exposing some uncomfortable truths about society's so-
called verities, and in particular as something which works to prise
apart ideas about 'woman's nature' rather than to confirm its existence.
It is thus particularly ironic that while accusations of actual witchcraft

did such damage to women, representations of fictional witchcraft may well be argued to have been part of the long cultural process which did in the end lead to an improvement in women's status. The real witch of Edmonton was executed, but the play to which she gave her name might prevent so sure a judgement in a future case; after all, many present and future members of the legal profession were regular attenders at the theatre, and a judge who had seen *The Witch of Edmonton* might well prove more sympathetic and enlightened than one who had not. Although *The Witch of Edmonton* initially suggests that literature is even more repressive than law and more likely to reinforce stereotypes than challenge them, it also shows that not all literature need not necessarily do so, since it can equally well work in the opposite direction. In so far as dramatic representations of female heroes in the period chart an increasing move towards liberalism, even these plays dealing with the apparently ultimately repressive influence of the law can be seen as a crucial part of that trajectory.

Who's the crocodile? *The White Devil*

In Webster's painfully learned preface 'To the Reader' at the beginning of *The White Devil*, we have that sadly rare thing in Renaissance drama, an author's comment on his own work. Amongst its other points of incidental interest, such as Webster's description of his admiration for Chapman, Jonson, Beaumont, Fletcher, Shakespeare, Dekker and Heywood (in that order), one thing in particular is strikingly clear: the discourse which the hurt playwright deploys to defend himself against the philistinism which he fears is that of classical learning, with allusions to Greek tragedy – 'I must answer them with that of Euripides to Alcestides' – and copious use of Latin quotations – '*nos haec novimus esse nihil*', '*Nec rhoncos metues, maligniorum, / Nec scombris tunicas, dabis molestas*'. We also hear something of the same technique in the play's first speech of any substance, spoken by Lodovico:

> Ha, ha, O Democritus thy gods
> That govern the whole world! – Courtly reward,
> And punishment! Fortune's a right whore.
> If she give aught, she deals it in small parcels,
> That she may take away all at one swoop.
> This 'tis to have great enemies, God quite them.
> Your wolf no longer seems to be a wolf
> Than when she's hungry.[10]

This speech also, though, enacts in miniature a larger cultural battle, for this is a world in which classical values, although still retaining cultural capital, are clearly revealed as residual rather than dominant, much as the play as a whole is going to stage a battle with more far-reaching implications about the forms and values of different cultures. Within the space of five lines from Lodovico's reference to Democritus, a rather different emphasis has begun to emerge. Instead of the elite men valorised by the classical tradition, such as Euripides and Democritus, some less securely individualised but considerably more menacing figures are beginning to emerge: first the 'whore' Fortune, and then a specifically female wolf. (Wolves will continue to be seen as female in the play when Flamineo later says of Zanche, 'I do love her, just as a man holds a wolf by the ears' [V.i.154–5] and Bracciano opines, 'Woman to man / Is either a god or a wolf' [IV.ii.91–2].) Moreover, while Lodovico laughs Democritus to scorn, the two feminised powers whom he invokes are ones which he cannot dismiss. Lodovico's speech thus sums up in miniature the battle which the whole play enacts between the designated forces of authority and the recalcitrant women who threaten and undercut them.

Lodovico himself is the first to introduce us to the most important of these women, and he does so in a way which proves typical of the strategies of the play as a whole. He rages,

> So, – but I wonder then some great men 'scape
> This banishment. There's Paulo Giordano Orsini,
> The Duke of Bracciano, now lives in Rome,
> And by close pandarism seeks to prostitute
> The honour of Vittoria Corombona –
> Vittoria, she that might have got my pardon
> For one kiss to the duke.
>
> (I.i.38–44)

At the outset of the speech, it is the unnamed 'great men' who are designated as culprits and are the target of Lodovico's wrath; at its close, a mere six lines later, it is Vittoria who, by dint merely of a sin of omission, is to be blamed, much as Bracciano will later deflect all responsibility for his own lust onto Cornelia when he accuses her,

> Uncharitable woman, thy rash tongue
> Hath raised a fearful and prodigious storm.
> Be thou the cause of all ensuing harm.
>
> (I.ii.306–8)

Flamineo too chooses to blame his mother rather than his extravagant father for his present poverty, saying to her, 'I would fain know where lies the mass of wealth / That you have hoarded for my maintenance' (I.ii.311–12). Lodovico here automatically assumes Vittoria's willingness to sleep with Bracciano, and so too does her brother Flamineo, who assures the Duke that 'The fair Vittoria, my happy sister / Shall give you present audience' (I.ii.6–7). Flamineo also silently concurs with Lodovico when he too uses the comfortable, established discourse of proverbs to liken women to animals when he tells Vittoria herself, 'Come sister, darkness hides your blush. Women are like curst dogs: civility keeps them tied all daytime, but they are let loose at midnight; then they do most good or most mischief' (I.ii.199–202).

The cause of this collective cultural rage against women and the feminised is clear, and it is no coincidence that it is against a mother that it is first seen to be directed. Its roots are made particularly apparent when Flamineo says to Vittoria, 'if woman do breed man / She ought to teach him manhood' (V.vi.242–3). A similar anger against the mother is visible in another exchange between the two:

> *Vittoria.*   Ha, are you drunk?
> *Flamineo.*   Yes, yes, with wormwood water. You shall taste
> Some of it presently.
> *Vittoria.*   What intends the fury?
> *Flamineo.*   You are my lord's executrix, and I claim
> Reward for my long service.
>
>   (V.vi.4–8)

Here Flamineo uses a strategy already familiar from *Hamlet*, where the prince declares that *The Mousetrap* is 'wormwood' to his mother and thus, especially in conjunction with the phrase 'treason in the breast', which also occurs in the mousetrap scene, suggests that what actuates him is an Oedipal wish for revenge for the first betrayal of applying wormwood to the nipple to wean the infant.[11] In Webster too, women are traitors, or at least treachery is gendered feminine when Francisco says, 'Treason, like spiders weaving nets for flies, / By her foul work is found, and in it dies' (III.iii.26–7). But even more alarmingly, women are mothers, and in the context of this overall contest for authority and cultural capital they thus emblematise an alternative site of origins to that represented by the patriarchal discourse of the classical past. It is always clear in Webster that it is men who own language, as I shall explore below, but here a woman contests that ownership when

Vittoria terms her brother a 'fury', a mythological monster normally gendered feminine. Flamineo in turn counters this with the bitter taunt of terming her an 'executrix', a word which inherently represents a deviation from the masculine norm of 'executor' – again a reminder of the uneasy and anomalous position of women in the eyes of the law. (There were, of course, no female lawyers.)

Men's ownership of language is certainly made clear in *The White Devil*, although the many references to dead or not universally comprehensible languages such as Latin and Welsh also make it clear that what men own is not any original language of Adam but something which is in itself belated and partial, and which indeed emblematises in its diversity not the gender-based ascendancy of Adam over Eve but the collective sin of mankind in general at Babel, which the King James Bible ascribes to 'the children of men' (Genesis 11:9). Women's words, unlike the collective cultural inheritance of male writers and speakers which is valorised in the forms of apophthegms, the *sententiae* of which Webster is so fond, and allusions, are dismissed: 'So now 'tis ended, like an old wives' story' (IV.i.116). But although it is clear that they are considered to be little better than animals, women are not in this play entirely debarred from using the humanist and humanising discourses of classical learning. Vittoria, whose real-life avatar was a famous Renaissance bluestocking, admits that she herself knows Latin, and her resonantly named mother Cornelia, whose classical namesakes included the wife of Pompey and the mother of the Gracchi, makes her first entrance invoking the classical past, exclaiming

> O that this fair garden
> Had with all poisoned herbs of Thessaly
> At first been planted, made a nursery
> For witchcraft, rather than a burial plot
> For both your honours.
>
> (I.ii.275–9)

When women speak such a language, however, it has rather different resonances from when men do. Cornelia, however innocently, here echoes Medea, suggesting that the discourse of classical learning holds traps for women, and she thus identifies herself with the demonised world of witchcraft, which always lies in wait to catch the transgressive woman.

Similar traps lie in wait elsewhere. When she decides that she herself will take the blame for the rupture of their marital relations, Isabella repeats the very words Bracciano has used to her, but with a difference. He says:

> Your hand I'll kiss, –
> This is the latest ceremony of my love;
> Henceforth I'll never lie with thee, by this,
> This wedding-ring; I'll ne'er more lie with thee.
> And this divorce shall be as truly kept
> As if the judge had doomed it. Fare you well,
> Our sleeps are severed.
>
> (II.i.192–8)

She says:

> Sir, let me borrow of you but one kiss,
> Henceforth I'll never lie with you, by this,
> This wedding-ring.
> *Francisco.*   How? Ne'er more lie with him?
> *Isabella.*   And this divorce shall be as truly kept
> As if in thronged court a thousand ears
> Had heard it and a thousand lawyers' hands
> Sealed to the separation.
>
> (II.i.253–9)

Bracciano figures one impersonal and hypostasised judge, but Isabella's imaginings are both more plural and more physical, as well as infinitely more public: a thousand ears, a thousand hands. Perhaps inevitably, while Bracciano's words are accepted by his appalled hearer as final, Isabella's are immediately dismissed as merely hysterical.

However, Isabella is right in so far as justice does indeed seem to be personal in this play, at least for women. The trial of Vittoria receives such prominence that the scene in which it occurs, III.ii, is assigned a separate heading, 'The Arraignment of Vittoria', a phenomenon of which I know no other instance in Renaissance drama. Gender dynamics are highlighted from the outset of the scene, as Bracciano says, 'An unbidden guest / Should travail as Dutch women go to church: / Bear their stools with them' (III.ii.5–7). Bracciano thus casts women as marginalised and needing to be self-reliant, while at the same time suggesting that their position is *not* an essential byproduct of their gender since he, a man, can inhabit and identify with it. Perhaps

Vittoria does something of the same when she responds to the lawyer's riposte that she understands Latin by saying,

> I do, sir, but amongst this auditory
> Which come to hear my cause, the half or more
> May be ignorant in't.
>
> (III.ii.15–17)

Who might the half of the audience be who are likely not to know Latin? Women seem to be a strong possibility, and if so, Vittoria has performed a rhetorical manoeuvre very similar to that of Bracciano earlier, because while he compared himself with women, she, as one who *can* speak Latin, seems to be implicitly aligning herself with men. The whole scene is thus imbued from the outset with a 'hic mulier' quality which suggests that it is gender roles as a whole which are at stake rather than merely the individual behaviour of Vittoria and of her brothers, who are also nominally in the dock with her – although they are soon abruptly and inexplicably discharged, further showing the extent to which the cards are stacked against a woman in a court.

The first target at whom we seem certainly invited to level disapprobation, however, is not Vittoria but the lawyer, who responds to the instruction to desist from using Latin by launching into the following:

> Most literated judges, please your lordships
> So to connive your judgements to the view
> Of this debauched and diversivolent woman,
> Who such a black concatenation
> Of mischief hath effected, that to extirp
> The memory of't must be the consummation
> Of her and her projections.
>
> (III.ii.26–32)

Even the Duke of Florence finds this *de trop*, and the suggestion is clearly that however morally superior the lawyer may be, he is a far less vital and attractive character than Vittoria, an impression confirmed when Monticelso likens whores to 'those brittle evidences of law / Which forfeit all a wretched man's estate / For leaving out one syllable' (III.ii.89–91), a simile which does at least at much damage to lawyers as to whores. Vittoria, on the other hand, certainly puts up a spirited defence, and does not hesitate to use her enemies' own weapons against them to considerable effect. When Monticelso attempts to tar her by association with the sin of Eve – 'I am resolved / Were there a second paradise to lose / This devil would betray it' (III.ii.68–70) – she ripostes, 'O poor charity! / Thou art seldom found in scarlet' (III.ii.70–1), which both draws on the almost equally strong popular tradition of anticlericalism, particularly when the cleric in question is a Catholic one, and also on the iconographic tradition which valorises the virtue charity and, by gendering it feminine, associates it with women rather than men. She similarly co-opts a mythologico-allegorical persona to shield her when she protests that she is 'So entangled in a cursed accusation, / That my defence, of force like Perseus, / Must personate masculine virtue' (III.ii.134–6). Perseus was indeed male and fought a female monster, the Gorgon, but equally he was defended by another woman, or at least goddess, Athene. All in all, we are surely likely to feel that when Monticelso accuses her 'Such a corrupted trial have you made' (III.ii.260) it is on him that the words rebound, and that Vittoria has a point when she declares 'you have ravished justice, / Forced her to do your pleasure' (III.ii.274–5). Here, moreover, she turns the dynamics of cultural assumptions about gender roles to her own advantage by presenting justice as the feminised victim of male aggression and lust.

This is so not least because her words so clearly echo those of the virtuous Katherine of Aragon in a play very close to this in date, Shakespeare's and Fletcher's *Henry VIII*, to another Cardinal, Wolsey. 'O, good my lord, no Latin!', cries Katherine, and she has earlier said,

> I do believe,
> Induced by potent circumstances, that
> You are mine enemy, and make my challenge
> You shall not be my judge.[12]

Moreover, the stress on Latin, the language of Rome, may well serve to remind us of two potential situational analogues here: first, the story of the woman taken in adultery and Jesus' plea for mercy for her, and second, the trial of Jesus himself before Pilate and the disbelief that attends his protestations of innocence. Perhaps Vittoria is indeed personating masculine virtue and using a more glorious model than Perseus to do so. In any case, these multiple echoes allow us to see clearly the extent to which the role of victim is culturally ascribed rather than inherent.

Certainly co-opting the masculine is women's most useful strategy in this play. Vittoria attempts to do so when she calls Flamineo a 'fury'

(V.vi.6), as if he as much as she is susceptible to the demonising effect of feminised mythological personae, and Cornelia does so too in her lines, '*But keep the wolf far thence, that's foe to men, / For with his nails he'll dig them up agen*' (V.iv.104–5), which undo the earlier insistent equation of women and wolves. It is true that in Flamineo's fable of the crocodile both the bird and the crocodile are gendered feminine:

> The crocodile, which lives in the river Nilus, hath a worm breeds i' th' teeth of 't, which puts it to extreme anguish: a little bird, no bigger than a wren, is barber-surgeon to this crocodile; flies into the jaws of't; picks out the worm; and brings present remedy. The fish, glad of ease but ingrateful to her that did it, that the bird may not talk largely of her abroad for non-payment, closeth her chaps intending to swallow her, and so put her to perpetual silence. But nature loathing such ingratitude, hath arm'd this bird with a quill or prick on the head, top o' th' which wounds the crocodile i' th' mouth; forceth her open her bloody prison; and away flies the pretty tooth-picker from her cruel patient.
>
> (IV.ii.222–35)

However, the double demonisation here in fact undoes itself, since if the crocodile is bad the bird must be good, and it is also part of Flamineo's point that the habitually feminised Nature is here to be seen as a beneficent and provident force. Moreover, Bracciano, neatly exposing the way that Flamineo here is attempting to co-opt the apparently natural for his own strictly material ends, makes it very clear that the applicability of a story lies in the meanings made of it rather than in any which are inherent:

> Your application is, I have not rewarded
> The service you have done me.
> (IV.ii.237–8)

The hypocrisy of Francisco in apprehending the matron of the convertites when the design was his (IV.ii.50–4) has already made it quite clear that blame should not always lie where it is ascribed. Thus by the time we reach Lodovico's accusation

> O the art,
> The modest form of greatness! that do sit
> Like brides at wedding dinners, with their looks turned

> From the least wanton jests, their puling stomach
> Sick of the modesty, when their thoughts are loose,
> Even acting of those hot and lustful sports
> Are to ensue about midnight
>
> (IV.iii.143–9)

we are well equipped to realise that this in fact tells us as much about the describer as about those whom he ostensibly describes, and that language is not ideologically neutral but may be carrying a payload of which we ought to be aware – especially since what has prompted Lodovico's simile denigrating women is actually what he takes to be the disingenousness and scheming of Monticelso.

Within *The White Devil*, however, such awareness of the ways in which language works can be of little avail to women, for ultimately the cards are too much stacked against them. As Flamineo says,

> We lay our souls to pawn to the devil for a little pleasure, and a woman makes the bill of sale. That ever man should marry! For one Hypermnestra that saved her lord and husband, forty-nine of her sisters cut their husbands' throats all in one night. There was a shoal of virtuous horse-leeches.
>
> (V.vi.161–6)

For every one positive story of a woman, there are forty-nine negative. The best that can be hoped for is actually silence:

> Know many glorious women that are famed
> For masculine virtue have been vicious,
> Only a happier silence did betide them
>
> (V.vi.244–6)

Extradiegetically, though, the picture is by no means so bleak, for the very reason that though all the women in the play have been defeated and killed, the audience has been made fully aware of how that has been effected. *The White Devil* shows lies, but it does not tell them.

And who's the witch? *The Witch of Edmonton*

If classical learning proves to be a fruiful source of misogynist ideas in *The White Devil*, reading in *The Witch of Edmonton* has even more pernicious effects. In several of his plays, John Ford represents the operations of both law and literature on the human psyche, and what he seems consistently to show is that while the force of law may be resisted or even subverted, the ideological conditioning effected by literature is indeed a powerful instrument of social control. This is true for many of his characters, but Ford's analyses of the workings of both internal and external modes of coercion are, typically, at their sharpest when he is representing the actions and situations of women. He represents women with great sympathy, consistently allotting to them what his culture as a whole did not, the position of reasoning and well-intentioned participants in his own world of the law. Ford presents women, almost invariably, as trapped – but it is usually not so much by actual facts or events as, initially at least, by expectations and assumptions promulgated by views and stereotypes, often derived from literature, which are shown as prominent in their cultures, and the subtlety of this ideological conditioning is highlighted by being counterpointed with the more obviously coercive mechanisms of the law.

Throughout his adult life, Ford seems to have been associated in some capacity (though precisely what, we cannot now establish) with the law.[13] Although never called to the bar, he seems to have lived throughout his adult life in the Middle Temple; he dedicated some of his works to his cousin and namesake John Ford of Gray's Inn and to other Graians; and he was, on his mother's side, the great-nephew of Elizabeth I's Lord Chief Justice, Sir John Popham, who presided over the trial of Sir Walter Ralegh and who had been held prisoner in Essex House in the early days of the Essex Rebellion. Another relative, Sir John Stradling, from whose translation of Justus Lipsius Ford borrowed,[14] wrote a history of the longstanding legal dispute over the ownership and tenantry rights of the Lower Burrows, Merthyr Mawr; Sir John was also a Member of Parliament, who in 1626 'formed one of the strong deputation sent by the House of Commons to the House of Lords to try to bring the duke of Buckingham to the bar of the house for questioning', and was chosen as one of the party who carried a remonstrance to Charles I after he had forbidden this manoeuvre.[15] Ford is, then, likely to have been both personally and professionally keenly interested and informed about legal matters, and this is reflected in many of his plays.[16]

In his early collaborative play *The Witch of Edmonton*, Ford worked with Dekker and Rowley to turn a real-life crime story into a fictionalised drama, and it is here that the potentially problematic relationship between law and its literary representation is most overtly thematised. The title-page of *The Witch of Edmonton* offers us several very interesting pieces of information about the play. In the first place, we are promised the titillation, usual in domestic tragedy, of knowing that what we are reading is a true story. Rather than any ephemeral piece of hastily written journalism, however, designed to capitalise on the interest of the moment, it has, we are told, been thoroughly shaped by art, since it has been 'composed into a tragicomedy by divers well-esteemed poets'. Emphasis is also placed on its favourable reception – 'Acted by the Princes Servants, often at the Cock-Pit in *Drury-Lane*, once at Court, with singular applause' – and on its novelty – 'never printed till now' – but both these pieces of information are conveyed in small print, and far more striking than cither is the engraving beneath them. This shows three figures who are presumably considered by the engraver to be the most prominent and memorable in the play: Cuddy Banks, Mother Sawyer and the Dog. In line with title-pages' frequent practice of asserting the truth of the story told by the play, all come from the witch-plot, believed to have been handled by Rowley and Dekker and based on the real case of Elizabeth Sawyer, who was executed for witchcraft, rather than from the fictional Frank Thorney section of the play, in which Ford seems to have had a large hand.

At the top left-hand corner is Tom, the talking dog, with a speech balloon containing his opening line of the play, 'Ho have I found thee cursing'; facing him is the witch herself, Mother Sawyer, speaking a line from slightly later in their first scene, 'Sanctabecetur nomen tuum'; and beneath Tom is Cuddy Banks, the clown of the play, floundering in a pond and saying – though with, apparently, considerable phlegm under the circumstances – 'Help help I am Drownd'.

Clearly the clown, the witch and the talking dog are considered to be the major selling points for the play, offering as they do entertainment, novelty, and the *frisson* associated with stage magic. Equally interesting, however, is their arrangement within this scene. Since all of the three moments occur separately in the play, the engraver had only his own artistic instincts to consult. Obviously Mother Sawyer and the Dog should be shown interacting, and probably it is only logical that the water into which Cuddy Banks has fallen should go at the foot of the picture, where it can simply 'fade out' into the frame. Nevertheless, while it may be dictated primarily by considerations of practicality, the arrangement adopted is susceptible of some highly suggestive readings. One thing that is immediately obvious is that the dog is placed directly above the man, subverting the normal hierarchies of the great chain of being, and the control which man was expected to exert over the animals. (Though the 'great chain of being' is now a critically unfashionable idea, I do think that it seems to be suggested here, and also that its invocation further underlines the idea that causality itself works like a chain which has already been suggested in the Argument of the play, and which forms so important a part of the authors' secularised perspective on events.) Moreover, while the Dog's speech shows him at his moment of greatest empowerment – those humans whom he does find cursing fall at once into his control – Cuddy's words are simply ridiculous: he is clearly *not* drowning, since he can speak, and he is, moreover, within a few inches of the bank. (Indeed, in the play itself he has emerged from the pond by the time he speaks this line.) Although it may seem pedantic to insist on so small a point, I do think that Cuddy's speech can in fact be read as an abuse, rather than a use, of language – and it is of course notable that not only does the Dog, unusually, possess the power of speech, but the line given to him in the caption is one which directly addresses uses and abuses of language in its reference to 'cursing', the improper deployment of words.

Between the elevated Dog and the debased man stands the woman. She occupies a middle ground between them, and is placed in opposition to both. Her speech caption is the phrase taught her by the Dog which she must use to summon him, but which she is unable properly to remember and which therefore appears here – in, appropriately enough, a kind of dog-Latin – as 'Sancatabecetur nomen tuum', instead of the correct form of 'Sanctibicetur nomen tuum'. Mother Sawyer may thus be open to mock for her inaccurate Latin, but nevertheless she is shown at a moment of empowerment, as she utters the words which will bring supernatural help to her aid. Above the beast in the great chain of being, but below the man, Mother Sawyer stands poised ambiguously, capable of inspiring both derision and fear – her culture's two most probable reactions to stories of witchcraft in general.

The play as a whole declines to decide between these two alternative responses, choosing instead to confirm this ambiguous treatment of Mother Sawyer. Taking what may, broadly speaking, be perhaps defined as a 'sociological' attitude to witchcraft, it very clearly shows that Mother Sawyer does not even contemplate becoming a witch until she has been repeatedly termed so by her neighbours, who can thus be seen as interpellating her as a passive subject into an ideological framework which must surely bear a large part of the blame for actions in which she is hardly more than a puppet:

And why on me? Why should the envious world
Throw all their scandalous malice upon me?
'Cause I am poor, deform'd and ignorant,
And like a bow buckl'd and bent together
By some more strong in mischiefs than myself?
Must I for that be made a common sink
For all the filth and rubbish of men's tongues
To fall and run into? Some call me witch,
And being ignorant of myself, they go
About to teach me how to be one; urging
That my bad tongue, by their bad usage made so,
Forespeaks their cattle, doth bewitch their corn,
Themselves, their servants, and their babes at nurse.
This they enforce upon me, and in part
Make me to credit it.

                                        (II.i.1–15)

This, our first introduction to her, immediately endows her with the dignity and status associated with soliloquy, and this adoption of a mode of speech primarily found in tragedy is further underlined by some slight but suggestive parallels between *The Witch of Edmonton* and Ford's later single-authored play *Perkin Warbeck*. Both share a character called Warbeck; *Perkin Warbeck* presents Margaret of Burgundy as a witchlike figure who has produced unnatural births; and most strikingly of all, Perkin's apparently completely genuine but totally delusional belief that he is the rightful king of England is clearly foreshadowed here in Mother Sawyer's suggestion that she may be led 'in part ... to credit' what she actually knows not to be true. Both Perkin and Mother Sawyer may be deluded, but they also make the same kinds of claim on our sympathy.

This strange mixture here on Mother Sawyer's part of clear-sighted perception of the precise processes of the social construction of individual subjectivity and simultaneous immersion in those processes comes very close to modern understandings of the workings of ideology and false consciousness. It invites the audience too to a similar awareness of the potentially pernicious role of awareness of the norm in the formation of their own apparently individual judgements; in Viviana Comensoli's formulation, 'the dramatists deliberately discredit supernatural causation by treating witchcraft as a complex social construction'.[17] Moreover, the evil which Mother Sawyer aims to achieve is expressly presented as something external to her rather than integral to her character:

> Would some power, good or bad,
> Instruct me which way I might be reveng'd
> Upon this churl, I'd go out of myself,
> And give this fury leave to dwell within
> This ruin'd cottage ready to fall with age
>
> (II.i.105–9)

'I'd go out of myself'; the words suggest a radical division between soul and body which is confirmed by the image of the body as a 'ruin'd cottage', which makes explicit the idea of the body as merely a form of housing for the soul.

A more unusual emphasis is also introduced here by the clear suggestion that when Mother Sawyer goes out of herself, she does not come back, and instead envisages her mortal frame as being in future tenanted by a being quite separate from herself, for whose actions she would, therefore, be only indirectly responsible. It even sounds as though she could be directly contemplating death; certainly at least a temporary departure from rationality and control must be envisaged, chiming interestingly with her earlier suggestion that she might be about to succumb to a delusion. At this, the last moment before her fateful encounter with the Dog, Mother Sawyer seems clearly to be divorcing self and soul from any future actions which the body may perform, and indeed she seems to be surprised when the Dog suggests otherwise: when he demands that she 'make a deed of gift / Of soul and body to me' she replies, 'Out, alas! / My soul and body?' (II.i.132–4), where we ought perhaps to hear an emphasis on the 'and' to stress the extent to which this contradicts her earlier supposition. Eventually the Dog has to force her to agree, and it is perhaps her sense that her compliance was not voluntary which provides the best explanation for why, even after she has agreed to this, and despite her self-confessed guilt, she dies defiantly proclaiming that 'My conscience / Is settled as it shall be' (V.iii.44–5) and striking a distinct note of piety as she says,

> Have I scarce breath enough to say my prayers,
> And would you force me to spend that in bawling?
> Bear witness, I repent all former evil;
> There is no damned conjuror like the devil.
>
> (V.iii.48–51)

We are therefore more likely to pity Mother Sawyer than to loathe her, and her obvious affection for her familiar the Dog may also move us.

The play, too, raises question marks about the extent of Mother Sawyer's actual guilt: although one of her victims, Anne Ratcliffe, kills herself, even at her execution Mother Sawyer resolutely denies that this was by her intention, and when it is put to her that it must have been the devil who urged Frank Thorney to kill his wife, she replies, 'Who doubts it? But is every devil mine?' (V.iii.28).

That every devil is *not* Mother Sawyer's is something of which the play leaves us in no doubt. The word 'devil' is one which recurs repeatedly, and it is, significantly, used most often to describe the actions or motivations of a human. In the first scene alone, there are three uses of it: Frank Thorney refers to 'The misery of beggary and want, / Two devils that are occasions to enforce / A shameful end' (I.i.18–20); Sir Arthur reproaches Frank that 'the nimble devil / That wanton'd in your blood rebell'd against / All rules of honest duty' (I.i.78–80); and Winnifride, pregnant by Sir Arthur, clandestinely married to Frank, and now resolved to turn honest, begs Sir Arthur, 'I was your devil! oh, be you my saint!' (I.i.218). Driven by lust, shame, need and greed, this is a trio hardly in need of any actual devils to prompt them further. The same analysis of evil as something internal rather than external to humanity is also furthered by Mother Sawyer, who, in a piece of social criticism worthy of King Lear himself, retorts to her judge's admonition of 'Know whom you speak to' with:

> A man. Perhaps no man. Men in gay clothes,
> Whose backs are laden with titles and honours,
> Are within far more crooked than I am,
> And if I be a witch, more witchlike.
>
> (IV.i.88–91)

When she later seems to accept the title of witch, and the scandalised judge demands in outrage 'Is the name of witch so pleasing to thine ear?' (IV.i.102), she goes on:

> A witch? Who is not?
> Hold not that universal name in scorn then.
> What are your painted things in princes' courts,
> Upon whose eyelids lust sits, blowing fires
> To burn men's souls in sensual, hot desires,
> Upon whose naked paps a letcher's thought
> Acts sin in fouler shapes than can be wrought?
>
> (IV.i.104–10)

Nor is it only women she indicts, as she later explains:

> Dare any swear I ever tempted maiden,
> With golden hooks flung at her chastity,
> To come and lose her honour, and being lost
> To pay not a denier for't? Some slaves have done it.
> Men-witches can, without the fangs of law
> Drawing once one drop of blood, put counterfeit pieces
> Away for true gold.
>
> (IV.i.141–7)

It is of course one of the great ironies of the play that this generalised tirade should touch a guilty chord in Sir Arthur, who immediately announces 'By one thing she speaks / I know now she's a witch, and dare no longer / Hold conference with the fury' (IV.i.147–9): her implicit castigation of *him* for a witch serves as proof enough for him that *she* is one. But striking though this is, the audience should not allow it to distract them from the wider implications of Mother Sawyer's speech (nor from the neat irony that her very name 'sawyer' suggests someone who utters saws or truths, though it was also the name of the historical figure on whom she was based rather than an invention of the dramatists'). And indeed the Justice himself can do no more than acknowledge the essential truth of her denunciations when he responds to her tirade with 'Yes, yes, but the law / Casts not an eye on these' (IV.i.120–1), which once again draws a damning distinction between that which is sinful and that which is illegal.

What is perhaps most remarkable about Mother Sawyer's unexpectedly articulate indictments of the society in which she lives is that, although the mouthpiece of a collaboration of male dramatists, she does not share the common early modern strategy of seeking to dislocate blame onto women. Equally obviously, she reads evil as a secular rather than a spiritual phenomenon, and so places still further emphasis on the social construction of the individual. Her analysis in this respect is supported by the events of the play's other plot, which centres on the bigamous wife-murderer Frank Thorney. Although the Dog crosses his path just before he decides to kill Susan, he is already clearly exasperated by her over-fondness, and a man who has already committed bigamy and made plans to flee the country and abandon his wife and his poverty-stricken father might well not stick at murder. Moreover, it is clear that the Dog works rather as an impartial agent in this, since he also appears just before

Frank's sister-in-law discovers the knife which provides the proof of his guilt; and since this revelation eventually leads Frank to genuine repentance and reconciliation, the Dog's action in this respect can indeed be seen as working in the ultimate interests of good. It would certainly not be possible to ascribe all the malice and the wrong-doing in the play to supernatural intervention of any kind, whether by devil or witch, and those who are genuinely pure at heart, like the clown Cuddy Banks, prove to be utterly impervious to all promptings of evil external influence. Both Cuddy and his father are, ultimately, beyond the reach of the Devil.

Guilt in *The Witch of Edmonton* is, then, very difficult to apportion and certainly cannot simply be offloaded onto the potential scapegoat figure of the witch. This is a phenomenon which may well seem to accord with the growing general scepticism about witchcraft which followed on James I's increasing disbelief in it, and on Reginald Scot's debunking of much witchcraft superstition in *The Discoverie of Witchcraft*.[18] In his early manhood James had been convinced of the witchcraft of an old woman who repeated to him the words he had spoken to Anne of Denmark on their wedding night (does Sir Arthur's moment of recognition come suggestively close to this?); later, though, he came increasingly to see 'witches' as harmless old women, dupes and scapegoats, rather than villainesses. The play may well be thought to follow him in this. Guilt cannot simply be attributed to Mother Sawyer or even to the Dog; rather, it is the whole social order, and especially its underpinning by money and by the exchange of women in marriage, which is called into question by the events of the play and the various characters' analyses of them. It is certainly marriage practices, which are so clearly identified throughout Renaissance drama as culturally specific, which sour the relationships between Frank and his father and between Warbeck and Old Carter. Equally, however, we are very directly led to see the inadequacy of the law in recognising the true complexity of situations: the judge is an ass, and Sir Arthur, the presiding magistrate, is at least as guilty as any of those he condemns, as Old Carter does not hesitate to remind him at the close of the play.

Certainly the inhabitants of Edmonton have no great opinion of the law. Mother Sawyer condemns

> The man of law
> Whose honeyed hopes the credulous client draws –
> As bees to tinkling basins – to swarm to him

From his own hive, to work the wax in his –
He is no witch, not he!

(IV.i.131–5)

Shortly after this, she meets her victim Anne Ratcliffe, whom the Dog
at her instigation has driven mad. Anne demands 'Are not you Mother
Sawyer' (IV.i.181–2), but receives the rhyming reply 'No, I am a lawyer'
(IV.i.183). To this Anne responds 'Art thou? I prithee let me scratch
thy face, for thy pen has flay'd off a great many men's skins. You'll
have brave doings in the vacation, for knaves and fools are at variance
in every village. I'll sue Mother Sawyer, and her own sow shall give
evidence against her'(IV.i.184–8). Lawyers, it seems, capitalise on
human misery, living on quarrels, their pens flaying off men's skins;
and when Anne Ratcliffe proposes bringing in a sow as a witness, we
may, perhaps, be meant to remember that lawyers in the Middle Ages
had indeed not shrunk from placing animals in the dock, nor even
from exercising capital punishment on them. For Mother Sawyer, it is
the lawyer who is the true witch.

If this play denounces the law, however, it is arguably equally
negative in its depiction of literature. It does, of course, go to some
trouble on its title-page precisely to claim literary status for itself,
with its references to 'poets' and to 'tragicomedy'; but it is rather
more ambivalent when it comes to its presentation of works other
than itself. Like many works of the late Jacobean theatre, *The Witch
of Edmonton* is extremely self-conscious about its place in a long
dramatic history, and its relationships to the works which precede
it. References to them pepper its lines and its events. The first lines
of the Prologue start by relating this play to another: 'The town of
Edmonton hath lent the stage / A devil and a witch, both in an age',
which refers to the play *The Merry Devil of Edmonton*. Anne Ratcliffe's
eventual suicide through beating out her own brains can perhaps be
compared with the well-known death of Marlowe's Bajazeth, in
Tamburlaine the Great, Part One, and Cuddy Banks promises the Dog
that if he will only reform, 'I think I could prefer you to Moll
Cutpurse' (V.i.164) – subject, of course, of another play by Rowley,
this time in collaboration with Middleton, *The Roaring Girl*. Indeed,
Cuddy's remark is only one of many which are indicative of a considerable knowledge of literature not only on the part of the authors,
but, perhaps more surprisingly, on that of their characters: Cuddy –
himself probably named for a character from folksong, Cloddie Banks
– refers elsewhere to Aesop's *Fables*, which he supposes the Dog to

have read (III.i.106), and recalls *Hamlet* when he is himself forgotten as the hobby-horse,[19] and Mother Sawyer announces in classic Petrarchan terms that 'I am on fire, even in the midst of ice' (V.i.10). Michael Hattaway further suggests that her 'A witch? Who is not?' speech also reinforces the strong sense of literary indebtedness in this play by being 'redolent of the indictment of conspicuous consumption in *The Revenger's Tragedy*'.[20]

Apart from this generalised knowledge, however, there are clear indications that in some at least of the characters' preferred reading matter, witchcraft has figured strongly. Mother Sawyer's own description of herself as 'like a bow buckl'd and bent together' (II.i.4) closely echoes what we are told of Sycorax in *The Tempest*. Anne Ratcliffe when mad exclaims that 'There's a Lancashire hornpipe in my throat' (IV.i.191), indicating, one assumes, familiarity with the story of the Lancashire witches; and Old Banks addresses Mother Sawyer as 'Mother Bumby' (IV.i.200), after the eponymous heroine of Lyly's play (he also calls her Gammer Gurton [IV.i.255]).[21] (Neither of these is a witch, but the casual lumping together of the names suggests that Old Banks is less concerned to differentiate amongst various types of old women than his son Cuddy is about breeds of dog [see IV.i.234–42].) What are we to make of such references? Are they to serve merely to reveal Banks as a relatively educated man? Or should we perhaps remember at this point that Banks is the first person in the play whom we see calling Mother Sawyer a witch, and that his eagerness to do so may perhaps have been in part at least induced by the cast of mind created in him by what he has read? In short, is the man who constructs Mother Sawyer as a witch himself the construct of ideologies which have traversed him all the more potently for being concealed in the relatively palatable form of literature? Perhaps, indeed, *The Witch of Edmonton*, a play which overtly criticises law and celebrates literature, in fact works to expose the fact that literature can merely convey in more subtle and permeating form the same casts of mind of which the characters are suspicious when they see them represented by the more obviously coercive power of the law.[22]

But not all books are bad, and indeed literature which reveals the deceits of literature is already halfway towards working to challenge ideologies instead of reinforce them. This is forcefully suggested in Ford's last play, *The Lady's Trial*. Here, the epilogue continues the conceit of the trial which has been working throughout the play:

The court's on rising. 'Tis too late
To wish the lady in her fate
Of trial now more fortunate.

A verdict in the jury's breast
Will be given up anon at least.
Till then 'tis fit we hope the best.

Else if there can be any stay,
Next sitting without more delay,
We will expect a gentle day.

(243)

'Court', 'trial', 'verdict', 'jury', 'stay' and 'sitting' all work together to suggest that the very experience of theatre may be closely analogous to the methodologies of forensic proceedings, with the audience weighing up and evaluating what passes before them just as the jury does. In his representations of women, literature and law throughout his plays Ford offers explorations of the human psyche that are markedly in tune with our own more modern interests in the workings and formation of ideology on the gendered subject. He shows how powerfully assumptions and conditioning may work to contain and entrap his female characters, but he also encourages his audience, like a jury, to understand and thus to gain an ideological purchase on those constrictions. The best kind of literature can, it seems, work with the fairness and rigour of law, if it can only encourage a properly critical attitude in its audience.

Both *The White Devil* and *The Witch of Edmonton*, then, stage events which they seem to invite us not only to deplore but also to find unjust. At the same time, Webster's virtually obsessive uses of *sententiae* and apophthegms and *The Witch of Edmonton*'s emphasis on the effects of reading both further invite us to consider the ways in which our mental landscapes have been conditioned. Although in both plays the application of the law produces injustice, both plays thus also work on an extradiegetic and metatheatrical level to educate their audiences and work towards a juster society.

4
Women's Souls: *The Duchess of Malfi* and *'Tis Pity She's a Whore*

The intensity of the early seventeenth-century interest in the body by no means precluded an equally eager interest in the soul. Even a work like Robert Burton's *Anatomy of Melancholy*, for all the resonances of the overtly medical underpinnings invoked by its title, postulated the mind as influenced by the body but by no means entirely constituted by it. In John Ford's 1629 tragicomedy *The Lover's Melancholy*, which openly acknowledges its debt to Burton,[1] the physician Corax explicitly denies that the primary cause of melancholy is physiological, or at least avers that it is so only in a highly complex way:

> Melancholy
> Is not as you conceive, indisposition
> Of body, but the mind's disease. So ecstasy,
> Fantastic dotage, madness, phrenzy, rapture
> Of mere imagination, differ partly
> From melancholy, which is briefly this:
> A mere commotion of the mind, o'ercharged
> With fear and sorrow, first begot i'th'brain,
> The seat of reason, and from thence derived
> As suddenly into the heart, the seat
> Of our affection.[2]

Similarly Bacon, also an influence on Ford (who used him as a source for his play *Perkin Warbeck*), argued that

> if any man of weak judgement do conceive that this suffering of the mind from the body doth either question the immortality, or derogate from the sovereignty of the soul, he may be taught in easy

instances, that the infant in the mother's womb is compatible with the mother and yet separable; and the most absolute monarch is sometimes led by his servants and yet without subjection. As for the reciprocal knowledge, which is the operation of the conceits and passions of the mind upon the body, we see all wise physicians, in the prescriptions of their regiments to their patients, do ever consider *accidentia animi* as of great force to further or hinder remedies or recoveries: and more specially it is an inquiry of great depth and worth concerning imagination, how and how far it altereth the body proper of the imaginant.[3]

Scientific interest in the nature of the relationship between the soul and the body was joined from the late 1620s by a markedly pseudo-scientific enquiry into the soul prompted by growing interest in neo-Platonism of Henrietta Maria, queen of Charles I, not to mention her devout Catholicism, which led to a spiritual tone at the court of Charles very different from that which had prevailed in the reign of his father.

It has often been postulated that Ford in particular was heavily influenced by this cult of Platonic love.[4] I have myself argued elsewhere that he was, moreover, personally sympathetic to Catholicism.[5] There are certainly some remarkable facts about his plays. Annabella in *'Tis Pity She's a Whore* behaves just as badly as the female heroes of either *The Changeling* or *Women Beware Women*, and indeed her story is closely modelled on the subplot of the latter, with the motif of incest resurfacing and Bergetto and Poggio clearly reprising the Ward and Sordido. However, unlike either of them, Annabella dies forgiven by a priest and with some distinct imagery of holiness and martyrdom clinging to her. To some extent this unusually lenient treatment of the female hero can perhaps be attributed to the novel phenomenon of the presence at court of a queen afforded respect and indeed devotion by her husband. Equally, however, it can be traced to the simple belief which Corax expounds in *The Lover's Melancholy*, that there is more to the soul than the body. This is also a belief found in Webster, to whom Ford's reuse of clearly Websterian motifs in *The Lover's Melancholy* loudly proclaims a debt almost as great as that to Burton.[6] In *'Tis Pity She's a Whore*, Ford's dramatic borrowings are more obviously from Marlowe and Shakespeare than from Webster, but nevertheless he shares with his more immediate predecessor the fact that both their female heroes, despite each at various times being visibly pregnant in a way that neither of Middleton's ever is, are ultimately defined less by their bodies than by their souls. Moreover, both playwrights underline this fact by a simple but extremely effective device: each borrows a motif from the Mystery plays. In Ford's case, this comes when the pregnant Annabella defies Soranzo's inquisition into the name of her child's father and assures that him an angel fathered her baby. In Webster's, a Mystery framework is less in evidence in *The Duchess of Malfi*, though the phenomenon of the Duchess's voice in a ruined monastic building, so marked a feature of the *English* rather than the Italian landscape, certainly points clearly enough to the post-Reformation confusion which has produced the situation in which, as Flamineo puts it, 'While we look up to heaven we confound / Knowledge with knowledge'.[7] In *The White Devil*, though, it is surely because the situation of Vittoria so closely resembles that of the woman taken in adultery, whom Christ pardons while rebuking the lawyers, that she is allowed so impressive and spirited a defence and that we are so little encouraged to judge her. Here, a deeper mystery than the merely literary forces the master to view all things *sub specie aeternatis*.

'With the skin side inside': *The Duchess of Malfi*

The Duchess of Malfi shares with *The Changeling* a strongly marked image-pattern of closets, wombs, interiors and secrets, but in Webster's play, men have interiors too, and inner nature is not a feminised threat, but an essential part of human make-up, which neither gender should ignore or seek to transcend. *The Duchess of Malfi* can thus be read as recuperating the popular image of women as governed by their bodies, and rehabilitating the fecund woman, by suggesting that bodies are in fact a vital part of all humans' understanding of their own condition, and indeed, paradoxically, a crucial tool and prerequisite for the apprehension of spirituality in ways which come closer to neo-Platonic ideas of ascension from the corporeal to the immanent than to early modern theories of anatomy as destiny. Indeed Maurice Hunt has suggested that the official medical practice of the play is made to seem notably ineffective beside 'the Duchess's acts of healing' and that '[b]y identifying vicious Bosola as a doctor, Webster devalues the medical profession'.[8] Along similar lines, William Kerwin has recently argued that the play is engaged in a deliberate critique of contemporary medical practice and attitudes:

> The play's medical theater displays how claims to ancient and disin-
> terested traditions can cover up base interests ... Webster's play can

help us understand how medical power legitimates itself – the pose of timelessness, similar to some late twentieth-century claims of scientific objectivity, masks the connections between medicine and society. Webster's representations of medicine point toward the configuration in early modern culture of theatrical, political, and medical discourses, and towards the tenuous demonstrations of power upon which the 'professions' often depend.[9]

Webster, Kerwin suggests, sees connections rather than separations between bodies and societies, and he seems to me to see a similar connection between bodies and minds. Women, as examples *par excellence* of creatures situated in the body, thus provide the ideal bridge from the material to the spiritual. Moroever, in what looks like an ironic echoing of the one-sex model, men are posited as essentially similar to women, but reluctant to realise it.

The Duchess of Malfi is a play rich in images of interiors. In his first exchange with Delio, Antonio insistently speaks about the insides of things. He says of Bosola,

> this foul melancholy
> Will poison all his goodness, for – I'll tell you –
> If too immoderate sleep be truly said
> To be an inward rust unto the soul,
> It then doth follow want of action
> Breeds all black malcontents, and their close rearing,
> Like moths in cloth, do hurt for want of wearing.[10]

Antonio's language here centres on inner qualities like goodness, that quintessence of interiority, the soul, the word 'inward' and an image of clothes folded away in a drawer or cupboard. Not only is Antonio thus immediately established as a man whose vision can penetrate past superficial outsides and probe what lies deeper, as when he later says directly to Bosola 'I do understand your inside' (II.i.82), but also we are firmly encouraged to subscribe to a belief in the existence of interiority and to regard it as relevant to this play. This is further underlined when Delio says, 'you promis'd me / To make me the partaker of the natures / Of some of your great courtiers' (I.i.83–5), and the motif of interiority surfaces again in Antonio's assertion that 'as out of the Grecian horse issued many famous princes, so out of brave horsemanship, arise the first sparks of growing resolution, that raise the mind to noble action' (I.i.143–6).

We continue to hear of interiors, as in Delio's bizarre description of Count Malateste, 'He has worn gunpowder in's hollow tooth / For the toothache' (III.ii.13–14), where we are offered a view inside the normally hidden parts of a man's mouth. Offered a ring, Antonio typically probes within it: 'There is a saucy, and ambitious devil / Is dancing in this circle' (I.i.412–13). The Duchess herself becomes, in Antonio's formulation, a sort of paradigmatic interior in which the absolute consonance between inside and outside means that her body functions not only as a window to her soul but also as a mirror:[11] 'Let all sweet ladies break their flatt'ring glasses, / And dress themselves in her' (I.i.204–5). The Duchess certainly shows herself acutely aware of interiors, saying to Cariola 'Leave me: but place thyself behind the arras' (I.i.357) and telling Antonio:

> Sir,
> This goodly roof of yours is too low built,
> I cannot stand upright in't, nor discourse,
> Without I raise it higher: raise yourself,
> Or if you please, my hand to help you: so.
> (I.i.415–19)

She also advises him,

> If you will know where breathes a complete man –
> I speak it without flattery – turn your eyes
> And progress through yourself.
> (I.i.435–7)

To the Duchess, interiors represent safety: 'All discord, without this circumference, / Is only to be pitied, and not fear'd' (I.i.469–70). Indeed she ceases to look outside at all, saying 'I now am blind' (I.i.494) and 'O, let me shroud my blushes in your bosom' (I.i.502). In danger, she flies to Loreto, where the supposed House of the Virgin Mary, said to have been carried there by angels, holds out hope of a reassuring domesticity.

It is therefore completely characteristic of the family formed by the Duchess both that danger should be imaged in terms of the outside, as when Antonio says of his wife in labour that 'She's expos'd / Unto the worst of torture, pain, and fear' (II.ii.66–7), with its telling image of *ex*posure, and that safety should be sought in a retreat to interiors:

Ant. Gentlemen,
We have lost much plate you know; and but this evening
Jewels, to the value of four thousand ducats
Are missing in the duchess' cabinet –
Are the gates shut?
Off. Yes.
Ant. 'Tis the duchess' pleasure
Each officer be lock'd into his chamber
Till the sun-rising; and to send the keys
Of all their chests, and of their outward doors,
Into her bedchamber – she is very sick.

(II.ii.51–9)

Gates, doors and chests must all be shut and locked before either
Antonio or the Duchess can begin to feel secure. Even Cariola
expresses her belief in the sacred inviolability of interiority when she
responds to Antonio's threat to stab her in the mistaken belief that she
has betrayed them to Ferdinand, 'Pray sir, do: and when / That you
have cleft my heart, you shall read there / Mine innocence'
(III.ii.144–6). Even towards the end of the play, Antonio still retains a
touching faith in what can be achieved by an appeal to interiority,
saying to Delio of the Cardinal:

I have got
Private access to his chamber, and intend
To visit him, about the mid of night,
As once his brother did our noble duchess.
It may be that the sudden apprehension
Of danger – for I'll go in mine own shape –
When he shall see it fraught with love and duty,
May draw the poison out of him, and work
A friendly reconcilement

(V.ii.64–72)

The discourse of interiority is not confined to Antonio, however.
Bosola too speaks it; indeed Celia Daileader speaks of him as governed
by a violent 'fantasy of visual penetration'.[12] He talks of 'th' inside of
my heart' (III.ii.302), of graves and cabinets (III.ii.291–6), and mice in
cat's ears (IV.ii.137–9), and often images interiority with a characteristic quirkiness which suggests the extent to which the perceptions of a
person's interior are themselves configured by the psychology of the

person doing the perceiving, thus opening up layers within layers of interiority:

> There was a lady in France, that having had the smallpox, flayed the skin off her face to make it more level; and whereas before she looked like a nutmeg-grater, after she resembled an abortive hedgehog.
>
> (II.i.26–9)

What Bosola wants to probe here, though, are specifically female mysteries and interiors, and indeed the Old Lady concedes, 'It seems you are well acquainted with my closet' (II.i.34). A similar impulse drives his efforts to probe the secrets of the Duchess' most protected interior space, her womb:

> I observe our duchess
> Is sick o'days, she pukes, her stomach seethes,
> The fins of her eyelids look most teeming blue,
> She wanes i' th' cheek, and waxes fat i' th' flank;
> And (contrary to our Italian fashion)
> Wears a loose-body'd gown – there's somewhat in't!
> I have a trick may chance discover it
>
> (II.i.63–9)

There's 'somewhat in't', but what it is defies discovery. The image of seeing into the womb is even more strongly stated shortly subsequently, as Bosola explains:

> A whirlwind strike off these bawd farthingales,
> For, but for that, and the loose-body'd gown,
> I should have discover'd apparently
> The young springal cutting a caper in her belly.
>
> (II.i.148–51)

To his eventual cost, however, Bosola pays no such attention to the contents of his own heart and mind, and thus finds himself led to perform acts which he will ultimately come bitterly to regret. For him, it seems, interiority is a space gendered feminine, and this idea of the sexualised nature of interiority is continued with the tale of the Switzer alleged to have been found in the duchess' chamber with the 'pistol in his cod-piece' (II.ii.36–41), and again with the obvious sexual symbolism of Ferdinand's

> Would I could be one,
> That I might toss her palace 'bout her ears,
> Root up her goodly forests, blast her meads,
> And lay her general territory as waste
> As she hath done her honours.
>
> (II.iv.17–21)

It is richly appropriate, moreover, that it is the lustful Julia's secreting of Bosola in her cabinet (V.ii.217) which leads directly to her death.

Bosola does, however, remember that men have interiors too, even if he neglects his own. He returns the compliment of character analysis paid him by Antonio when he assures the Duchess that the latter was

> a soldier that thought it
> As beastly to know his own value too little
> As devilish to acknowledge it too much:
> Both his virtue and form deserv'd a far better fortune.
> His discourse rather delighted to judge itself, than show itself.
> His breast was fill'd with all perfection,
> And yet it seem'd a private whisp'ring-room,
> It made so little noise of't.
>
> (III.ii.251–8)

Bosola asks 'What thing is in this outward form of man / To be belov'd?' (II.i.45–6), to which the implicit answer is that any cause for such love can therefore only lie in internal qualities. Most importantly, Bosola shares with Antonio a decided interest in the interior make-up of the Duchess' two brothers. Antonio is the first to pronounce on the subject. Delio wishes particularly to be informed of the internal qualities of the Cardinal.

> *Delio.* Now, sir, your promise: what's that cardinal?
> I mean his temper? they say he's a brave fellow,
> Will play his five thousand crowns at tennis, dance,
> Court ladies, and one that hath fought single combats.
> *Ant.* Some such flashes superficially hang on him, for form; but
> observe his inward character: – he is a melancholy churchman; the
> spring in his face is nothing but the engendering of toads
>
> (I.i.152–9)

Delio is careful to qualify his initial query 'what's that cardinal?' with 'I mean his temper', specifically asserting his belief in the possibility of a lack of congruity between inside and outside, and Antonio replies that this is indeed so, both in the Cardinal's case and in that of his brother, Ferdinand, since 'What appears in him mirth, is merely outside' (I.i.170), whereupon Delio offers another striking image of what lies beneath surfaces:

> Then the law to him
> Is like a foul black cobweb to a spider –
> He makes it his dwelling, and a prison
> To entangle those shall feed him.
>   (I.i.177–80)

Later, Bosola too discusses what lurks behind the façades of the Cardinal and his brother:

> I have known many travel far for it, and yet return as arrant knaves as they went forth, because they carried themselves always along with them; – Are you gone? Some fellows, they say, are possessed with the devil, but this great fellow were able to possess the greatest devil, and make him worse.
>   (I.i.42–7)

Bosola's language of interiority, though, has the ultimate effect of leaving Ferdinand's own interior oddly opaque; what we hear is not of how any devil is inside him, but how *he* is inside a devil. Bosola's further elaboration of the Aragonian brothers' character equally fails to illuminate what in fact lies within:

> He, and his brother, are like plum-trees, that grow crooked over standing pools; they are rich, and o'erladen with fruit, but none but crows, pies, and caterpillars feed on them
>   (I.i.49–52)

We see them only from outside; we can only guess at what is emblematised by that crooked growth.

It is in fact richly appropriate that Bosola should fail to convey any real sense of the Aragonian brethren's interiority, for just as he neglects his own inner self and conscience (which is perhaps what disables him in the attempted observation of theirs), so the two brothers themselves do not believe that they have any inner self, and cultivate that which they think also lacks it.[13] Ferdinand exclaims,

> Damn her! that body of hers,
> While that my blood ran pure in't, was more worth
> Than that which thou wouldst comfort, call'd a soul
> (IV.i.121–3)

Earlier, he has told his sister,

> For they whose faces do belie their hearts
> Are witches, ere they arrive at twenty years –
> Ay: and give the devil suck.
> *Duch.* This is terrible good counsel:–
> *Ferd.* Hypocrisy is woven of a fine small thread,
> Subtler than Vulcan's engine: yet, believ't,
> Your darkest actions – nay, your privat'st thoughts –
> Will come to light.
>
> (I.i.309–16)

Ferdinand fiercely resents any idea that the face might not faithfully mirror the heart, but is sure that such a state of affairs could never continue: things cannot be kept hidden. Ferdinand's belief that all interiors can be made transparent is also illustrated in his injunction to Bosola that 'I give you that / To live i' th' court, here; and observe the duchess' (I.i.251–2) because 'this will gain / Access to private lodgings' (I.i.280–1).

The Cardinal, by contrast, does believe that some secrets can be kept, telling his brother 'Be sure you entertain that Bosola / For your intelligence: I would not be seen in't' (I.i.224–5). The Cardinal is also able to parrot the language of interiority, as Julia reveals when she reminds him that

> You told me of a piteous wound i' th' heart,
> And a sick liver, when you woo'd me first,
> And spake like one in physic.
>
> (II.iv.37–9)

But the Cardinal too believes, like Ferdinand, that he can penetrate the secrets of hearts, and women's hearts in particular. He tells Julia, 'You fear / My constancy, because you have approv'd / Those giddy and wild turnings in yourself' (II.iv.10–12). The Cardinal also believes that his own interior qualities can be effectively rendered exterior: 'There is a kind of pity in mine eye, / I'll give it to my handkercher' (II.v.27–8).

As the play progresses, however, it is interiority which returns to haunt both the Aragonian brethren as much as it does Bosola. Ferdinand finds his rage turned strangely inwards when he tells the Cardinal, 'I could kill her now, / In you, or in myself' (II.v.63–4), and his hell is notably characterised in terms of enclosure when he rants,

> I would have their bodies
> Burnt in a coal-pit, with the ventage stopp'd.
> That their curs'd smoke might not ascend to heaven:
> Or dip the sheets they lie in, in pitch or sulphur,
> Wrap them in't, and then light them like a match;
> Or else to boil their bastard to a cullis,
> And give't his lecherous father, to renew
> The sin of his back.
>
> (II.v.66–73)

Onto images of the enclosed pit crowd those of a Thyestean banquet, with the parent monstrously reincorporating the child into the bodily interior from which the infant once originated. Ferdinand continues to think in terms of immuring and imprisoning his sister and her husband:

> And for thee, vile woman,
> If thou do wish thy lecher may grow old
> In thy embracements, I would have thee build
> Such a room for him as our anchorites
> To holier use inhabit: let not the sun
> Shine on him, till he's dead; let dogs and monkeys
> Only converse with him, and such dumb things
> To whom nature denies use to sound his name;
> Do not keep a parquito, lest she learn it.
> If thou do love him, cut out thine own tongue
> Lest it bewray him.
>
> (III.ii.99–109)

Ferdinand not only wishes to condemn Antonio to the inside of a hellish prison, he believes that the Duchess could not sufficiently control her own internally held knowledge to prevent herself giving an external signal of it. (Notably, the interior offered by Ferdinand is the only one which the Duchess ever resists, protesting 'Why should only I / . . . Be cas'd up, like a holy relic?' [III.ii.137–9]).

What Ferdinand actually finds, however, is not only that the horror cannot be thus rendered external and distinct from him, but also that it has taken possession of his own inside, of the interiority which his resolute denial of conscience has led him not even to know that he possessed. Robert Rentoul Reed argues that '[t]he study of Ferdinand appears to be inconsistent primarily because there is no obvious external cause for his obstinate determination that his widowed sister, the duchess, shall never marry again',[14] but it is surely the main point that the cause lies not in any exterior source, but inside Ferdinand himself. Earlier, the Duchess has warned him, 'You violate a sacrament o' th' church / Shall make you howl in hell for 't' (IV.i.39–40), and howl he does indeed, in the private hell of his own interiority:

> In those that are possess'd with't there o'erflows
> Such melancholy humour, they imagine
> Themselves to be transformed into wolves,
> Steal forth to churchyards in the dead of night,
> And dig dead bodies up: as two nights since
> One met the duke, 'bout midnight in a lane
> Behind Saint Mark's church, with the leg of a man
> Upon his shoulder; and he howl'd fearfully;
> Said he was a wolf, only the difference
> Was, a wolf's skin was hairy on the outside,
> His on the inside; bade them take their swords,
> Rip up his flesh, and try
>
> (V.ii.8–19)

Hairy on the inside, Ferdinand pays the price for having ignored his conscience, and for never having thought in terms of the spiritual values expressed by Bosola when he urges his employer to 'Send her a penitential garment to put on / Next to her delicate skin' (IV.i.119–20), which is remembered and inverted here just as the Duchess's prophecy about howling is.[15] And the Cardinal, who has equally neglected his interior, is horrified, in a gloriously pre-Gothic moment of reflective dualism, to find himself staring into it:

> I am puzzled in a question about hell:
> He says, in hell there's one material fire,
> And yet it shall not burn all men alike.
> Lay him by:–how tedious is a guilty conscience!
> When I look into the fish-ponds, in my garden,
> Methinks I see a thing, arm'd with a rake
> That seems to strike at me
>
> (V.v.1–7)

The Cardinal may wish that he could 'Be laid by, and never thought of' (V.v.90), but the balance of the play's evidence does seem to suggest that there actually is an afterlife, because however much the Duchess may lament that the stars do not seem to hear her curses, we are perhaps invited to believe that she has successfully penetrated to the ultimate interior, heaven. When she stirs from her apparent death, she says 'Antonio!', to which Bosola replies, 'Yes, madam, he is living' (IV.ii.350). The 'yes' seems almost to imply that Bosola is answering a question, and if so, the question apparently concerns Antonio. One possible reading of this might perhaps be that the Duchess has discovered that Antonio's spirit is not waiting for her beyond the grave, and has come back to enquire about it.[16] Perhaps, then, there is an afterlife, as is indeed further suggested by the apparent survival of the Duchess' voice and personality in Act V, and if so, neither the Cardinal nor Ferdinand can be expected to prosper in it. Both men have paid the price for ignoring the simple truth eventually learned and expressed by Bosola, that 'I would not change my peace of conscience / For all the wealth of Europe' (IV.ii.350–1), because, as he tells the Duchess:

> Didst thou ever see a lark in a cage? such is the soul in the body: this world is like her little turf of grass, and the heaven o'er our heads, like her looking-glass, only gives us a miserable knowledge of the small compass of our prison.
>
> (IV.iii.128–33)

Bosola by the end has indeed finally plucked out the heart of both brothers, and can at last describe them: 'You have a pair of hearts are hollow graves, / Rotten, and rotting others' (IV.ii.319–20). He himself renounces exterior shows altogether – 'off my painted honour' (IV.ii.36) – just as the Duchess has earlier told him that it is futile to 'wrap thy poison'd pills / In gold and sugar' (IV.i.19–20) because, in the end, it is only the insides that matter.

If this is so, it may, perhaps, help to explain a mystery about the play which has often puzzled scholars. The fact that the play is named after the Duchess leaves us in no doubt that she is its central focus, and yet, violating the norm for a tragic protagonist, she dies in the fourth act. Webster, a painstaking dramatist who is always careful to display his learning and his familiarity with classical culture, must surely have been well aware of the magnitude of his departure from tradition here. The fact that the entire last act unfolds without her has been seen as effectively relegating the Duchess to the status of lesser player, an incidental hero rather than someone whose consciousness, as with Hamlet, is the centre and fundamental condition of the drama which bears her name. And yet of course the Duchess's consciousness does *not* disappear from the play; it merely ceases to possess any form of external wrapping. Her much-fetishised and objectified body may have gone, but her voice and thoughts have not. Throughout the play, men – even Antonio – have sought to classify, describe, box and penetrate her; but she has already hinted at the potential for a radical divorce between external body and internal mind when she tellingly reminds Antonio that she is not 'the figure cut in alabaster / Kneels at my husband's tomb' (I.i.454–5), any more than the wax figures represent the true being of Antonio and her children or than the bodies of Sophonisba or of the Lady of *The Lady's Tragedy* represent the full truths of their being. When the Duchess kneels down to enter the small, enclosed space which she imagines heaven as being, she escapes for ever from the world of exteriors; and the fact that she dies in Act IV rather than Act V thus serves not to marginalise her, but to confirm her status as encapsulation of the ethos of interiority which the play has so energetically propounded. Like Middleton, Webster has centred his tragedy round a mysterious core of nature and instinct emblematised as a woman's womb, but for Webster that space is not a threat, but the only hope for humanity.

The anatomy of love: *'Tis Pity She's a Whore*

The womb also proves crucial in *'Tis Pity She's a Whore*. Throughout his work John Ford shows a pronounced interest in concepts and structures of interiority. *The Lover's Melancholy*, which may perhaps have been Ford's earliest independently written play and was certainly the first to be published, in 1629, centres on the attempts of a variety of those at court, including a doctor, to probe the innermost feelings of their prince, Palador. *The Broken Heart* and *Love's Sacrifice*, both published in the same year as *'Tis Pity She's a Whore*, both focus on emotions which, for a variety of reasons, cannot find open expression in the society of the plays, and although the medical is not neglected, with the breaking of Calantha's heart in particular described in notably physicalised terms, the perspective is predominantly psychological, with the emphasis being above all on the relationship between feeling and speech. In *Perkin Warbeck*, published the following year, the stress is again on the disjunction between public and private and the primacy of affection, and in Ford's two final plays, *The Fancies Chaste and Noble* and *The Lady's Trial*, both tragicomedies, the probing of silence and repression has become so much intensified that we have a highly perverse dramaturgy where the most sensitive and interesting characters are those who have the least to say – an apotheosis of interiority but also one which is inherently unstageable.

'Tis Pity She's a Whore* retains the medicalised perspective on human nature found in Middleton and explored in Ford's own *The Lover's Melancholy*, but by making its doctor Richardetto a self-confessed fake, the play develops the scepticism of *The Duchess of Malfi* into a fully-blown interrogation into the power and origins of claims to knowledge about humanity, with a false doctor and a nervous priest jostling for epistemological authority with a sceptic, Giovanni, a believer, Annabella, and two self-styled experienced observers of people, Putana and Vasques. The whole drama is played out on a human battlefield where we are continually reminded that the common currency of descriptors of the body, words like 'heart' and 'blood', have also a variety of other meanings and resonances, spiritual, affective, and metaphorical, whose connotations may well be the more pertinent and the more urgent,[17] but we are also constantly reminded of the difficulties attendant on knowing whether this is so or not.

Ever since Brian Morris remarked in his introduction to the New Mermaids edition of *'Tis Pity She's a Whore* that 'the word "blood" ... occurs more than thirty times in the course of the play',[18] critical attention has been paid to Ford's complex uses of the term.[19] In terms of sheer frequency, however, there is another word which figures far more prominently than 'blood' in the play, yet which has received much less sustained examination, and that is the verb 'know' and its related forms.[20] 'Know' itself occurs 76 times, 'knowledge' three, 'know 't' six, 'known' four, 'knows' three, 'knew' five and 'know'st' four, giving a total of 101 instances. Such frequency of use should certainly alert us to the fact that knowledge, and indeed epistemology itself, as well as their literal and metaphorical corollaries blindness and ignorance, form an important part of the play's thematic structure. Moreover, 'knowing' words are, as one might expect, not distributed uniformly through the text; they cluster around particular issues, and, very strikingly, demarcate the speech- and thought-patterns of particular characters, most especially Vasques and the Friar. To use John S. Wilks's term for *Doctor Faustus* and *The Atheist's Tragedy*, plays with which *'Tis Pity* shares interests in incest and in atheism, this is 'a tragedy of knowledge',[21] whose incestuous love-story proves a site for the exploration of some of the key discourses of Renaissance knowledges and their demarcations and is, most importantly for my purposes, centrally concerned not only with knowledge about gender but also with the gendering of ways of knowing. As Bruce Boehrer argues, 'Ford drew the intellectual conflict of *'Tis Pity* from the very issues that were beginning to distinguish modern European society from its medieval origins',[22] and he dramatised it in ways which tapped into the most urgent of contemporary issues of consciousness and epistemology.

One repeated feature of Ford's use of 'knowing' words is, as so often in Renaissance drama, a sustained pun on the idea of 'carnal knowledge'. *'Tis Pity She's a Whore* very obviously derives much of its source material from a reworking of *Romeo and Juliet*,[23] but there is a striking difference in the presentation of the two main characters and those who surround them: instead of a nurse, a figure who serves overtly to link Juliet with the childhood comforts she leaves behind during the course of her story, Annabella is attended by a 'tut'ress'. The female servant whose role is explicitly referred to as an educational one is a rare phenomenon in Renaissance drama, and serves further to underline the idea of the importance and imparting of knowledge. Ironically, however, this particular 'tut'ress', the ominously named Putana (meaning 'whore'), proves disconcertingly like Juliet's nurse in her farmyard morality. What she teaches Annabella is nothing more than a radically debased view of human sexuality, and it implicitly serves as a shocking indictment of the ideas which we must assume to have informed Florio's choice of her as a guardian for his daughter (in marked contrast to the extensive education at Bologna that has been provided for Giovanni), since Florio's assumption seems to have been that all women need to know is sex and that women even of the Renaissance need know no more than the members of the generation which preceded them. Putana's eventual punishment for her misleading of her charge is a fitting one: like Oedipus and like Gloucester, she pays the price for her sexual sin by forfeiting her eyes. 'Knowing' what one should not and being ignorant of what one should know are rewarded by a blindness which, in Putana's case, proves to be a literal, not a redemptive one – no 'cloud of unknowing' but a state of terrifying vulnerability and disempowerment in which she can be led unresisting to her death.

The specifically sexual nature of Putana's knowledge is amply illustrated. In her summing up of Annabella's suitors, she describes Soranzo as 'liberal, that I know; loving, that you know' (I.ii.91–2), which directly links knowledge both with felt experience and, explicitly, with love. Moreover, unlike Juliet's nurse, Putana is never said to have had a husband and child of her own, yet she can demand indignantly of Giovanni, 'How do I know't? Am I at these years ignorant what the meanings of qualms and water-pangs be?' (III.iii.10–11).[24] And she is finally indicted by her own half-boast to Vasques, 'I know a little, Vasques' (IV.iii.195), in a context charged with knowing sexuality not only by the explicit fact that it is the father of Annabella's child who is under discussion but by the possibility of an all/awl pun in Vasques' expression of his wish that Annabella would reveal its paternity: 'Well, I could wish she would in plain terms tell all' (IV.iii.188–9).

Other characters also make the link between loving and knowing. Giovanni does so repeatedly. Of his eight uses of 'know', one of 'knew', four of 'know't' and two of 'know'st' (giving an overall total of fifteen), several hover around the love/knowledge pun. ''Tis not, I know, / My lust, but 'tis my fate that leads me on', he says at I.ii.153–4. The statement is in various ways a highly dubious one. Giovanni is always anxious to allocate responsibility for his own actions to fate; here his rationale seems especially suspect, since our awareness of the habitual secondary meaning of the word 'know' serves merely to reinforce the suggestion of lust. Later, when Annabella, showing him the jewel given her by Donado and playfully terming its donor 'a lusty youth' (II.vi.127), asks him if he is jealous, he replies:

> That you shall know anon, at better leisure.
> Welcome, sweet night! The evening crowns the day.
> (II.vi.131–2)

The evening crowns the day, presumably, because it brings with it the promise of sexual activity, which is what will make the night sweet; what Annabella will know, then, is carnal knowledge.

The same idea recurs when Giovanni is reproaching her for her altered attitude in V.v:

What, changed so soon? Hath your new sprightly lord
Found out a trick in night-games more than we
Could know in our simplicity?

(V.v.1–3)

It even colours his passionate defence of their actions:

If ever after-times should hear
Of our fast-knit affections, though perhaps
The laws of conscience and of civil use
May justly blame us, yet when they but know
Our loves, that love will wipe away that rigour
Which would in other incests be abhorred.

(V.v.68–73)

But others can of course precisely not 'know' the love of Giovanni and
Annabella in the sense in which Giovanni customarily employs the
word; such knowledge can only be directly experiential, not vicarious.
The terms on which Giovanni has previously predicated the acquisition of knowledge must make it for ever incommunicable.

A literal inability to communicate marks Giovanni's penultimate use
of the word 'know':

Yes, father; and that times to come may know
How as my fate I honoured my revenge,
List, father, to your ears I will yield up
How much I have deserved to be your son.

(V.vi.36–9)

What does this mean? The abstract nouns 'fate' and 'revenge' serve, as
so often in Ford,[25] to dissipate the sense of direct and unambiguous
meaning, nor is the tone clear: what effect does Giovanni intend to
produce upon his father by apparently explaining his horrific actions
in terms of 'how much I have deserved to be your son'? It is at least
arguable that Giovanni is in fact mad here – functioning under the
clearly mistaken belief that it is possible to identify a person by their
heart, and using words and phrases in a similarly idiosyncratic and
ideolectal manner.[26] His final use of the word 'know' certainly reveals
an odd kind of logic:

> For nine months' space in secret I enjoyed
> Sweet Annabella's sheets; nine months I lived
> A happy monarch of her heart and her.
> Soranzo, thou know'st this; thy paler cheek
> Bears the confounding print of thy disgrace,
> For her too fruitful womb too soon bewrayed
> The happy passage of our stol'n delights,
> And made her mother to a child unborn.
>
> (V.vi.44–51)

Soranzo's knowledge here is, once again, envisaged by Giovanni as having an essentially physical basis. Manifesting itself in the bodily sign of the pale cheek, what Soranzo 'knows' seems to be profoundly connected with what is 'bewrayed' by Annabella's womb, which Giovanni has himself so recently 'ploughed up' (V.vi.32).

Giovanni's own need to uncover the secrets of Annabella's womb by direct contact with it raises the whole issue of what Luke Wilson has called 'the problem of knowledge about the inside of the body',[27] and a more rarely dissected female body at that. This may well be seen as lending a similarly experiential colouring to Giovanni's use of 'know' here, as it perhaps did to his earlier demand to Putana, 'With child? How dost thou know't?' (III.iii.9); Giovanni in his quest for knowledge will violate not only the traditionally female, private space of the birth chamber,[28] but the secrets of the womb itself, making of himself 'a tragicall midwife'.[29] His act echoes and ironically inverts our first glimpse of Hippolita, who enters, as Nathaniel Strout points out, 'having forced her way into her lover Soranzo's private room';[30] both stand as desperate attempts to find out what is hidden inside, and indeed William Dyer refers to Giovanni's treatment of his sister as 'his nine-month pursuit of interiority'.[31] Both violations of space may, moreover, remind us that Ford had both family and literary links to the history of St Carlo Borromeo,[32] whose invention of the confession box, apparently intended originally only for women, can be argued to have performed an analogous function of serving to demarcate sexual knowledge as an area of investigation.[33]

The question of knowledge of God does indeed bulk almost as large in the play as knowledge of love. Giovanni presents himself as absolutely confident of his own knowledge, rooted as it is in his physical experiences. An impression of far less certainty is conveyed by the Friar's very different pattern of usage of words denoting knowledge, which indeed brings him very much into line with what John Wilks has called the 'epistemological uncertainty' of Ford's own non-dramatic writing.[34] The Friar is responsible for two of the three uses of the word 'knowledge' in the play (and also, at I.i.75, for an occurrence of its near-homonym 'acknowledge'). To the Friar – appropriately given his recent position at Bologna – knowledge appears to be an absolute, unquestionable good; and yet his actual use of the words 'know' and 'knowledge' often works to undercut the very certainties he apparently articulates. His first use of 'knowledge' has him crying:

> O Giovanni, hast thou left the schools
> Of knowledge to converse with lust and death?
> (I.i.57–8)

Here the proximity of 'knowledge' to 'lust' threatens to pull the word in precisely the direction so markedly favoured by Giovanni, tending to merge the two rather than sustaining the opposition ostensibly created between them. The Friar's second use of the word destabilises it even further, as he stigmatises Giovanni's reasoning as 'O ignorance in knowledge' (II.v.27). Here knowledge is not an absolute at all, but something that can, with alarming rapidity, be seen to contain its own opposite.[35]

Even more striking is the fact that during the entire scene in which the Friar convinces Annabella to marry Soranzo he uses the word 'know' only once, and then not in connection with the heavenly things of which he is presumed to have special knowledge, but, with apparent perversity, in relation to the secular:

> Sigh not; I know the baits of sin
> Are hard to leave. O, 'tis a death to do't.
> (III.vi.39–40)

When it comes to hell and heaven, the Friar claims no knowledge; when it comes to 'the baits of sin' from which he seeks to dissuade Annabella, he does. The Friar is in fact remarkably reluctant to claim knowledge in his own sphere, and Ford, whatever the precise nature of his involvement with the law may have been,[36] will certainly have been well aware of the important legal distinction between what is within one's own personal knowledge and what is merely hearsay,[37] and thus of the fact that when the Friar does in fact claim knowledge he is actually merely relying on hearsay. The Friar uses 'know' only three times in the play, 'knowledge' twice, and 'known' once.

Moreover, two of these uses are actually within the specific context of denying or refusing knowledge:

> I must not stay
> To know thy fall; back to Bononia I
> With speed will haste, and shun this coming blow.
> Parma, farewell; would I had never known thee,
> Or aught of thine.
>
> (V.iii.65–9)

This reluctance to know is prefigured in his opening speech:

> Dispute no more in this, for know, young man,
> These are no school-points; nice philosophy
> May tolerate unlikely arguments,
> But Heaven admits no jest: wits that presumed
> On wit too much, by striving how to prove
> There was no God, with foolish grounds of art,
> Discovered first the nearest way to hell,
> And filled the world with devilish atheism.
> Such questions, youth, are fond; for better 'tis
> To bless the sun than reason why it shines;
> Yet He thou talk'st of is above the sun.
> No more; I may not hear it.
>
> (I.i.1–12)

For all the Friar's official status as educator, this entire speech is imbued with an aesthetic and indeed an ethic of ignorance; all that can be known is that it is better not to know, and beyond this it is better not to hear. The whole effect is reinforced by the condescension of the 'young man' which disables Giovanni's entire perspective by suggesting accumulated (although presumably strictly circumscribed) experience rather than ratiocination as the appropriate basis for knowledge. It is of course ironic that the speech's obvious allusion to Marlowe, most famous of the 'wits who presumed',[38] issues the audience with an appeal to their own knowledge, to be used in spotting and applying the reference. To have the Friar by definition deaf to this metatheatrical level on which his words operate underlines his willed blindness; at the same time, however, the choice of the verb 'discovered', with its suggestion of inappropriate revelation, may prompt us towards an application of the Marlowe story which would at least in part endorse the Friar's perspective on it.

A similar desire not to know powers the Friar's admonition to Giovanni in II.v:

> Peace. Thou hast told a tale, whose every word
> Threatens eternal slaughter to the soul.
> I'm sorry I have heard it; would mine ears
> Had been one minute deaf, before the hour
> That thou cam'st to me.
>
> (II.v.1–5)

Here it is not only Giovanni's actual deeds but his very words which are seen as having the power to defile, and the Friar ends his gesture of recoil by a wish for deafness which provides a clear counterpart to the literal blindness eventually inflicted on his educative counterpart, Putana. It is gloriously ironic that one of the very few occasions on which the Friar does assume knowledge and pronounce with certainty should be such a ludicrous one: he pontificates that 'that marriage seldom's good, / Where the bride-banquet so begins in blood' (IV.i.109–10), asserting a wide experience of bloody bride-banquets which neither he nor very many other people can seriously be expected to possess.

Ironically, Friar Bonaventura's name echoes that of the famous Franciscan author of the *Lignum Vitae*, and thus works to associate him with the pronounced Franciscan interest in epistemology: as Charles Harrison observes, 'at its origins, the Franciscan movement had what we might now consider a revolutionary character, and revolutions produce changes in knowledge and in thought, notably about the nature of human relations and about the determining conditions of human life'.[39] The possibility of a deliberate allusion to St Bonaventure here is enhanced by the fact that in Whetstone's *An Heptameron of Civill Discourses* a Monsieur Bergetto, who bears the same name as the foolish ward of Ford's play, reports a tale set '[i]n a little village among the Apennine mountaines, not far from the place where S. Fraunces lieth intombed'. (Whetstone also features a character called Soranso, the name of Annabella's husband.)[40] Faustus, transgressing in ways notably similar to the modes of Giovanni's rebellion, had specifically requested that Mephostophilis should appear in the robes of a Franciscan friar; perhaps, if the stage image of Giovanni with Friar Bonaventura may recall that of Faustus and Mephostophilis, the cagey nature of Friar Bonaventura's proselytising may similarly echo Mephostophilis's question-begging, niggardly imparting of information on things celestial. Both Friar Bonaventura and Mephostophilis, however, stand in sharp contrast to the questioning spirit of Franciscan thought, and both, too, insert into their respective plays a reminder of the anti-materialist commitment of the Franciscans which sharply critiques the worldly values which so many of the characters espouse. Moreover, an allusion to St Bonaventure becomes a particularly pointed one in a play about incest, since his model of a harmonious relationship between God and the soul was one which a recent critic has termed 'spritually incestuous'.[41]

There is also a striking contrast between the Friar's own reticence about his authority and the evidence for popular Christian beliefs and practices which we see in the play, and to which the Franciscans as an order were traditionally sympathetic. When the Friar expounds his vision of hell to Annabella, he prefaces it with the injunction, 'weep faster yet, / Whiles I do read a lecture' (III.vi.5–6). To call it a 'lecture', and to stress its status as something which he reads, deliberately situates it within the realm of human, book-based knowledge rather than of divine wisdom, something which is underlined by the existence of copious literary antecedents for the picture he paints. Giovanni adopts exactly the same position when he speculates on the after-life: 'The schoolmen teach that all this globe of earth / Shall be consumed to ashes in a minute' (V.v.30–1). Annabella, however, has no such qualms about authority: she replies to her brother's questions with 'That's most certain' (V.v.35), and 'For certain' (V.v.38). The lack of experiential basis for her claim to knowledge seems sharply underlined when she eventually acknowledges that she has reached its limits:[42]

> *Giovanni.*   But d'ee think
>   That I shall see you there? – You look on me?
>   May we kiss one another, prate or laugh,
>   Or do as we do here?
> *Annabella.*   I know not that.
>
>   (V.v.38–41)

Here 'know' seems once again to flirt with its habitual sexual meaning; Annabella disclaims knowledge of kissing or laughing not only in the abstract but, presumably, in the present, because the entire scene seems to be unfolding in the aftermath of her implied refusal to resume sexual relations with her brother. For all that Annabella and Giovanni enter 'lying on a bed' (V.v.s.d.), Giovanni's opening accusation 'What, changed so soon?' (V.v.1) appears to leave little doubt that relations between them have dramatically altered. The resulting emotional dynamic charges the whole scene with a particularly forceful sense of the connections between 'knowing' and carnally knowing.

As in this scene, Annabella, unlike the Friar, is generally characterised by a remarkable confidence in her own knowledge, and her uses of the word knowledge and its cognates tend to be tellingly nuanced by ideas of faith and belief. There is a suggestive exchange with Soranzo which plays with precisely such ideas:

> *Soranzo.*   Do you not know
>   What I should tell you?
> *Annabella.*   Yes, you'll say you love me.
> *Soranzo.* And I'll swear it, too; will you believe it?
> *Annabella.* 'Tis no point of faith.
>
> (III.ii.15–18)

When Giovanni, about to broach his passion to her, says 'I think you love me, sister' (I.ii.182), she replies unhesitatingly, 'Yes, you know I do' (I.ii.183), and Giovanni concedes 'I know't indeed' (I.ii.184). Annabella can feel sure even of what other people know; she disables Giovanni's claim to 'thought' by the counter-assertion that the idea of her love is not a product of his own ratiocination but a pre-existing absolute to which he merely has access. A similar distinction underlines her notable defiance of Soranzo, which tellingly reprises and inverts their earlier exchange:

> *Annabella.*   Alas, alas, there's all.
>   Will you believe?
> *Soranzo.*   What?
> *Annabella.*   You shall never know.
>
> (IV.iii.50–1)

Immediately before this Annabella has announced to her husband that 'This noble creature was in every part / So angel-like, so glorious' (IV.iii.36–7), and taunted him:

> Let it suffice that you shall have the glory
> To father what so brave a father got.
>
> (IV.iii.44–5)

The idea of 'glory', the suggestion that there is merit attached merely to being perceived as the father of this mysteriously begotten infant, and above all the resonant appellation of 'angel' all serve to invest the scene with parodic echoes of the traditional Mystery Play revelation of the divine responsibility for the pre-marital pregnancy of Mary and the unworthy nature of Joseph's suspicions;[43] and the idea is reinforced when Annabella sings '*Morendo in gratia Dei, morirei senza dolore*' (IV.iii.63) ('Dying in the grace of God, I shall die without pain').

In such a context Annabella's juggling of the twin poles of knowledge and belief becomes doubly charged. What she actually says is ambivalent in its meaning. Soranzo's 'What?' interrupts the syntax of her sentence and makes it ultimately unclear whether the verb 'believe' is to be taken as transitive or intransitive. Soranzo's questioning 'What?' could be meant completely literally, as requesting clarification of the object of 'believe', and this could be precisely what he is offered in the second half of the sentence: Annabella wants him to believe that he will never know, that is, to accept that his hounding of her is futile since she will never tell him the name of her child's father. Equally, though, the sentence seems to set up a powerful opposition between knowing and believing which makes one more than merely the object of the other, and this takes on a particular force if it is read within the template of Annabella as an analogue of Mary, possessed of special, divinely imparted knowledge, and Soranzo as the ignorant Joseph from whom an act of faith is required. With her customary certainty, Annabella denies absolutely the possibility of Soranzo ever possessing her own knowledge, but she does offer him the alternative position of belief – the same sort of belief that will later characterise her own attitude in her exchange with Giovanni about the afterlife. What would remain unclear in this second reading is *what* Soranzo is invited to believe, unless he is being recommended to the blindest of faiths. Earlier, Annabella has told him, with a strange mixture of insult and seeming ingenuousness, 'Would you be patient yet, and hide your shame, / I'd see whether I could love you' (IV.iii.24–5); she could be seen as extending a similar sort of invitation here, offering fidelity in exchange for faith. Alternatively, the religious connotations of the preceding section of the dialogue might spill over to invite a Christian approach of forgiveness from Soranzo, though either of these interpretations might well seem subject to the charge of strain. Ultimately, the only person who can ever be fully confident of Annabella's meaning is herself, since she seems to be guided throughout by an absolute confidence in her own ability to control the hermeneutics of her pregnancy.[44] To this extent, at least, the Friar's distrust of knowledge seems justified, since Annabella, who has had so much less formal education than her brother, has so markedly greater a spiritual certainty than he.

The other character in the play who displays a notably high level of confidence in his own knowledge is Vasques. Indeed, in terms of the depiction of knowledge and igorance, Vasques and the Friar emerge as the structural poles of the play, situated at precisely opposite extremes. Whereas the Friar, an ostensible authority-figure, utters only six of the play's 101 uses of 'know' and its derivatives, Vasques is responsible for 23. Admittedly, he has a larger part: of the play's total of 2,281 lines, Vasques speaks 296 and the Friar 181 (figures which are complicated by the fact that all Vasques' lines are in prose, and may therefore be either significantly longer or significantly shorter than an iambic pentameter, and all the Friar's are in verse). Nevertheless, the discrepancy seems to me striking, and it may well be taken as telling that the society of Parma is one in which a servant – albeit a Spanish one, and thus a member of the group which was, at the time when Ford wrote, effectively colonising much of Italy – feels more epistemologically secure than an honoured representative of the state-sponsored religious system.

Unburdened by worries about the status of knowledge, Vasques is far more concerned with its functions. When he is speaking to Putana, he represents knowledge not as an absolute, but as a transitory object of gratification, at least for Soranzo:

> I durst be sworn, all his madness is for that she will not confess whose 'tis, which he will know, and when he doth know it, I am so well acquainted with his humour, that he will forget all straight. Well, I could wish she would in plain terms tell all, for that's the way indeed.
>
> (IV.iii.185–9)

For the Friar, to know is to be irrevocably tainted; for Vasques, though, knowledge is not a permanent enlightenment but a temporary acquisition, a process that is valued for its own sake rather than for what it represents. It is interesting to plot Vasques' trajectory through the play in these terms. Seeing through Hippolyta, suspecting Annabella, anticipating Giovanni, Vasques is 'knowing' indeed, and his confidence in his own knowledge may well seem justified when he departs the play alive, unpunished, and with an exit line which expresses nothing but self-satisfaction: ''Tis well; this conquest is mine, and I rejoice that a Spaniard outwent an Italian in revenge' (V.vi.146–7). The Friar leaves in order that he may *not* know; Vasques stays until he is in full possession of all the facts so that he shares with the audience the possession of narrative satisfaction at least, even if events have not unfolded entirely in accordance with his wishes.

A similarly functional attitude to knowledge is shared with Vasques by the man who pardons him, the Cardinal. Unlike the Friar, the Cardinal is not at all hesitant to lay claim to authority on the basis of knowledge, though like the Friar, he ironically does so largely in secular matters. When Grimaldi is pursued to his door, there is an enactment of the pursuit of knowledge, too, to its borders. Ignorance of a variety of things is the keystone of the Cardinal's counter-charges against Grimaldi's accusers:

> Why, how now, friends! What saucy mates are you
> That know nor duty nor civility?
> Are we a person fit to be your host,
> Or is our house become your common inn,
> To beat our doors at pleasure? What such haste
> Is yours as that it cannot wait fit times?
> Are you the masters of this commonwealth,
> And know no more discretion?
>
> (III.ix.28–35)

Passing on after this disabling preamble to the substance of their complaint, he is able to dismiss it slickly on the grounds of his own superior knowledge:

> you have lost a nephew,
> Donado, last night by Grimaldi slain:
> Is that your business? Well, sir, we have knowledge on't.
> Let that suffice.
>
> (III.ix.36–9)

And he continues to harp on the theme when he warns them:

> know, as nuncio from the Pope,
> For this offence I here receive Grimaldi
> Into his holiness' protection.
>
> (III.ix.52–4)

The ambiguity of the syntax here serves only too clearly to point up that it is the sub-text rather than the text which is important: the abrupt imperative 'know' is empowered by its immediate proximity to the declaration of the Cardinal's status as 'nuncio from the Pope', while the initial placing of 'For this offence' provocatively invites a reading in which Grimaldi is afforded protection *because* he has committed the offence, with the murder acting as positive stimulus for papal interest rather than merely rendering it necessary. It is hardly surprising that the Cardinal should conclude his dismissal with the injunction 'learn more wit, for shame' (III.ix.59): when 'wit' – a part of the process of cognition itself – is seen as the object of 'learning', rather than any specific piece of information, it becomes quite clear that, as in Vasques' epistemological model, what is important is not the subject of knowledge but the politics of its processes.

A similar awareness imbues the comical exchange between Donado, Bergetto and Florio:

> *Florio.*   Sure 'twas the doctor's niece, that was last day with us here.
> *Bergetto.*   'Twas she, 'twas she.
> *Donado.*   How do you know that, simplicity?
> *Bergetto.*   Why, does not he say so? If I should have said no, I should have given him the lie, uncle, and so have deserved a dry beating again; I'll none of that.
>
> (II.vi.96–101)

Bergetto may be simple, but he is wise enough to realise that what he needs to know is the social and political origin of any claim to knowledge rather than the veracity of its content. Donado's oxymoronic coupling of knowledge and simplicity serves to reinforce our sense of the lack of wisdom that may be entailed in society's privileging of the status of the knower over the status of what is known, while Bergetto's blunt reference to a 'dry beating' merely offers a simple statement of the power relations governing knowledge which are expressed so much more knowingly by the Cardinal. Moreover, the phrase 'dry beating', not suggested by anything in the preceding dialogue, may well recall the phrase 'dry basting', used in *The Comedy of Errors* by Dromio of Syracuse to his master during a long discussion of the whys, wherefores, rhymes and reasons of a beating which, as the audience know, was actually administered on the basis of a mistaken identity and as an apparently natural effect of the power-relation between the two.[45]

The inescapability of politics is something which Ford himself underlines when he gives the Cardinal the closing speech of the play and allows that final dismissive summing-up, ''tis pity she's a whore', to stand as his own title. Although the greater part of the play has been concerned with the domestic affairs of Parma, the dramatist shows himself acutely aware that however peripheral the Cardinal may be to the events of the plot, his social position is enough to ensure that though his experiences may correlate only indirectly with those of the rest of the characters, the language in which he chooses to describe events will always be what passes for the normative and formative. The Cardinal is also allowed to dispense justice on Putana,[46] and chooses a punishment which seems to label her crime as witchcraft when he decrees that she shall be burned to ashes.[47] His epistemological counterpart Vasques, has, however, perhaps acted more judiciously when, on his own initiative, he inflicted on Putana the traditional mythological punishment for inappropriate and particularly sexual knowledge, the blinding which was the fate of Gloucester and the choice of Oedipus.[48] Oedipus is a figure with whom Orgilus in Ford's *The Broken Heart* explicitly compares himself – 'Dark sentences are for Apollo's priests; / I am not Oedipus'[49] (an allusion picked up in the 1994–5 Stratford-upon-Avon production by making Tecnicus blind) – and the connection here is made particularly potent in the terms of Vasques' instruction, 'You shall know presently. Come sirs, take me this old damnable hag, gag her instantly, and put out her eyes' (IV.iii.224–5). With its obvious literal and symbolic links to the processes and politics of knowing, this literal disablement also bodies forth the symbolic disabling strategies which have punctuated the attempts of the Friar and the Cardinal to maintain control over knowledge, and thus serves to align the Cardinal with his religious *confrère* as well as with Vasques. Such a doubling of doublings serves as a powerful emblem for the radical instability with which Ford has imbued his complex depictions of knowledge, its cognitive mechanisms and its social meanings. If we agree with Giovanni, we are forced to recognise that our own responses to the play must always be devalued because of our merely vicarious experience of it; if we agree with the Friar, we may well conclude that the very act of viewing the story has been an essentially corrupting one, and that vicarious experience, far from being insufficient, is therefore in itself too much. Paradoxically, the perspective we are most likely to adopt is in fact that shared by the two characters whom we may well like the least, the Cardinal and Vasques, whose awareness of the uses of knowledge we are surely likely to share.

As our 'discovery' of that initial allusion to Marlowe suggests, a play which concentrates so much on dramatisation of the dangers of knowledge never ceases to remind us that we are always already implicated in it.[50]

And yet for all this highly sophisticated, complex, self-conscious meditation on epistemology, the play also shows up that the entire paraphernalia of the processes and politics of cognition can be simply side-stepped and shortcircuited by Annabella and also, to a lesser but no means insignificant extent, by Philotis. Though they may know nothing but how to make marmalade and play instruments (a skill which almost invariably has bawdy connotations on the Renaissance stage), both these women nevertheless end the play spiritually whole, and are indeed, apart from the equally untutored Bergetto, the only characters who unequivocally do so. Philotis, who has not sinned at all, departs in safety for a convent, and Annabella, who has, is so far absolved by her conversation with the Friar and her simple faith in him that she is allowed once again to inhabit the symbolically significant region of the upper stage from which her love for Giovanni had initially banished her. Once again, women seem to be afforded a privileged access to a secure and interior realm to which men find it much more difficult to enter, not, this time, because they ignore it, but because they have attempted to construct an over-elaborate route to it. In both *The Duchess of Malfi* and *'Tis Pity She's a Whore*, then, women remain associated with nature, but that association is triumphantly vindicated and redeemed because it also gives them a closer connection not only with the body but also, far more importantly, with the soul.

5
Women and History: *The Tragedy of Mariam, The Broken Heart* and *The Concealed Fancies*

The death of Elizabeth I on 24 March 1603, and the subsequent accession of James of Scotland, prompted many reflections not only on Elizabeth's performance as queen but also on the likely prospects, if any, for the future political role of women in Britain. Once she was dead, the queen had become, in every sense, history, and one of the principal uses of the study of history in the late sixteenth and early seventeenth centuries was to evoke it as a precedent, in an attempt to shape and predict not only the present but the future; thus the French Ambassador, for instance, reported that he felt the English were so relieved to see an end to petticoat government that they would never tolerate it again.

The process of co-opting the history or ostensible history of queens for ideological purposes centred on present-day rule had already begun well before the death of Elizabeth, though, with the radical Huguenot François Hotman, in his *Francogallia* (1573), claiming that 'if ever women acquired control of the administration of the kingdom in the times of our ancestors, they always caused extraordinary calamities and subsequently a vast crop of troubles in our commonwealth ... As Cato used to say, "If you loose the reins with women, as with an unruly nature and a untamed beast, you must expect uncontrolled actions"'.[1] Along similar lines, the Venetian Ambassador to France, Michele Suriano, declared in 1561 that 'women are excluded by the Salic law, as they call it, or by an established custom which has the force of law. And therefore the king of France is always a Frenchman and can never be of another nationality. For this reason there never happens here what often happens in other kingdoms where the succession through women causes uncertainty as to who will become king, and where often the king comes from a hated and hostile people'.[2] Though British writers gamely battled back with the legendary precedent of Queen Cordelia,[3] the work of Polydore Vergil had cast too much doubt on the supposed history of pre-Roman Britain offered by Geoffrey of Monmouth for Cordelia to carry much argumentative weight any more.

What is particularly notable in the conduct of the debate is the implicit emphasis on origins and antiquity which is offered by those on both sides of the argument. Hotman appeals to Cato, and Suriano to the Salic law and to questions of national origins; similarly, the English writers' references to Queen Cordelia tap into the bitter debate between traditionalist and progressive historians about the accuracy of Geoffrey of Monmouth's descriptions of pre-Roman Britain. In this chapter I want to examine how issues of origins and the effect of precedent are examined by Renaissance dramatists, including women ones. As the references to the Salic law and to Queen Cordelia show, accounts of historical women exerted considerable pressure on the lives of contemporary women, but women themselves were nevertheless culturally prohibited from writing such accounts, or did so only with risk to their reputations. Nevertheless, some persevered, and two of the three plays at which I shall look in this chapter were written by women. I will focus mainly on only two, the first surviving tragedy by a woman, Elizabeth Cary's *The Tragedy of Mariam*, and John Ford's *The Broken Heart*, but I also want to invoke *The Concealed Fancies*, by Lady Jane Cavendish and Lady Elizabeth Brackley, as a coda to my story, because I want in this chapter to chart not only indebtedness but also development.

Elizabeth Cary was unusual in actually publishing her play, but she drew the line at having it publicly acted. For her, negotiation both with previous male writers and with historical or mythical women is dangerous, constantly presenting her with the pitfall of forced identification with inappropriate or distasteful analogues; the perils which writing holds for her are consistently imaged by her persistent use of imagery focusing on whiteness, darkness, staining, and spotting, with its clear relationship to the black marks made by print on white paper, and by the fate which befalls her heroine, Mariam, even though her only fault is inappropriately frank speech. Thirty years later, however, Jane Cavendish and Elizabeth Brackley, literally under siege by Parliamentarian troops, use many of the same analogues and precedents as Cary had done, but they find these liberating rather than constricting. Although the Cavendish sisters too envisaged only a private, household performance for their work, they nevertheless figure the act of performance as inspiring and enabling.

One of the reasons why the Cavendish sisters find their reading of texts about women recuperative rather than restrictive is simply that, for them, there were more such texts to be read. Although the intent of these texts may not always, or indeed ever, have been to celebrate women, the energy of the female characters they created had a dynamic of its own, leaching into inadvertent magnetism. Escaping from the meanings of its makers to those of its recipients, representation inevitably allows re-presentation, which is above all what the Cavendish sisters are able to achieve. To see how this is made possible, I shall have to glance not only at plays but also, at least in passing, at selected poetry and prose, and works other than those on which I am focusing will therefore be recurred to throughout the chapter, because as the period progresses and texts accumulate, so new plays take on meaning not only in relation to themselves but also in relation to what has gone before – above all to the works of prestigious male writers, foremost amongst them Sir Philip Sidney and Shakespeare.

'The faire queen of Jewry' and 'the brown Egyptian': *The Tragedy of Mariam*

Elizabeth Cary seems to have been particularly sensitive to the issue of how women had been previously represented, especially in traditional modes of historiography. *The History of the Life, Reign and Death of Edward II*, which is now tentatively attributed to her, is notably sympathetic in its attitude to Edward's queen, Isabella.[4] Whether she wrote this or not, however, it is clear that in her second (and only surviving) play *The Tragedy of Mariam* she attempted to probe the dyamics of the cultural construction of the past in order to offer a genuinely recuperative view of female heroism – but found herself beset at every turn by the prejudices and difficulties surrounding a woman's right to speak at all. It is Elizabeth Cary's negotiations of Renaissance women's difficulties in speaking and writing that I wish to examine, but I want to begin not with Mariam, but with a figure who had already been used by more than one playwright to explore the problematics of women's representation in historiography, Cleopatra. My choice is prompted by the fact that Mariam and Cleopatra, who are repeatedly counterpointed in Cary's text, emblematise two competing traditions, Judaeo-Christian and classical, each of which is connected to a myth of origins which possessed considerable cultural capital in Jacobean England. It is by pitting the two against each other that Cary, always aware of society's denigration (a word I use advisedly) of writing women, is able to carve a space into which to write her own narrative, presenting in the process a play which is not only in itself the *fons et origo* of original tragic drama by women in England but a sustained meditation on discourses of origins.

But first, Cleopatra. 'How very unlike the home life of our own dear queen!' famously exclaimed a nineteenth-century theatre-goer attending a performance of Shakespeare's *Antony and Cleopatra*. For all that Shakespeare stresses the exoticism of his Egyptian queen, however, for Renaissance audiences Cleopatra was not necessarily all that alien from themselves and their traditions; indeed Mary Sidney, translating Garnier, makes her not dark and mysterious but blonde and an adherent of surprisingly conventional wifely values.[5] For one thing, Renaissance audiences, or at least their educated members, were perhaps rather more likely than nineteenth-century ones to be sufficiently in touch with classical culture and historiography to remember that Cleopatra was not actually of indigenous Egyptian origin, but was descended from Ptolemy, the Greek general who had conquered Egypt in the time of Alexander. This brings her very close to the revered classical cultures from which many Renaissance ideas derived. For another thing, both the central episodes of Cleopatra's career involved her with men who were at other times engaged in the colonisation of Britain (indeed Antony compares himself to the supposed *ur*-coloniser, Aeneas, whose grandson Brutus allegedly founded Britain, when he says 'Dido and her Aeneas shall want troops, / And all the haunt be ours').[6] The first of these men is Julius Caesar, who was, as *Antony and Cleopatra* recalls, Cleopatra's first lover; the second is her nemesis, Augustus, whose army's attempts to bring a recalcitrant Britain to heel provide the background for Shakespeare's later play *Cymbeline*. Cleopatra can thus be seen as emblematising in her own person the weight and tradition of classical culture and its ongoing effects on Renaissance Britain.

As *Cymbeline* also recalls, however, Augustus was famous for another reason too: it was during his reign that Christ was born. While the presence of allusion to Christ's nativity in *Cymbeline* has often been recognised,[7] it has been much less remarked that *Antony and Cleopatra* shows equal signs of such an awareness.[8] There is, however, a host of suggestive allusions to the nativity story. Early in the play, Charmian beseeches the soothsayer, 'Good now, some excellent fortune! Let me be married to three kings in a forenoon and widow them all. Let me have a child at fifty, to whom Herod of Jewry may do homage' (I.2.27–30). Antony recurs to motifs associated with the nativity when he excuses himself to Caesar by saying, 'Three kings I had newly feasted' (II.2.80); Cleopatra pretends the fish she catches are Antony as if she were one of the fishers of men (II.5.10–15); and it is suggested that Cleopatra, like the Pharaoh of the Bible, might be stricken by leprosy (III.10.9–11). Other things also point firmly in the same direction, such as the constant references to trinities and triples, Antony's caution that Cleopatra will have to 'find out new heaven, new earth' (I.i.17), the parallel between Enobarbus and Judas, and Pompey's comment about Caesar getting money (II.1.13–14) (indeed, the whole play could in one sense be seen as centring on giving unto Caesar the things that are Caesar's). There is also Antony's apparent recollection of the Psalms when he speaks of the hill of Basan (III.13.126–8), the parodic Last Supper on the night of Cleopatra's birthday, and Caesar's assurance that 'The time of universal peace is near' (IV.6.5–7).[9]

Shakespeare's emphasis on the synchronicity of classical and Christian stories is not found in the other contemporary or near-contemporary treatments of the Cleopatra story by Samuel Daniel, Samuel Brandon or Mary Sidney. We do find in *Antonie*, Mary Sidney's translation of Robert Garnier's *Antoine*, Agrippa's comment on Antony that 'In like proud sort he caused his head to lose / The Jewish king Antigonus',[10] but this entirely lacks the very specific resonances of the name Herod. Mention of Herod recurs in *Antony and Cleopatra*, however, sometimes in contexts which are by no means confined to the birth of Christ, where his presence would have been understandable, but also in less obvious ones where allusion to him therefore appears to be calculated as a deliberate effect. Alexas says, 'Good majesty, / Herod of Jewry dare not look on you / But when you are well pleased', to which Cleopatra replies, 'That Herod's head / I'll have; but how, when Antony is gone, / Through whom I might command it?' (III.3.2–6). A brief but briskly sketched vignette of jockeying is played out here, with Herod first postulated as a figure of fear only for it to be revealed that both Antony and Cleopatra are, in their own ways, more alarming still. The strife thus imagined actually materialises during the course of the play; initially Caesar lists 'Herod of Jewry' as one of Antony's allies (III.6.73), but later Enobarbus tells us that

> Alexas did revolt and went to Jewry on
> Affairs of Antony; there did dissuade
> Great Herod to incline himself to Caesar
> And leave his master Antony.
>
> (IV.6.12–15)

The descriptions of these manoeuvrings remind us that the relationship between the historical Antony and Herod was configured not spiritually by the imminent arrival of the Christ-child, of which neither had any knowledge, but by political and material considerations informed by the neighbourhood of Egypt and Judaea.

This reminder may in turn encode a consciousness that the recounting of classical and legendary stories, especially when they are myths of origin, is never ideologically neutral, or free from political implications, any more than the events themselves originally were. At the end of *Antony and Cleopatra*, Octavius may be about to walk into history as Augustus Caesar and be able to sponsor Livy and Virgil to hymn his career, but the play's subtle allusions to Christ, whose ideological pull would be so much longer-lasting and would in the end even convert Rome, qualify our sense of Octavius' triumph, just as Cleopatra's and Antony's rapturous anticipations of a very differently conceived afterlife invite us to read the political events of the play *sub specie aeternatis*. The result is a typically Shakespearean effect of ambiguity and offsetting of gains and losses, while Cleopatra's nervousness about possible future reenactments of her story reminds us that any account of an event can only ever give a partial version of its truth.

There is a similar counterpointing of classical and Christian, and a similar competition between myths of origin, in Elizabeth Cary's *The Tragedy of Mariam*, and once again the reminder of the two traditions encourages the reader to be acutely aware both of the continuing pressures exerted on the present by history, and that at the same time, history may not be true. However, while Shakespeare, as so often, seems to me to be most interested in the creation of ambiguity and a dual perspective on events, Elizabeth Cary, I shall argue, not only sets up a competition but does, in the end, make a definite choice.

In Cary's play, the story centres on the family of Herod, and it is Antony and Cleopatra who make the guest appearances, serving not as heroic or romantic exemplars but as figures of promiscuity who can be contrasted with the heroine Mariam to facilitate her exculpation. Indeed Antony and Cleopatra virtually frame the events of *The Tragedy of Mariam*. We hear of Antony as early as the Argument, where we are told that 'In this mean time Herod was again necessarily to visit Rome, for Caesar having overthrown Antony, his great friend, was likely to make an alteration of his fortune',[11] while later Constabarus demands 'who can think that in Antonius' fall, / Herod, his bosom friend, should 'scape unbruised?' (II.ii.83–4). We are repeatedly encouraged, therefore, to think of Herod's destiny as intimately and irrevocably bound up with Antony's. Another key member of the cast of *Antony and Cleopatra* also gets a mention when Baba's second son recalls how when in Rome 'I did see Octavius, then a page' (II.ii.97). If Shakespeare's play invites us to read the classical tradition against the christian, Cary's seems to be inviting us to read itself against Shakespeare.

This effect is all the more pronounced because although *The Tragedy of Mariam* makes so many references to characters also found in *Antony and Cleopatra*, it also proclaims loudly and clearly that it takes a very different view of them. This is made clear from the opening lines of *The Tragedy of Mariam*, when Mariam recalls another figure central to the events of *Antony and Cleopatra* as she says:

> How oft have I, with public voice run on
> To censure Rome's last hero for deceit?
> Because he wept when Pompey's life was gone,
> Yet when he lived, he thought his name too great.
>
> (I.i.1–4)

Mariam here alludes to both Gnaeus Pompey and Julius Caesar, both of whom figured prominently in the story of Cleopatra. Rather than aligning herself with Cleopatra, however, Mariam opposes herself to her by casting herself as implicitly Pompeian, and thus an adherent of a man who had been killed by Cleopatra's brother Ptolemy. Given what I shall be suggesting about the contemporary overtones of *The Tragedy of Mariam*, it is perhaps worth noting that Shakespeare uses a character called Pompey to critique and interrogate Jacobean authority in *Measure for Measure*. Pompey there is a tapster and bawd, answering to the name of Pompey Bum, but though he is a poor speaker and no doubt a reprehensible figure, we are left in no doubt that he does have a point: the resolution made intra-diegetically by the ruler in the play (and shared extra-diegetically by the ruler outside the play, James I himself) to enforce the laws strictly and suppress all brothels will not only rob people like Pompey of their livelihood, but will ultimately prove unenforceable. Like Pompey Bum, Mariam too will develop a voice that will puncture and deflate the pretensions and authority of the male ruler, and her association of herself with Pompey in her opening lines forms a suitable introduction to her oppositional role.

Unlike Pompey Bum, however, Mariam will mount her critique by encoding and referring to debates about the origins of the ruler's authority rather than about the mode in which it is currently being exercised. Questions of origins lie at the heart of the story of *The Tragedy of Mariam*. The repeated stress on the temporal adjacency and political alliance of Herod and Antony is already enough in itself to point up the competing claims to originary status of classical and Christian traditions, but we are almost immediately made aware that there are in fact still further divisions within Jewry itself, as Mariam's mother Alexandra declares of Herod,

> My curse pursue his breathless trunk and spirit,
> Base Edomite, the damnèd Esau's heir.
> Must he ere Jacob's child the crown inherit?
>   (I.ii.5–8)

Alexandra, like the inhabitants of post-Reformation England, can only look back longingly to a golden time of unity encapsulated in the person of Aristobulus, whose 'birth anointed him both priest and king' (I.ii.40) – a phrase whose importance is reiterated since it has already occurred in the Argument, where we hear of 'Mariam the daughter of Hircanus, the rightful king and priest'. This clearly suggests that countries where temporal and spiritual authority are institutionally divided – as, of course, in Cary's post-Reformation England – are at a disadvantage.[12] (Though Cary had not yet converted to Catholicism at the time when she wrote *The Tragedy of Mariam*, her awareness of the difficulties under which she and women like her laboured was hardly calculated to make her an eager adherent of the patriarchal values of Jacobean England, that land in which James VI and I was suggestively claimed to have made 'Israel and Juda one'.)[13]

Moreover, choice between authority systems of the kind which has now been forced upon Israel (and by implication England) is seen as inherently dangerous, confusing, and likely to lead either to no decisions or to poor ones, as Alexandra rather daringly reveals when she reminisces about her dealings with Antony, and how she had confused the issue by sending him pictures of both her son and her daughter. She had hoped to be sure of captivating his fancy, but in fact the embarrassment of riches thus proffered had plunged him into an agony of indecision and made him incapable of choosing at all, as Alexandra laments:

> So I, that sought felicity to have,
> Did with her minion Antony begin.
> With double sleight I sought to captivate

> The warlike lover, but I did not right.
> For if my gift had borne but half the rate,
> The Roman had been over-taken quite.
> But now he fared like a hungry guest,
> That to some plenteous festival is gone;
> Now this, now that, he deems to eat were best,
> Such choice doth make him let them all alone.
>
> (I.ii.91–100)

As the Chorus gloomily avers, 'no content attends a wavering mind' (I.vi.6).

Questions of choice are therefore seen to lie at the heart of this play, and it is thus of particular significance that Herod and Mariam, then, are presented in the play not only as man and wife but, as we are insistently reminded, as representatives of two rival traditions and family lines: Herod is descended from Esau, and is thus, in the eyes of Alexandra, merely a 'base Edomite', while Mariam, on the other hand, is descended from Esau's more favoured brother, Jacob. Indeed we later discover from Mariam's taunts to Salome that to be an Edomite is not merely to be a lesser kind of Jew, but not really to be Jewish at all. Told that women far better than she would have been delighted to be married to Herod, Mariam retorts:

> Though I thy brother's face had never seen,
> My birth thy baser birth so far excelled,
> I had to both of you the princess been.
> Thou parti-Jew, and parti-Edomite,
> Thou mongrel, issued from rejected race!
> Thy ancestors against the heavens did fight,
> And thou like them wilt heavenly birth disgrace.
>
> (I.iii.26–32)

Salome herself is not unnaturally inclined to be dismissive of this perspective:

> Still twit you me with nothing but my birth?
> What odds betwixt your ancestors and mine?
> Both born of Adam, both were made of earth,
> And both did come from holy Abr'ham's line.
>
> (I.iii.33–6)

Even in our own egalitarian age, however, we are likely to feel that it is Mariam who is supposed to have the right of it in this debate, and in the acutely ancestry-conscious Jacobean period, that would have been far more readily apparent. The idea is further reinforced later when Constabarus declares

> The sons of Baba have it by descent,
> In all their thoughts each action to excel,
> Boldly to act, and wisely to invent.
>
> (II.ii.42–4)

Since Constabarus, like Mariam, is virtuous, the point seems clearly to be made that descent does indeed matter.

However, although it insists that origins are crucial, this play, like the society it depicts, is at odds with its past; indeed its repeated insistence on the previous death of a character called Josephus may make us recall its own relationship to a source-text authored by another man named Josephus, from whose account it diverges in a number of details, most notably the timescale and the physical locations of Salome, Mariam and Alexandra.[14] Nor is this the only text from which it visibly differs. Though critics have been more prone to stress Cary's debt to (and differences from) Mary Sidney's *Antonie*,[15] where Cleopatra is a timid, faithful blonde, there can be no doubt that Cary's references to Cleopatra also respond directly and thoughtfully to Shakespeare's treatment of the character. Far from being a role model, though, Cleopatra functions as merely a negative exemplar for Mariam. Early in the play, Mariam exclaims, 'Yet had I rather much a milkmaid be, / Than be the monarch of Judea's queen' (I.i.57–8), which, as Dympna Callaghan points out, recalls Cleopatra's similar protestation[16] (and, as I shall show later in this chapter, anticipates that of Penthea in Ford's *The Broken Heart*). But though Mariam's desires thus prove consonant with those of Cleopatra, Mariam and those on her side are in all other ways at pains to put distance between herself and the Egyptian queen. Mariam's mother, Alexandra, pursuing her train of thought about the two pictures of her son and daughter which she sent to Antony, laments his failure to fall in love with the portrait of Mariam:

> He would have loved thee, and thee alone,
> And left the brown Egyptian clean forsaken.
> And Cleopatra then to seek had been

So firm a lover of her waned face;
Then great Antonius' fall we had not seen,
By her that fled to have him hold the chase.
(I.ii.111–16)

Here the events of Shakespeare's play are, one by one, imaginatively undone, as we imagine a counterfactual world in which Antony did not fall in love with Cleopatra, so that she was left entirely deserted after Caesar's death and the battle of Actium never took place.

There is also a further inflection of a Shakespearean source audible here. 'By her that fled to have him hold the chase' clearly recalls Helena's line in *A Midsummer Night's Dream*, 'Apollo flies, and Daphne holds the chase',[17] which is itself a musing on a radical rewriting of a source text. *A Midsummer Night's Dream*, too, is a play with a classical setting (indeed it is set in the very Athens to which Antony begs Caesar to be allowed to retire). Like *Antony and Cleopatra* and *The Tragedy of Mariam*, also, *A Midsummer Night's Dream* is much interested in discourses of race and blackness – Titania and Oberon are at odds over an Indian boy, Lysander abusing Hermia calls her a 'tawny Tartar' (III.2.263) – so its intertextual presence in a discussion of 'the brown Egyptian' is particularly suggestive,[18] indicating that questions of race and hence of individual and national origins are indeed at the forefront of Cary's nexus of concerns. Nor is this the only allusion to *A Midsummer Night's Dream* in *The Tragedy of Mariam*. Later in the same scene, Alexandra seems to echo *Dream* again, when she dismisses Herod's passion for her daughter as 'And yet not love, but raging lunacy' (I.ii.46), recalling Theseus' linking of 'The lunatic, the lover, and the poet' (V.i.7). *A Midsummer Night's Dream* might well have been of particular interest to Cary, since both she and her sister-in-law and dedicatee (also called Elizabeth Cary, though it is not clear which of the two possible women of this name was meant) shared a name, or at least a homonym, with the Elizabeth Carey whose wedding to Thomas Berkeley is often thought to have been the occasion of *A Midsummer Night's Dream*'s first performance.[19] There was, however, no relationship between the Elizabeth Carey who married Thomas Berkeley and the Elizabeth Cary who wrote the play, so that once again, an apparent similarity of origins seems to be evoked only to be denied.

Moreover, *A Midsummer Night's Dream* is being subtly reworked in *The Tragedy of Mariam* rather than simply revisited. Just as *A Midsummer Night's Dream* rewrites *Romeo and Juliet* as comic, so *The Tragedy of Mariam* rewrites *Dream* itself and inserts it once more into the realms of tragedy from which it had escaped. In *Dream*, colour is relative – a lover who is sufficiently besotted 'Sees Helen's beauty in a brow of Egypt' (V.i.11–12) – but in *Mariam* the polarities of race and pigmentation remain absolute: the 'brown Egyptian' Cleopatra is a bad woman, and remains so. Indeed Cleopatra is not even beautiful, as we see in Mariam's long speech criticising her:

> The wanton queen that never loved for love,
> False Cleopatra, wholly set on gain,
> With all her sleights did prove, yet vainly prove,
> For her the love of Herod to obtain.
> Yet her allurements, all her courtly guile,
> Her smiles, her favours, and her smooth deceit,
> Could not my face from Herod's mind exile,
> But were with him of less than little weight.
> That face and person that in Asia late
> For beauty's goddess, Paphos' queen, was ta'en,
> That face that did captive great Julius' fate,
> That very face that was Antonius' bane,
> That face that to be Egypt's pride was born,
> That face that all the world esteemed so rare,
> Did Herod hate, despise, neglect, and scorn,
> When with the same he Mariam's did compare.
> (IV.viii.13–28)

We are indeed a long way here from the lively, enchanting figure of Shakespeare's play or the biddable, affectionate creature of Mary Sidney's translation of Garnier.

However, Cary's play also registers considerable unease at being thus at odds with its source. The 'custom-breaker' (I.iv.49), Salome, is undoubtedly the play's worst character, and both the importance of literary origins and an unease about revisiting them are signalled in Herod's declaration that

> For neither shall my love prolong thy breath,
> Nor shall thy loss of breath my love remove.
> I might have seen thy falsehood in thy face –
> Where could'st thou get thy stars that served for eyes
> Except by theft?
> (IV.iv.59–63)

The answer to Herod's rhetorical question inevitably entails the Petrarchan tradition, the most obvious locus of the equation of stars with eyes. To borrow from this is indeed, in one sense, theft – and yet Herod is also clearly indicating that he himself cannot think in any other terms, for here he directly echoes both the sense and the wording of one of the earliest of English translations of Petrarch, 'Love that liveth and reigneth within my thought' by Henry Howard, Earl of Surrey, first cousin of Anne Boleyn. This concludes with the couplet, 'Yet from my lord shall not my foot remove: / Sweet is the death that taketh end by love'.[20] The phrasing, rhythm and idea of the Surrey poem all recur in Herod's words, and we might notice too that when Constabarus believes that the death of Herod means freedom at last for the imprisoned sons of Baba, he says to them 'enough is left' (II.ii.40). The phrase is, amongst its other meanings, a direct translation of 'Sat superest', the Latin motto of Surrey. As such, it may recall not only the death of Surrey himself, beheaded in 1536, but also the story of Surrey's father, Norfolk, who was due to be executed on the day of Henry VIII's own death, and who was thus reprieved. The apparent allusion to Surrey's motto here may further remind us that Surrey's crime had in itself been to do with origins, in that he was accused of displaying too prominently on his armorial bearings the indication of his descent from Edward III. Surrey had also been careful to figure himself in his translation of the *Aeneid* as 'the sole survivor, like Aeneas, of a special genealogy'.[21]

Nor was Surrey alone in using Petrarchan verse to interrogate questions of origins. His friend Sir Thomas Wyatt's figuring of Anne Boleyn as a possession of Caesar's in his sonnet 'Whoso list to hunt' comes close to presenting her as a modern Cleopatra:

> And graven with diamonds in letters plain
> There is written her fair neck round about:
> '*Noli me tangere* for Caesar's I am,
> And wild for to hold though I seem tame.'[22]

Wyatt also uses a Caesar figure in another sonnet, referring to 'Caesar, when that the traitor of Egypt / With th'honourable head did him present' (p. 76). This alludes to precisely the episode in Caesar's career which Mariam herself (in what Marta Straznicky terms 'a fascinating gender switch')[23] recalls in the opening lines of the play (I.i.1–4), Caesar's being presented with the head of Pompey by Cleopatra's brother Ptolemy and surprising the onlookers by manifesting grief

rather than triumph. In *The Tragedy of Mariam*, therefore, Cary seems
to be recollecting both Wyatt and Surrey, and using them to reinforce
her own preferred view of Cleopatra as not only dangerous and disrup-
tive, but also as a figure closely associated with Anne Boleyn, whose
involvement with Henry VIII precipitated the English Reformation,
which seems to be remembered in this play as a source of fragmenta-
tion and confusion. Moreover, in the wake of Wyatt and Surrey
themselves comes the entire Petrarchan tradition of which they
were the earliest and most prominent representatives, and its clearly
established codes for figuring women in tropes derived from their
actual and ascribed colour. These codes are also further recalled in the
intertextual presences of *Antony and Cleopatra* and *A Midsummer
Night's Dream*. At the same time, however, the spectral presences of
these two plays and of Wyatt's poetry pull against the main thrust
of Cary's project by reminding us that both Shakespeare and Wyatt
figured Cleopatra as magnetic and dynamic rather than merely
destructive.

Cary's allusions to Cleopatra in particular and literary tropes for
figuring women in general thus do more than simply revisit either
Shakespeare or the Petrarchan tradition. Her recollections of previous
literary treatments of Cleopatra set up a system of competition which
operates both extra-diegetically, by pitting the various source texts of
The Tragedy of Mariam against each other, and intradiegetically, by
instantiating a binary opposition not only between Mariam and
Cleopatra themselves but also between the different poles of womanhood which Cary figures them as representing. (Cary's strategy here
may be compared with her equally problematic treatment of race: as
Kim Hall has argued, the only culturally available strategies for figuring one woman as 'white' necessitated figuring another as 'black',
because 'women are only fair or black in comparison with one
another'.)[24] By writing Cleopatra as a 'brown Egyptian' and evoking
the 'tawny tartar' Hermia, Cary strongly reminds the reader of the
tradition, enshrined in Petrarchan poetry, that women's beauty was
dependent on fairness of complexion. In one sense, the extradiegetic
darkness of Cleopatra and Hermia thus serves merely the same function as the intradiegetic darkness of Salome, to point up Mariam's own
beauty, just as the 'white' beauty of Vittoria in *The White Devil* is offset
by the darkness of her Moorish maid Zanche or as the goddess Diana
in Renaissance painting is often depicted accompanied by a black
attendant whose colour contrasts with and highlights her own.[25] It is
certainly much easier to read the Jewish Mariam as suitably 'white' in

the context of the 'brown' Egyptian Cleopatra. At the same time, though, whiteness was not the only trait praised by Petrarchan poetry: the black eyes of both Anne Boleyn and of her great-niece Penelope Rich, the model for Sidney's Stella, led to a sustained strand of the language of blackness amongst the dominant red and white of Petrarchan discourse. Perhaps, moreover, we need to hear in *The Tragedy of Mariam* not only Petrarchan discourses themselves but, behind them, a meditation on the historical moment of their first introduction to England, the court of Henry VIII at the time when Anne Boleyn, cousin of Surrey and muse of Wyatt, was in the ascendant – and the last moment before the English Reformation.

That Anne Boleyn might be an influence on *The Tragedy of Mariam* was first suggested by Margaret Ferguson and Barry Weller, who in their edition of the play argued very convincingly that it was influenced by Cary's interest in the first and second marriages of Henry VIII.[26] There certainly seem to be strong suggestions that this is so, and indeed I think Ferguson's and Weller's case is actually a much stronger one than they suggested. Early in *The Tragedy of Mariam*, Mariam expresses her hopes for her son by declaring that

> My Alexander, if he live, shall sit
> In the majestic seat of Solomon.[27]

Henry VIII was often identified with Solomon. John King comments that '[l]ike his father, Henry VIII received praise as a second Solomon', and King describes a Holbein portrait showing

> the king as Solomon receiving the gifts of the queen of Sheba, who kneels at the head of her retinue ... The composition of this miniature in the same period as the break with Rome suggests an allusion to the Reformation. After all, the queen of Sheba is a traditional type for the church, and her kneeling homage and submission to an omnicompetent monarch carry every suggestion that the picture commemorates the recent submission of the Church of England to Henry as the head of the church.[28]

Many aspects of *The Tragedy of Mariam* do indeed work to underline this parallel between the Judaea of Herod's return and an England trembling on the brink of Henry VIII's divorce and of the Reformation – not such an unlikely context as the chronological distance of the Henrician era might initially make it appear, since, as Jasper Ridley points out, even in 'the second half of the seventeenth century ... the divorce of Catherine of Aragon and the Reformation of Henry VIII's reign were not yet history – they were still politics'.[29] The seat of Solomon, then, may indeed seem to suggest the seat of Henry VIII too.

If Henry was Solomon, his second wife Anne Boleyn might well make a fitting candidate for Sheba, since she was repeatedly associated with the iconography of blackness. In 1522, Anne and her sister Mary appeared in a Shrove Tuesday masque hosted by Cardinal Wolsey at York Place, in which eight choristers of the Chapel Royal dressed up as Indian women with names like Disdain and Unkindness.[30] Wyatt called her 'Brunet',[31] and in Shakespeare and Fletcher's *Henry VIII*, the Second Gentleman observes of Anne that 'Our King has all the Indies in his arms, / And more, and richer, when he strains that lady';[32] later in the play, Anne's daughter Elizabeth I is directly associated with the figure of Sheba when Cranmer prophesies, 'Saba was never / More covetous of wisdom and fair virtue / Than this pure soul shall be' (V.5.23–5). Physical descriptions of Anne Boleyn, moreover, emphasise her darkness, particularly the blackness of her eyes,[33] and Sheba is often imaged as racially other.[34]

Although contemporary Catholic propagandists identified Anne not with Mariam, but with Salome – albeit the Salome of the John the Baptist story, who was also alleged to have been beheaded, rather than that of the play[35] – Mariam of the 'ebon-hewed' eyes (IV.vii.98) does indeed thus seem to recall Anne Boleyn. Anne, though, was hardly a happy role model, not least because of the disruption she wreaked not only to the actual Tudor succession, by first precipitating the divorce of Catherine of Aragon and the consquent bastardisation of the latter's daughter Mary, and second failing to produce a son, but also to the dynasty's myths and ideologies of its own origins. Much Tudor iconography stressed the Tudors' reputed descent from King Arthur, who was himself the supposed descendant of the Trojan Brutus, and the dynasty's consequent status as emblem of continuity with the classical world and also the much-prophesied agent of national British revival. Henry VII called his eldest son Arthur, though the boy died shortly after his marriage to Catherine of Aragon and left his younger brother, the future Henry VIII, to succeed to the possession of both his wife and his throne; and under Henry VII's auspices Tudor emblems were added to the so-called Round Table at Winchester. The legendary King Arthur, however, whatever his personal achievements and greatness had been, had also been sadly undermined by his unfaithful wife, Guinevere – a haunting parallel to the marital tribulations of Henry

VIII himself. Thus, while Mariam's descent so notably outshines Herod's, Anne, whose thousand days began and ended with quasi-Arthurian tournaments (events whose very name was supposed to derive from Turnus, a character in the *Aeneid*),[36] was not only herself lower-born than the king, but can also serve as an encoding and remembrance of some of the darker aspects of dynastic history, especially since Anne was also reputed to be the name of Arthur's sister, on whom he incestuously begot Mordred, who then, in turn, slept with his stepmother Guinevere.[37] Given that Henry VIII before his marriage to Anne Boleyn had already slept with her sister Mary – and, according to Catholic propagandists, with her mother too – the suggestion of incest encoded in the Arthur story was dangerously close to the bone, especially since Anne herself was subsequently charged with incest and adultery with her brother George.

Anne Boleyn, therefore, was a figure who featured prominently in the event which originated the English Reformation, who personally inspired both the poets who originated the immensely influential tradition of English Petrarchan poetry, and whose iconography touched on the two most culturally influential myths and ideas of English national origins and contemporary spiritual identities. Mariam is also a figure around whom discourses and myths of origin cluster, together with associated issues of belief systems. Indeed it is remarkable how much Mariam's fall is constructed in terms of competing discourses of origins and related issues of ultimate spiritual destiny; even the emphasis on her colouring can be read in such terms, since Michael Drayton in his great chorographical poem *Poly-Olbion* had explicitly raised the question of the link between colour and national origins, declaring that 'Esau' and 'Edom' both meant 'red' and that 'Nile' meant 'black', while 'Britain' itself signified 'the coloured Isle'; Drayton also relates the story of Merlin seeing Britain in terms of the white dragon of the Saxons, the red dragon of the Britons and the black dragon of the Normans,[38] which is also found in William Rowley's *The Birth of Merlin*. Most notably, a surprisingly large part of Herod's lament for her focuses precisely on this issue, as he apostrophises the sun:

> You could but shine, if some Egyptian blowse,
> Or Ethiopian dowdy lose her life.
> This was (then wherefore bend you not your brows?)
> The king of Jewry's fair and spotless wife.
> Deny thy beams, and moon refuse thy light,
> Let all the stars be dark, let Jewry's eye

No more distinguish which is day and night,
Since her best birth did in her bosom die.
Those fond idolaters, the men of Greece,
Maintain these orbs are safely governèd,
That each within themselves have gods apiece
By whom their steadfast course is justly led.
But were it so, as so it cannot be,
They all would put their mourning garments on.
Not one of them would yield a light to me,
To me that is the cause that Mariam's gone.
For though they fame their Saturn melancholy,
Of sour behaviours, and of angry mood,
They fame him likewise to be just and holy,
And justice needs must seek revenge for blood.
Their Jove, if Jove he were, would sure desire
To punish him that slew so fair a lass,
For Leda's beauty set his heart on fire,
Yet she not half so fair as Mariam was.

(V.i.195–218)

Here Herod directly pits the traditions and belief systems of Jewry against those of classical Greece before deciding that 'these are fictions, they are void of sense, / The Greeks but dream, and dreaming, falsehoods tell' (V.i.235–6).

Questions of origins are equally stressed in Herod's use of a different element of the Petrarchan formula:

on the brow of Mariam hangs a fleece,
Whose slenderest twine is strong enough to bind
The hearts of kings; the pride and shame of Greece,
Troy-flaming Helen's, not so fairly shined.

(IV.vii.57–60)

Herod appears to think that he is comparing Mariam here to Helen of Troy, but the word 'fleece' has already pointed quite unmistakably in the direction of the deceitful and murderous Medea. In Herod's words, then, Asiatic Medea and Greek Helen morph eerily into each other in ways which suggest both how difficult and important it is to discriminate between women. As the inclusion of Salome in this play works forcibly to point out, women are *not* all the same, and we cannot, with Hamlet, generalisingly conclude that 'Frailty, thy name is woman', while the intertextual presences of Cleopatra and of Anne Boleyn further remind us not only of the differences between individual women but of the cultural differences between the two dominant traditions in which the women of Cary's culture had been most influentially inscribed.

Anne Boleyn and Cleopatra thus encode a number of competing myths of origin and also emblematise the two literary traditions of most direct importance for Cary's own text, Petrarchan poetry and English Renaissance drama. At the same time, Anne Boleyn and Cleopatra might well seem to threaten to provide two originary stories of bad women so powerful and magnetic that they might in fact overshadow Cary's story of the virtuous Mariam and blunt her point. But when Cary stresses the literariness of her own text, inviting the reader to recognise echoes and demonstrating familiarity with Petrarchan discourses, she does not simply reduplicate the ideological strategies of the works to which she alludes. By stressing Judaeo-Christian traditions as well as the classical ones which Cleopatra's Greek ancestry and Anne's Arthurian and hence ultimately Trojan associations both recall, Cary prises apart the authority of the various accounts of individual and national origins available to her culture, pitting them against each other to reveal the instability of 'history' and the subjectivity inevitably attendant on the processes of inscription. This process is assisted by Cary's analogous stress on the differing ethnic origins and consequent competing dynastic claims of Herod and Mariam, which reminds us that stories of national origins are never simple and are invariably written by the winner.

Moreover, *The Tragedy of Mariam* also shows itself aware that all truth is relative, that presentation is all and that the same events can be quite differently slanted and have quite different effects if they are recounted by different narrators. Salome sends Pheroras to Herod with the news that Constabarus has kept the sons of Baba alive rather than going herself, because she knows that 'This will be Constabarus' quick dispatch, / Which from my mouth would lesser credit find' (III.ii.49–50). Salome may be wicked, but she is not stupid: she knows that narratives persuade best when they are not obviously self-interested, although she simultaneously reminds us that even narratives which are not obviously self-interested may be so covertly, further fostering our distrust of the uses of history and precedent. Similarly, Herod reveals an acute awareness of the ways in which truth can be distorted when he says of Alexandra

from the accumulated knowledge of previous thinkers contained in the world of books, but that is also imagined as being, in the end, to their advantage.

The Broken Heart goes even further than *'Tis Pity She's a Whore* towards examining the relationship between lived emotional experience and literary representations of it. In particular, *The Broken Heart* concurs with much of Ford's other work in seeming to suggest that some at least of the growing body of medical and paramedical works examining the relationship between the mind and the body could in fact offer a viable understanding of the human condition which might even help to effect improvement in it. *The Broken Heart* revisits the physicalised perspective on human nature and events which we encountered in *The Changeling* and *Women Beware Women*, but this time the playwright is introducing these ideas not in order to endorse them but to critique them. Texts which have focused solely on bodies seem to have nothing to teach, but texts which have focused on the heart and mind can, if they are allowed to, communicate with the hearts and minds of others – only, in *The Broken Heart*, none of the characters will read or heed them.

From the outset of *The Broken Heart*, books themselves are posited as a probable and primary object of desire. Crotolon, seeking to dissuade his son Orgilus from wishing to travel to Athens, prefaces his persuasions with 'if books and love of knowledge / Inflame you to this travel ... '.[39] Unlike Florio, Crotolon here figures books not as in opposition to desire but as a likely, and particularly intense, source of desire, eliciting such strongly affective language as 'love' and 'inflame'. Soon afterwards, Orgilus himself speaks to Tecnicus of how the latter is 'applying to my hidden wounds the balm / Of thy oraculous lectures' (I.iii.10–11); although Orgilus also observes that 'Physic yet hath never found / A remedy to cure a lover's wound' (I.iii.40–1), he imagines that learning, in the specifically literary form of 'lectures', whose very name is derived from reading, can at least afford 'balm', in marked contrast to the damage to health it is figured as effecting by Florio. It is notable too that the most secluded and romantic place to be found at the Spartan court is also designated as a domain of learning, as Prophilus explains to Euphranea:

> None have access into these private pleasures
> Except some near in court, or bosom student
> From Tecnicus his oratory, granted
> By special favour lately from the king
> Unto the grave philosopher.
>
> (I.iii.95–9)

Here, love and learning prove to occupy the same ground spatially as well as emotionally.

In this private pleasure-garden, the two lovers Euphranea and Prophilus meet Euphranea's brother Orgilus, who is disguised as Aplotes. When they first encounter him, the supposed Aplotes is talking to himself, saying,

> I'll baulk illiterate sauciness, submitting
> My sole opinion to the touch of writers.
>
> (I.iii.122–3)

In this play of divided minds, Orgilus/Aplotes pits a self apparently confident of its own opinion against one who defers to the written authority of others. He thus neatly emblematises the distinction between personally experienced emotion and culturally prescribed modes of thought and feeling which overarches the play's representations of bodies and books. Interrupting this dialogue of ventriloquised selves, Euphranea and Prophilus ask the supposed scholar the question which would later prove so resonant for Freud, what he wants. To this he replies, 'Books, Venus, books' (I.iii.143), in which the name of Venus, goddess of love, is sandwiched between the repetition of the word 'books' as though in apposition in this list rather than functioning, as syntactically it must, as a vocative by which the disguised Orgilus addresses his sister. It is little wonder that Prophilus responds, 'I will furnish / Thy study, or what else thou canst desire' (I.iii.158–9), for study has indeed been conceived of so far as the probable object of desire, just as later Orgilus will refer to 'a strain my younger days / Have studied for delight' (III.v.86–7). Books, though, may prescribe in a positive as well as a negative sense, and the audience, who know that Orgilus's desire for books is in fact feigned, may well be encouraged to ask at this point whether it might not be wise for it to be genuine. Are books really in opposition to desire, or might some of them at least not be able to illuminate its workings?

Orgilus, though, is not actually interested in reading books at all; what he is concerned about is writing, or rather a resistance to writing, as we see when he assures Penthea,

> Time can never
> On the white table of unguilty faith
> Write counterfeit dishonour.
>
> (II.iii.25–7)

For Orgilus here, a person truly in love is like a 'table' – as Hamlet reminds us, a writing surface – but it is a curiously blank writing surface, and one on which indeed nothing can be written. Similarly in the song sung about Penthea, we hear the simile 'Pure as are unwritten papers' (IV.iii.145), as if the essence in purity lies in an antithesis of writing.

It is true that Orgilus' assumptions are not wholly shared by Penthea. For her, narrative is a mode to procure sympathy, as we see when she says, 'I hope thy wife, / Hearing my story, will not scorn my fall' (II.iii.93–4). And it is language which Penthea figures as the vital currency and which she threatens to use as a tool with which to punish Orgilus:

> If ever henceforth thou appear in language,
> Message or letter to betray my frailty,
> I'll call thy former protestations lust
>
> > (II.iii.113–15)

Rather than reading a text, or as resisting the inscription of one, Penthea figures herself here as authoring one. It is, however, one which very clearly does not correspond with her own emotional truth, since she really does love Orgilus, and is resisting him purely for social rather than for emotional reasons. While for Orgilus, then, emotion is antithetical to writing, for Penthea writing is a thing to be feared, and language is ultimately a thing more likely to conceal than to reveal the truth of the emotions.

Moreover, the sense of a real divorce between books and bodies is heightened by the play's creation of another insistent divide. This is between a minority of characters, who talk about books (though without necessarily reading them), but actually work for death, and the majority, who talk about bodies and health, and are focused on their plans (or fears) for the future. It is thus not only emotional states but bodily well-being which are figured as being in tension with books. Again, though, it is important to note that it is not in fact books themselves which are thus being indicted, but the mere pretence of reading them, which is being used by Orgilus to cloak a very different form of activity.

The Broken Heart is a play in which we hear a great deal about health and illness. Bassanes, explaining to Prophilus why they have not visited Ithocles before, says,

> We had not needed
> An invitation if his sister's health
> Had not fallen into question.
>
> (II.i.142–4)

Ithocles himself is not well, and sees no easy means of becoming so:

> Morality applied
> To timely practice keeps the soul in tune,
> At whose sweet music all our actions dance.
> But this is form of books, and school tradition;
> It physics not the sickness of a mind
> Broken with griefs. Strong fevers are not eas'd
> With counsel but with best receipts and means.
>
> (II.ii.8–14)

As one might expect in a play where the names of the speakers are concretised representations of normally transient emotional states here conceived of as permanently reified identities, Ithocles in this passage accepts a relationship between bodies and minds, but, unlike Orgilus, he does not figure learning as being able to effect a genuine transformation of mental states. Ithocles in fact comes closer to Florio in *'Tis Pity She's a Whore* when he dismisses traditional knowledge and recorded ideas as 'form of books, and school tradition'. For Ithocles, experience can only be acquired personally, not vicariously, and history and observation thus have nothing at all to teach. This is ironically revealed when he says,

> then I could not dive
> Into the secrets of commanding love;
> Since when, experience by the extremeties – in others –
> Hath forc'd me to collect.
>
> (II.ii.50–3)

The irony is created by the fact that Ithocles is lying – he has not learned about love by the extremities 'in others' but because he has himself fallen hopelessly in love with Calantha – so that just as Orgilus lies about desiring books, Ithocles lies about his observations of others. Both thus resolutely shut themselves off from the nearest available means of learning, and blunder on, refusing to learn from any outside source. Moreover, since we observe that this is what they are doing, this parallel between their strategies works to reinforce our sense that the sources they neglect are of the same type and that what is to be learned from books is therefore emotional wisdom.

When Ithocles really is taken ill, presumably as a result of the pressure of his unexpressed love for Calantha (though there is no sign that Ithocles realises this himself), Prophilus advises Penthea, 'Lady, come. Your brother / I carried to his closet. You must thither' (II.iii.139–40). The closet, as we saw in *The Changeling*, is the private space, the inner sanctum, and, interestingly, a place where either books or medicine might well be found. (Later, the mad Penthea will say of Ithocles, 'Alas, his heart / Is crept into the cabinet of the princess' [IV.ii.117–18], further figuring closets, by analogy with their close relatives cabinets, as site of privacy.) Although his malady would seem to be a clear case of the mind affecting the body, however, Ithocles turns neither to medicine, the traditional cure of the mind, nor books, the traditional cure of the body. Instead he relieves his feelings by confessing them to his sister. This may suggest that Ithocles is in fact just beginning to apprehend physical illness in terms of a state of mind, but if so he almost immediately reverts to his earlier mode of imagining bodies and their experiences in purely medicalised terms when he instructs Penthea on their interruption by the angry Bassanes, 'Purge not his griefs, Penthea' (III.iii.139) – an expression, moreover, which suggests a notably old-fashioned and unsubtle view of the physicalised basis of emotion.

The male characters in particular continue throughout the play to represent their experiences in resolutely physicalised terms, ignoring the possible impact of any other element. Bassanes says, 'Diseases desperate must find cures alike' (III.iii.168), as though there needed to be some quasi-mathematical congruence between illness and treatment. Orgilus tells his father that Ithocles

> Too humbly hath descended from that height
> Of arrogance and spleen which wrought the rape
> Of griev'd Penthea's purity.
>
> (III.v.25–7)

Here the spleen seems credited almost with independent agency of its own, controlling functions of the mind which one would hope would be guided by more rational forces, and thus effectively governing human behaviour. The conversation between Orgilus and his father continues along similar lines, as Orgilus pretends to explain why he did not in fact go to Athens:

> *Orgilus.*   'Twas care, sir, of my health cut short my
> journey;
> For there a general infection
> Threatens a desolation.
> *Crotolon.*   And I fear
> Thou hast brought back a worse infection with thee,
> Infection of thy mind; which, as thou sayst,
> Threatens the desolation of our family.
>
> (III.v.40–5)

Ironically, Crotolon here attempts to introduce a less physicalised
perspective with his idea of 'infection of the mind', but Orgilus again
is deaf to new ideas. So this mental plague continues to rage:

> *Armostes.*   Quiet
> These vain unruly passions, which will render ye
> Into a madness.
> *Orgilus.*   Griefs will have their vent.
> *Armostes.*   Welcome. Thou com'st in season, reverend man,
> To pour the balsam of a suppling patience
> Into the festering wound of ill-spent fury.
>
> (IV.i.117–22)

Orgilus persists in a purely physicalised viewpoint in which griefs work
like steam, and continues with his plan undeterred by anything that
anyone older or more experienced may say. Ignoring any idea of
'quiet' and 'control', Orgilus works on the theory that emotion cannot
be calmed or rechannelled, but must explode. Orgilus' dogged pursuit
of this idea will of course mean that events will indeed proceed to a
violent and tragic outcome.

   Not until towards the end of the play do the male characters finally
begin to realise the nature of the unstoppable spiral towards violence
in which they have embroiled themselves, and the kinds of mechanism that might have been able to prevent it. Grausis and Phulas tell
the recovering Bassanes, 'Thou art the very honeycomb of honesty ...
The garland of goodwill' (IV.ii.14–15), where, suggestively, the terms
they choose to praise him with are titles of popular books. Bassanes
himself says:

> But men, endow'd with reason and the use
> Of reason to distinguish from the chaff

Of abject scarcity the quintessence,
Soul, and elixir of the earth's abundance
The treasures of the sea, the air, nay heaven,
Repining at these glories of creation,
Are verier beasts than beasts.

(IV.ii.22–8)

Here Bassanes finally shows that he realises that one must look beyond the physical, and goes on: 'No tempests of commotion shall disquiet / The calms of my composure' (IV.ii.38–9). Moreover Bassanes here, in one of Ford's characteristically Shakespearean moments, echoes the rhetoric of Othello just as he has earlier done his jealousy. Othello says to Desdemona,

O my soul's joy,
If after every tempest come such calms
May the winds blow till they have wakened death,
And let the labouring bark climb hills of seas,
Olympus-high, and duck again as low
As hell's from heaven.

(2.1.182–7)

For Othello here winds are fearsome, with great power over humans. Iago by contrast blasphemously inverts the familiar idea of man as God's creature in the Garden of Eden to figure a world in which the human will is absolutely paramount:

Virtue? a fig! 'tis in ourselves that we are thus, or thus. Our bodies are our gardens, to the which our wills are gardeners. So that if we will plant nettles or sow lettuce, set hyssop and weed up thyme, supply it with one gender of herbs, or distract it with many, either to have it sterile with idleness or manured with industry – why, the power and corrigible authority of this lies in our wills. If the balance of our lives had not one scale of reason to poise another of sensuality, the blood and baseness of our natures would conduct us to most preposterous conclusions. But we have reason to cool our raging motions, our carnal stings, our unbitted lusts; whereof I take this, that you call love, to be a sect or scion.

(I.3.320–33)

For Iago here, the body is merely the casing and ultimately the servant of the mind. Ford is unlikely to have preferred Iago to Othello any more than any other reader or audience member every has. However, Ford's repeated reworkings of motifs from *Othello*, culminating in the thoroughgoing inversion of it in his last play, the tragicomedy *The Lady's Trial*, suggests that he was extremely interested in the emotional states represented in *Othello*, and in ways of avoiding that play's tragic outcome. Iago, who entirely ignores the possibility of love, may go too far in his theory of the parmountcy of the mind over the body, but that does not mean that his idea has no truth in it, and he is certainly able to carry out some very skilful emotional manipulation on that basis.

A similar contrast to that thus made between Iago and Othello is playcd out in *The Broken Heart*. Wc can sec a small-scale version of it an encounter between Orgilus and Bassanes. For Bassanes, as for Iago, the world is inside him: he says 'No tempests of commotion shall disquiet / The calms of my composure' (IV.ii.38–9). Orgilus by contrast echoes Othello in seeing his mentality as physicalised and reified. He tells Bassanes, 'Play not with misery / Past cure' (IV.ii.46–7), as if his own misery had an external existence and was not amenable to the normal laws of nature which might permit of a cure. Ithocles too imagines his own emotions as externalised and concretised:

> On my soul
> Lies such an infinite clog of massy dulness,
> As that I have not sense enough to feel it.
> See, uncle, th'augury thing reutrns again.
> Shall's welcome him with thunder? We are haunted
> And must use exorcism to conjure down
> This spirit of malevolence.
>
> (IV.ii.174–80)

Some editions change 'augury' to 'angry', but the suggestion of divination and of the supernatural, and of the heavens overarching the human, is continued in Nearchus' comment,

> Amelus, I perceive Calantha's bosom
> Is warm'd with other fires than such as can
> Take strength from any fuel of the love
> I might address to her. Young Ithocles,
> Or ever I mistake, is lord ascendant
> Of her devotions
>
> (IV.ii.196–201)

This retains, however, the material perspective; astral forces are merely larger and stronger physical bodies governing human ones, and consultation of them was indeed a standard part of Renaissance medical practice.

It is only fitting that what should precipitate the crisis of this thoroughly medicalised play is an illness, as Nearchus announces, 'The king is on a sudden indispos'd' (IV.ii.193). Now this play in which there has been so much talk of whether people can be helped and cured or not faces a crisis in which a radically physicalised view of humanity as almost on a continuum which the plant kingdom disables any possibility of hope, as Armostes relays the words of Tecnicus:

> *The plot in which the vine takes root*
> *Begins to dry from head to foot;*
> *The stock soon withering, want of sap*
> *Doth cause to quail the budding grape;*
> *But from the neighbouring elm, a dew*
> *Shall drop and feed the plot anew.*
>
> (IV.iii.11–16)

Amyclas takes a similarly materialist and physicalised view of people when he declares:

> There is no physic
> So cunningly restorative to cherish
> The fall of age, or call back youth and vigour
>
> (IV.iii.51–3)

Indeed, the process of physicalisation becomes increasingly grotesque, as Bassanes says,

> Armostes, rend not
> Thine arteries with hearing the bare circumstances
> Of these calamities.
>
> (V.ii.53–5)

This is a horrific image. However, Orgilus for one revels in this new language of extremes:

> *Nearchus.*   Now, Orgilus, thy choice?
> *Orgilus.*   To bleed to death.
> *Armostes.*   The executioner?
> *Orgilus.*   Myself, no surgeon;
> I am well skill'd in letting blood. Bind fast
> This arm, that so the pipes may from their conduits
> Convey a full stream. Here's a skilful instrument
>   (V.ii.97–102)

For Orgilus here, humans are effectively nothing more than a
conglomeration of pipes. Indeed he takes pride in his own espousal of
a totally physicalised perspective: 'Thus I show cunning / In opening
of a vein too full, too lively' (V.ii.121–2). This leads to a bizarrely
detailed medical discourse superseding that of passion, as Bassanes
says of Orgilus' blood,

> It sparkles like a lusty wine new broach'd;
> The vessel must be sound from which it issues.
>   (V.ii.124–5)

Calantha too subscribes to the physicalised view of humanity which
would see women as inherently different:

> A woman has enough to govern wisely
> Her own demeanours, passions, and divisions.
>   (V.iii.8–9)

And Calantha even describes her own death in medicalised terms
when she says, 'They are the silent griefs which cut the heartstrings'
(V.iii.75).

   Penthea, however, introduces the possibility of a quite different
perspective. For her, it is mental as well as physical states which
matter, as we see when, developing Cleopatra's and Mariam's idea of
the milkmaid, she says,

> The handmaid to the wages
> Of country toil drinks the untroubled streams
> With leaping kids and with the bleating lambs,
> And so allays her thirst secure, whiles I
> Quench my hot sighs with fleetings of my tears.
>   (III.iii.22–6)

Striking a balance between external and internal landscapes, Penthea here images a world configured equally by the material and the mental, just as she will later speak of 'the unguarded castle of the mind' (III.vi.23). Notably, too, she uses the imagery of the pastoral to do it, suggesting that for this woman, at least, pastoral is a literary genre which offers her a means of expressing her feelings. (This is an idea which also seems to be implicit in Sir Philip Sidney's dedication of his pastoral romance *The Countess of Pembroke's Arcadia* to his sister Mary, and *The Countess of Pembroke's Arcadia*, as I shall discuss below, was clearly an influence on *The Broken Heart*.) It is only in her madness that Penthea reverts to the medicalised view, which thus becomes clearly identified *with* madness, as she says of herself,

> since her blood was season'd by the forfeit
> Of noble shame with mixtures of pollution,
> Her blood – 'tis just – be henceforth never heighten'd
> With taste of sustenance. Starve; let that fullness
> Whose pleurisy hath fever'd faith and modesty –
> Forgive me; Oh, I faint!
>
> (IV.ii.149–54)

Now Penthea thinks that there are 'Nor cure nor comforts for a leprous soul' (IV.ii.169), as though the soul needed to be treated with medicine like the body. This chimes fully with Bassanes' claim that

> There is a mastery
> In art to fatten and keep smooth the outside;
> Yes, and to comfort up the vital spirits
> Without the help of food: fumes or perfumes,
> Perfumes or fumes.
>
> (IV.ii.162–6)

Before this, however, Penthea knows better, and what she knows is not so much medicine as what we would now call psychiatry. And what is remarkable about Penthea's description of her own feelings is the extent to which her imaging of them is mediated through what she has read.

Most obviously, Penthea here uses the Petrarchan discourse of sighs and tears. Petrarchan language is risky for a woman, as we see in the ways in which it sets up a competition between women in *The Tragedy of Mariam*, and also in the embattled reputation of Sir Philip Sidney's niece Lady Mary Wroth, famous almost equally for her writing and for her adulterous affair with her cousin William Herbert, Earl of Pembroke. Petrarchism, for women, then, is marked as dangerous, but that it is also potentially fruitful and recuperative is clearly shown by its insistent use by a poet like Lady Mary Wroth.[40] Penthea also demonstrates two further sets of literary affiliations. She echoes both Cleopatra and Mariam when she contrasts her own position with that of a pastoral figure, and she also makes clear her grasp of the extent to which the pastoral is a state of mind, a *locus* in the literary as well as the literal sense, by that seamless transition to the quasi-Petrarchan idea of quenching sighs with tears. Moreover, Penthea's use of pastoral discourse further aligns her not only with Wroth again, but, more tellingly in this context, with Wroth's uncle, Sir Philip Sidney. There are strong parallels between the *Arcadia*, Ford's work in general, and *The Broken Heart* in particular. Sidney is indebted to Sannazaro,[41] whom Ford mentions by name in *'Tis Pity*, while Pyrocles in the *Arcadia* anticipates Giovanni's curiosity about the nature of the after-life when he speculates that 'I perceive we shall have a debate in the other world, if at least there remain anything of remembrance in that place' (*Arcadia*, p. 804). In *The Old Arcadia*, Pyrocles' name when in disguise is Cleophila, in honour of Philoclea, and this is the name of the heroine's sister in *The Lover's Melancholy* (set in Cyprus, original home of Sidney's Gynecia); Pamphilus in the new version of the *Arcadia* womanises in the same way as Ferentes in *Love's Sacrifice*, and suffers the same fate of death at the hands of those he has deceived.

Most obviously, the Prologue to *The Broken Heart* asserts that

> What may be here thought a fiction, when time's youth
> Wanted some riper years, was known a truth.[42]

This has often been taken to refer to the real-life relationship between Sidney and Penelope Rich, sister of the Earl of Essex and the 'Stella' of *Astrophil and Stella*,[43] and, as her blonde hair and black eyes (*Arcadia*, p. 146) and Pyrocles' reference to her as 'my only star' (*Arcadia*, p. 741) make plain, the model for Philoclea. (The black eyes of Penelope Rich also helped perpetuate the emphasis on darkness introduced to English Petrarchan poetry by the black eyes of her mother's cousin Anne Boleyn.) The story of Orgilus and Penthea certainly does have elements in common with that of Sidney and his Stella, while the names of Ford's characters may well seem to echo those of Argalus and Parthenia, who feature in one of the numerous sub-plots of the new

Arcadia. In the *Arcadia*, the King of Laconia is called Amiclas, matching Ford's Amyclas; Parthenia when deformed refuses to marry Argalus, just as Penthea refuses Orgilus, though Parthenia later, in disguise, tries to trick Argalus into marrying her with a ring, rather as Calantha asserts her wedding to Ithocles. There are other parallels, too. When Pyrocles tells Philoclea his identity she has 'a divided mind' (*Arcadia*, p. 329), just as Euphranea has when Prophilus proposes marriage to her. Argalus, like Orgilus, bleeds to death and finds 'each thing beginning to turn round in the dance of death before his eyes' (*Arcadia*, p. 507) just as the execution of Orgilus forms the conclusion to Calantha's literalised dance of death, and Argalus also has bleeding hearts, a favourite Ford idea, embroidered by Parthenia upon his sleeve (*Arcadia*, p. 504). Cecropia, like Nearchus, is the child of the King of Argos, and hopes that her son Amphialus will succeed his uncle Basileus as king, as Nearchus succeeds his uncle Amyclas. The *Arcadia*'s posthumous prologue 'To the Reader' contains the plea 'if they may be entreated not to define which are unfurnished of means to discern, the rest, it is hoped, will favourably censure', just as the epilogue to *Broken Heart* sternly declares 'Those censures may command / Belief which talk not till they understand' (3–4).

Even more interestingly, the prologue 'To the Reader' also disables other judges by exclaiming 'What talk they of flowers! They are roses not flowers must do them good' (p. 59). This might well shed new light on Ford's celebrated lines about roses in *The Broken Heart*,

> When we last gather'd roses in the garden,
> I found my wits, but truly you lost yours.
> (IV.ii.120–1)

Perhaps these lines are more than simply elegiac; perhaps they do posit a causal relationship between the gathering of roses – often seen as a cordial in seventeenth-century medicine – and the loss of wits. If Ford is thinking here in medicalised terms, though, he is not positing a simple link between bodies and minds. If roses are medicinal and the absence or presence of them induces or banishes madness, then the mind and the body must certainly be linked, but it is also impossible to overlook the strongly affective connotations of roses which makes the process more than simply a physiological one. Indeed Ford's representation of the relationship between body and psyche is generally a subtle one, and in *The Broken Heart* it is one of the most savage of the play's ironies that while everyone around her is taking such a relentlessly physicalised perspective on events, Penthea, though her body is cosseted, should go quietly and irreversibly insane.

'*Tis Pity She's a Whore* goes even further than *The Broken Heart* towards underlining the importance of a psychiatric as well as a purely medical perspective. Of course this was not new – as early as the first half of the sixteenth century the Italian humanist practitioner Giovanni Manardi (1462–1536) noted how 'Galen's psychiatry cure[d] melancholic correspondents in both Hungary and Italy'[44] – but Ford's interest in disorders of the mind ranges beyond common complaints to delusion about one's own identity (as is apparently the case in *Perkin Warbeck*) and to psychosexual disorders of the sort explored in *The Fancies Chaste and Noble*. Even the incest of '*Tis Pity She's a Whore* can be seen as presented in psychiatrised terms, since Ford's depiction of the relationship of Giovanni and Annabella may well have been influenced by early diagnoses of the psychiatric syndrome *folie à deux*. Although the term *folie à deux* was not used until the 1870s, the condition itself had been commented on long before that, by James Primrose in 1638, William Harvey in 1651 and Sir Kenelm Digby in 1658. Although the publication of all these discussions postdates that of Ford's plays, this does not preclude the possibility that the ideas themselves had been previously publicised; Harvey, for example, did not publish his discovery of the circulation of the blood until 1628, although he had been referring to it in his lectures since 1615. If the ideas had indeed been previously aired, Ford could certainly have heard of them, since both Harvey and Digby were friendly with several of his dedicatees.[45] Certainly Digby's description of the delusion of two sisters, of whom one is cured when separated from the other, comes very close to '*Tis Pity*'s story of a shared indifference to the values of the world which then changes to repentance on Annabella's part when she is removed from the orbit of Giovanni.

Above all, while medicalisation proved a conservative and restricting discourse for women, that of psychiatry could be enabling (and perhaps provided one of the reasons why Kenelm Digby, in an age which fetishised virginity, could unquestioningly adore a wife who, at least according to John Aubrey, had very publicly fallen).[46] The seismic shift in attitudes which this new perspective permitted can be clearly seen by charting the differences between and Shakespeare's *Othello* and Ford's own *The Lady's Trial*, in which a woman successfully pleads her innocence to a suspicious husband. It can be seen, too, in the differences between plays like *The Insatiate Countess* and Shirley's *The Lady of Pleasure*, in which the adulterous heroine Aretina goes

unpunished and indeed undetected because she has genuinely
reformed, moving from a consciousness of her own sin in which she
says 'My soul is miserable' to a confident aside that

> Already
> I feel a cure upon my soul, and promise
> My after life to virtue; pardon, heaven,
> My shame yet hid from the world's eye.[47]

Of course, Shirley's play is a comedy, but that in itself is not enough
to account for so dramatic a difference, and it is particularly suggestive
that Bornwell, Aretina's unusually inventive and understanding
husband, specifically refers to himself as having seen plays and as
having thought about their effect on the audience:

> There was a play on't,
> And had the poet not been bribed to a modest
> Expression of your antic gambols in't,
> Some darks had been discovered, and the deeds too;
> In time he may repent and make some blush
> To see the second part danced on the stage.
>
> (I.i.119–24)

Drama here is clearly marked as educative.

Ford's Penthea and Calantha are not able to share the kind of cure
and reformation which Bornwell's tolerance and cunning play on her
psychology eventually allow Aretina to attain. For them, as for
Parthenia in the *Arcadia*, it is already far too late. Death is the only
possible balm for the crippling emotional wounds they have sustained,
as it was too for Penelope Rich herself, who died relatively young very
soon after she had been widowed (and after Ford had dedicated to her
his first published work, condoling on her loss). Nevertheless, by
recalling her history, Ford's play, like Cary's, does not simply reduplicate the events of the past which it recounts; it contests them. Ford
does not actually illustrate here, as he was to do in *The Lady's Trial*,
how a different outcome could have been achieved, but he leaves us in
no doubt that it would have been possible for that to have happened.
Ithocles and Orgilus take no note either of books or of the emotions of
others. Calantha and Penthea are not shown as having any access
to books, and we see very clearly that, ignorant of history, they are
thus condemned to repeat it. Above all, none of these characters

demonstrates any sort of metatheatrical awareness. Ford himself is one of the most consistently allusive of writers, but his characters are presented as unaware of any form of literary or theatrical tradition, and consequently as tragically trapped. Even Penthea appears unconscious that the emotions she expresses echo any previously expressed. Not until *The Concealed Fancies* – a play itself very obviously influenced by Ford, and unafraid to proclaim so – are women shows as knowing the writing of the past, and therefore able to avoid duplicating the mistakes it describes.

The Concealed Fancies: the real female heroes

The Concealed Fancies is centred on two sisters, Luceny and Tattiney, and their suitors Courtley and Presumption (who, despite his unprepossessing name, is by no means a bad character – perhaps 'assumption' comes closer to his mode of behaviour). The girls' father, Monsieur Calsindow, who is away, is also being courted, by the vulgar Lady Tranquillity; and the two girls' brothers, known only as Elder Stellow and Younger Stellow, are in amorous pursuit of two of their three cousins, who are besieged in the castle of Ballamo. (The eldest of these is called Cicilley; the two youngest are known only by the speech prefixes of Sh. and Is.) The Stellows eventually rescue the besieged women and, in a grand, masque-like finale, Monsieur Calsindow returns and gives his consent to the marriages of his sons and daughters. He himself announces his intention to marry a waiting-maid, but is dissuaded by an angel, and the play closes with an epilogue in which Luceny and Tattiney discuss the unexpectedly satisfactory state of their marriages. It is not clear whether the play was ever performed – the absence until after the end of the civil war of the sisters' father, who so clearly forms a major part of the intended audience, may have deterred them from staging it – but it would have been eminently stageable.

What distinguishes *The Concealed Fancies* is above all its intense and sustained quality both of saturation in other dramas and of intelligent reflection both on these earlier plays and on their cultural positions. Its authors, Lady Jane Cavendish (1616–69) and Lady Elizabeth Brackley (1621–63), were the daughters of William Cavendish, first Earl of Newcastle, and of his first wife Elizabeth; their grandfather had been Bess of Hardwick's younger son Charles Cavendish, builder of the neo-chivalric fantasy castle of Bolsover. Newcastle's cousins on his father's side included Lady Arbella Stuart, whose mother had been Bess of Hardwick's daughter,[48] and Lady Mary Talbot, whose husband William Herbert, 3rd Earl of Pembroke, was one of the two 'incomparable brethren' to whom Shakespeare's First Folio was dedicated.[49] Pembroke was also the nephew of Sir Philip Sidney, the son of Mary Sidney, Countess of Pembroke, and the lover of his cousin Lady Mary Wroth.

The Cavendish sisters were thus part of an extended family circle with copious and intimate knowledge of the dramatic productions and conventions of the thirty or so years which had preceded the start of the Civil War.[50] Newcastle, in addition to being an amateur dramatist himself,[51] had been the patron of Jonson, Shirley, Brome and Ford, and had specially commissioned Jonson's *Love's Welcome to Bolsover* (1634) for the reception of Charles I at one of the Cavendish family seats; and the woman with whom he may, at the time of the play's composition, already have been emotionally involved, Margaret Lucas (who is sometimes suggested as the model for Lady Tranquillity in his daughters' play) was also distinguished for her literary interests, and was later, as Margaret Cavendish, to become a celebrated, if derided, producer of fiction, plays, poetry and scientific writing. The younger of Newcastle's two daughters, Lady Elizabeth, had also married into a similarly theatrical tradition, for in 1642 she had become the wife of John Egerton, Viscount Brackley (Earl of Bridgewater after 1649),[52] who had been one of the children for whom Milton's *Comus* (1634) was originally written, and had acted the Elder Brother. It is hardly surprising, therefore, that the Cavendish sisters' own work should prove to be densely metatheatrical, full of references not only to the playing of parts in general but to particular and specific Renaissance plays, including plays by Shakespeare.

It is also unsurprising that their work, like Ford's, should show signs of a psychiatrised perspective, for this was implicit in the very fabric of their lives. In the first place, their father's cousin Arbella had ended her life insane, starving herself to death, which must surely have heightened awareness of mental health in the family in general. In the second, the decorative scheme of the ground floor of the Little Castle at Bolsover was based entirely on the idea of the interplay between passions and body. In the Hall, frescoes depicted the animal labours of Hercules, representing man subduing his animal passions, while in the Marble Closet, a painting shows Patience crushing a heart in a press to demonstrate her superiority to emotion.[53] These are, moreover, images which work in very different ways from the prescriptions of conventional iconography, with its restricted range: here the image is accommodated to the measure of the human rather than the human having to fit him or herself into the preshaped dimensions of the image. And when in the most private area of the castle we find ourselves being offered a choice between two closets, one symbolising the fleshly delights of the pagan Elysium and the other the spiritual blessings of the Christian Heaven, it seems to be clearly suggested that the mind need not be conditioned by the body, but may act independently of it.

All the drama produced by and for the Cavendish household is remarkable for the extent of its interplay with its physical surroundings, and *The Concealed Fancies* is no exception. As well as working firmly within the traditions of drama associated with the Cavendish family – Alison Findlay suggests that the girls had most likely seen the two Jonson pieces, and that costumes from them might even have been still available[54] – *The Concealed Fancies* also shows clear marks of its location. Written when the two sisters were under siege by Parliamentary troops, most probably at Welbeck,[55] it alludes repeatedly to both its historical moment and its geographical setting. A character identified only by the speech-heading 'Sh', who, like the authors, is besieged by the Parliamentarians, asks her sisters, 'Pray, how did I look in the posture of a delinquent?';[56] Tattiney's references to her 'dark parlour room' (p. 150) and Luceny's to walking in the 'nuns' gallery' look like specific allusions to features of the abbey; and the two sisters, appropriately enough for a play conceived in a former abbey (doorways from which can still be seen today in the lower portions of the building), dress up as nuns.[57] Most intriguingly, there seems to be a reference to the elaborate decorative schemes characteristic of Cavendish houses when Luceny says that 'Each chamber ceiling doth create true sad, / Yet tempered so as I am quiet, glad' (p. 149). Welbeck has been much altered since the seventeenth century, and the only painted ceiling known to be still preserved, in the Duke of Newcastle's riding school (built in 1623), is nineteenth-century (and currently invisible, hidden behind a plaster barrel-vault ceiling, though a small door in this still gives access to the roof-space),[58] but Cavendish propensities might well have meant that there would originally have been others.

This interplay with the physical and material details of Welbeck's past is matched by an acute awareness of those of its present. We are constantly reminded that Ballamo Castle – the Welbeck of the play – is under siege, not only by the insistent use of military language such as 'the magazine of love' but also by a sustained emphasis on the difficulty of preserving private space inviolate. Though much is made of the sisters' neglect of household affairs – 'those wits will ne'er be housewives' (p. 134) – the two girls are very aware of the house itself, and what it means both literally and metaphorically: Luceny asks Courtley to 'make an honourable retreat out of the house' or she would 'cause Mr Steward to make him make his retreat with more confusion' (p. 135) Just as we hear in technical detail about the defensibility of the siege works at Ballamo (pp. 140–1), so we have a clear sense here of the physical and psychological importance of the house's boundaries. It is not a space in which women are allowed to move freely, as we see in Luceny's imagined dependence on the intervention of the Steward, and Presumption's threat that Tattiney will not be able to speak to a male servant when they are married, 'were it but to know who it was that came last into the house' (p. 142). Nevertheless, it is the only one which they can possibly inhabit, and to be in it boosts their status: Presumption threatens that if Tattiney 'do not give respect to my mother and sisters, I will tell her she hath not deserved to enter into my honourable old house' (p. 142), striking a similar note to William Cavendish's *A Debauched Gallant*, where there is an acute consciousness of how a woman who is not legitimately married may end up having to give birth literally in the street, since her seducer has barred his door.[59] The Cavendish sisters' play, then, never loses sight of the interdependence of the material and the mental.

Moreover, the crossover between reality and fiction in *The Concealed Fancies* is doubly appropriate because the text shows itself perpetually aware of the performed and theatrical nature not just of conventional social intercourse but of *all* selfhood. In only the second line of the play, Presumption uses an extremely suggestive phrase: commenting on Tattiney's behaviour to him, he says, 'Faith, my misfortune is, she knows her scene-self too well' (p. 133). To think of one's self as something that is played seems indeed to be second nature to the more intelligent characters of the play, as is the use of theatrical and metatheatrical metaphors: Presumption counsels Courtley, 'Come let's go to them and see how they will act their scenes' (p. 133), while both girls separately affect to assume that the courtships of Presumption and Courtley are not genuinely intended but are either dress-rehearsals or action replays of some similar scene in which they have been or will be in earnest. The awareness is, however, particularly acute for the two sisters Luceny and Tattiney, since, as for their authors, language and performance are the only arenas of action currently open to them. But then, the play's intense self-reflexiveness and metatheatrical allusions have already served to suggest that actually that is *always* so, and that it need not necessarily be a limiting thing.

The most immediately obvious of the play's allusions to other drama comes in Act III, scene iv. While the three cousins, Cicilley, Is., and Sh., are besieged in Ballamo Castle, the following conversation takes place:

> *SH.* Pray, how did I look in the posture of a delinquent?
> *Cicilley.* You mean how did you behave yourself in the posture of a delinquent? Faith, as though you thought the scene would change again, and you would be happy though you suffered misery for a time. And how did I look?
> *SH.* As yourself; that's great, though in misfortune.
> *Cicilley.* So did you.
> *SH.* How should I do otherwise, for I practised Cleopatra when she was in her captivity, and could they have thought me worthy to have adorned her triumphs[,] I would have performed his gallant tragedy and so have made myself glorious for time to come.[60]

There seems little doubt that an allusion to Shakespeare is intended here – who else can the referent of 'his' be, unless conceivably Garnier or Fulke Greville? – particularly in the light of an earlier scene (III.iii) in which Courtley and Presumption have discussed techniques of wife-taming very similar to those employed by Petruchio; they, however, will meet with markedly less success than he, since their wives, like Fletcher's heroine in *The Woman's Prize*, have ideas of their own on the subject.

Nor is this the only pointer to Shakespeare. Sophie Tomlinson characterises Luceny and Tattiney as 'tormenting [their suitors], Beatrice-like, on the rack of their language',[61] and it is also tempting to see a reference to Shakespeare in the prologue of *The Concealed Fancies*, where the desirability of having a woman introduce the play is discussed in terms which Cerasano and Wynne-Davies find suggestive of the epilogue of *As You Like It* (note, p. 209):

> Ladies, I beseech you not to see
> That I speak a prologue, being a she;
> For it becomes as well if votes cry, aye,
> Why then should I, a petticoat, cry, fie!
> Gentlemen if so you allow, is wit,
> Why then not speak, I pray your patience, sit;

And now to tell you truth of our new play:
It doth become a woman's wit the very way,
And I did tell the poet plainly truth,
It looks like eighteen or twenty-two youth,
Or else it would not be, as 'tis but well;
I'll say no more until your hand-plays tell.

(A prologue to the stage)

This, the first of three prologues to the play, offers at the least a fruitful comparison with, and arguably a direct reworking of, Rosalind's famous lines:

It is not the fashion to see the lady the epilogue; but it is no more unhandsome than to see the lord the prologue. If it be true that good wine needs no bush, 'tis true that a good play needs no epilogue. Yet to good wine they do use good bushes; and good plays prove the better by the help of good epilogues. What a case am I in then, that am neither a good epilogue, nor cannot insinuate with you in the behalf of a good play? I am not furnished like a beggar, therefore to beg will not become me. My way is to conjure you, and I'll begin with the women ... [62]

In both, the woman's voice becomes both speaker and subject of the dramatic language, and both highlight the nature of female presence and response within the theatrical tradition, as the woman who really appears on stage (and who also highlights the issue of female authorship) echoes the male-authored, male-actored simulacrum of 'Rosalind'. Once again, it seems, women writers find the discourse of the pastoral enabling (and indeed the Cavendish sisters' other surviving joint-authored work is entitled simply *A Pastoral*).

But although this prologue may seem to have something of the character of a rejoinder to Rosalind, what is most notable, perhaps, is that for the fictional women of *The Concealed Fancies*, and by extension, presumably, for the real women who wrote it, Shakespeare is primarily depicted as empowering. Knowledge of him and remembrance of his works offers spiritual support when under siege; Cleopatra is invoked as a positive and very relevant role model. This surely counts as invaluable first-hand testimony in the debates about the position of women in the late Renaissance audience and about the representation of women on the Shakespearean stage. It also helps us see the ways in which the Cavendish sisters' construction of voices for their fictional heroines depend on the recollection and appropriation of earlier dramatic voices.

Shakespeare, moreover, is not the only famous author evoked in the play. After their discussion of Cleopatra, Sh., Is. and Cicilley move on to a new topic: they decide to open the private closet of their uncle Lord Calsindow, to see what cordials he keeps in it. In itself, this may well be reminiscent of the scene in *The Changeling* in which Beatrice-Joanna similarly rifles the medicine chest of her newly married husband, although the play also suggests an alternative context by its overt reference to 'my Lady Kent's cordials' (III.iv.56–7), an allusion to the herbal knowledge of the Cavendish sisters' aunt Elizabeth Grey, Countess of Kent, who in 1653 was to publish *A Choice Manuall of Rare and Select Secrets of Physick and Chirurgery* (Cerasano and Wynne-Davies, p. 212). Additionally, though, Sh. wants her pleasure enhanced, in a species of reverse voyeurism, by the thought that her uncle might be able to see them; although she knows that he is in France, she comments, 'I wish he saw us in a prospective' (III.iv.46). When Is. replies rather mundanely 'But 'tis a great way for him to look in a prospective' (III.iv.47–8), Cicilley answers ''Tis no matter, 'tis a wish' (III.iv.49). I suspect a joke here about a similar exchange in *The Duchess of Malfi*, where Bosola tells the Duchess that her curse on the stars has not been effective – 'Look you, the stars shine still' – and she replies, 'O, but you must / Remember, my curse hath a great way to go'.[63] Is. seems to show a similar literal-mindedness; what Cicilley does is effectively point out to her the difference that context and convention make to the decoding of meaning. The exchange must surely be meant to be comical, a sophisticated juggling with codes, allusions and tone, of a piece with the play's pervasive concern with discourse; and as such it serves as a good pointer to the complex self-referentiality and play of metatheatrical allusion which structures so much of Renaissance drama and allows us to see in each play an informed engagement with its predecessors. Moreover, the Duchess of Malfi is, surely, a suitable companion for Cleopatra in the catalogue of the play's allusions, and an appropriate figure for these resolute young women, since she, too, refuses to bow to male pressure and stays true to her own values. Webster's tragedy has sometimes been seen as influenced by the story of Lady Arbella Stuart, who was Newcastle's first cousin, in which case the allusion would be a family one.[64] The whole effect is, moreover, highlighted by drawing attention to the self-conscious metatheatricality of the scene, a quality which in itself serves to underline that even if no actual allusions are detected, the dramaturgical principles here are certainly comparable with those informing the work of Shakespeare and his contemporaries.

Other allusions in *The Concealed Fancies* are clearly less specific, but nevertheless cumulatively important. The Angel evokes the genre of the mystery play rather than any particular example of it, and this is also the case with the masque ending[65] – an appropriately defiant generic feature to find in a work written shortly after the closing of the theatres by royalist authors. The idea evoked when Care says to the maid that 'thy very name, Pretty, hath undone thee' (V.v.23–4) points, by its use of names, in the direction of both moralities and masques, without scoring a square hit on either, but does suggests that the allegorical mode once used to restrict women can now be definitively suborned by them. Similarly, the two brothers who are so determined to rescue their imprisoned mistresses may be reminiscent of the two brothers of *Comus* (one of whom had, after all, originally been acted by Lady Elizabeth's husband), but for that matter it would be equally possible to argue for a similarity with the heroics of Pyrocles and Musidorus when Pamela and Philoclea are kidnapped by Amphialus; and the general motif of the imprisoned beauty can also be clearly related to courtly allegories of the castle of love.

One playwright, however, does seem to me to be consistently alluded to. John Ford had dedicated his *Chronicle History of Perkin Warbeck* (1634), a play about the celebrated impostor, to the girls' father, Newcastle. The sisters' use of the word 'imposture' (I.iv.59) might seem suggestive in this context, as might the fact that the comment 'I'll have a lady of the times' (IV.v.76–7) directly echoes a phrase very pointedly and self-consciously used in Ford's part of *The Welsh Embassador*, which he co-authored with Dekker. The highly sophisticated remark that 'we have been brought up in the creation of good languages, which will make us ever ourselves' (II.iii.142–4) is also closely comparable with the twin emphases in *Perkin Warbeck* on language and selfhood, quite apart from its obvious applicability to contemporary concepts of Renaissance self-fashioning. Toy, referring to the heroines, says 'this lady that I mean will have her several scenes, now wife, then mistress, then my sweet Platonic soul' (IV.v.55–7), a clear reference to the Platonic love cult of Henrietta Maria with which Ford has been so often associated. The very title of the play, *The Concealed Fancies*, could be taken as an allusion to Ford's own *The Fancies Chaste and Noble*, which, like *The Concealed Fancies*, features three cousins forced to live in seclusion. Finally, when the two girls accuse their suitors of adopting conventional poses, they are echoing the only known description of Ford's own appearance and behaviour. 'Now, will not your next posture be to stand with folded arms? But that posture now grows much out of fashion' (I.iv.67–9) says Luceny to Courtley barely six lines after the imposture reference, while Tattiney asks Presumption, 'Now, do you think the pulling down your hat and looking sad, shall make me believe your speech for truth?' (II.ii.20–2). In William Hemminge's *Elegy on Randolph's Finger*, Ford is thus described:

> Deep in a dump Jack Ford alone was gat,
> With folded arms and melancholy hat.[66]

Maybe, then, this system of references to Ford serves not only to point to an author intimately associated with the sisters' own family tradition but also to point up the striking self-consciousness and metatheatricality of their own drama in comparison with his.

Certainly *The Concealed Fancies* as a whole is full of metatheatrical references. It opens with not one but three highly self-conscious Prologues, the first two of which explicitly raise the issue of gender: as the second prologue jestingly remarks, ''tis woman all the way; / For you'll not see a plot in any act' (The second prologue, ll.14–15). And Presumption's line 'Faith, my misfortune is, she knows her scene-self too well' (I.i.3–4) is not only a pun on 'seen' – the sisters throughout the play show themselves intensely aware of the constitutive and erotic power of the gaze – but also, as the many later references to such a concept make clear, an acknowledgement of the position into which Tattiney has been so self-consciously interpellated by dramatic and Petrarchan convention. What the play reveals is not only the force of the interpellative processes and positions but also the extent to which their occupiers are aware of them: as Courtley ruefully exclaims, 'What a misfortune's this to me, / To court a wench that doth so truly see' (I.iv.110–11). Both real and fictional sets of sisters fashion, through their self-consciously fashionable art, an image of the ways in which selves both fashion and are fashioned within a shaping framework of art.

In short, Jane Cavendish and Elizabeth Brackley have created a sophisticated work which needs to be read with strong awareness of both generic convention and specific allusion if the fancies concealed within it are to be revealed and properly understood. Most striking of all the sisters' reshapings of generic conventions is the simple fact that, although it draws on so many tragedies about women, this play is not itself a tragedy. Its masque-like ending offers us the besieged cousins rescued, and the two sisters settled down into marriages which, we learn from the final scene, are working, if anything, rather better than they expected. Not only is Cleopatra deployed here as an empowering figure, but the very genre of tragedies about women is here recuperated as essentially enabling and indeed inspirational, since by offering more and more discourses about women and modes of understanding them, it has effectively allowed them to choose one they like.

Equally noteworthy is the tolerance and liberalism of the perspective offered by this play. Although it was written when the sisters were actually besieged by the Parliamentarians and in imminent danger from them, it has no villains, with the arguable exception of Lady Tranquillity. Even then, the girls' father is pointedly exculpated from any taint by association; his notorious philandering is cheerfully accepted as a simple byproduct of that sanguine humour for which he was so famous that in the Anteroom of Bolsover Castle, paintings of three of the four humours were accompanied by merely the background for a representation of the sanguine, since the effect was intended to be completed by the presence of William Cavendish himself. Similarly both Courtley and Presumption, despite the apparent opposition implied by their names, are accepted with equal readiness into the family structure. Cleopatra may have started life as 'the brown Egyptian', but to 'practise' her has, it now seems, opened the door to a new acceptance of a proliferation and diversity of roles far beyond the dichotomised ones which exerted such a stranglehold over *The Tragedy of Mariam,* and the agent which has effected this change is essentially the repeated representation and re-presentation of even negatively intended dramatic images of women. Locked inside the closet, women have finally looked round to see what was in it, and in so doing, they have found the means to get out of it.

Notes

Introduction

1. Arthur Little, *Shakespeare Jungle Fever: National-Imperial Re-Visions of Race, Rape, and Sacrifice* (Stanford: Stanford University Press, 2000), p. 2.
2. Margaret Cavendish, *Bell in Campo* (1662), *dramatis personae*.
3. See for instance Andreas Mahler, 'Italian Vices: Cross-cultural Constructions of Temptation and Desire in English Renaissance Drama', in *Shakespeare's Italy: Functions of Italian Locations in Renaissance Drama*, edited by Michele Marrapodi, A.J. Hoenselaars, Marcello Cappuzzo and L. Falzon Santucci (Manchester: Manchester University Press, 1993), pp. 49–68, p. 64; and Eileen Allman, *Jacobean Revenge Tragedy and the Politics of Virtue* (Newark: University of Delaware Press, 1999), p. 104.
4. See for instance Judith Butler, *Bodies That Matter: On the Discursive Limits of 'Sex'* (New York and London: Routledge, 1993), p. 5.

Chapter 1

1. See Thomas Laqueur, *Making Sex: Body and Gender from the Greeks to Freud* (Cambridge, Mass.: Harvard University Press, 1990), p. 64.
2. Katharine Park and Robert A. Nye, review of Thomas Laqueur, *Making Sex: Body and Gender from the Greeks to Freud*, *New Republic* 18:2 (1991), pp. 53–5, p. 54.
3. For discussion of Fallopius' residual allegiance to the one-sex model, see Winifred Schleiner, 'Early Modern Controversies about the One-Sex Model', *Renaissance Quarterly* 53:1 (Spring 2000), pp. 180–91, p. 183. Schleiner traces the first serious challenge to the one-sex model to André Dulaurens, personal physician to Henri IV (p. 188).
4. See Kate Aughterson, *Renaissance Woman: A Sourcebook* (London: Routledge, 1995), p. 42.
5. Jonathan Sawday, *The Body Emblazoned* (London: Routledge, 1995), p. 222.
6. Jane Sharp, *The Midwives Book, Or the Whole Art of Midwifery Discovered*, edited by Elaine Hobby (Oxford: Oxford University Press, 1999), introduction, p. xvi.
7. See Dale J. B. Randall, 'Some New Perspectives on the Spanish Setting of *The Changeling* and its Source', *Medieval and Renaissance Drama in England* 3 (1986), pp. 189–216, appendix.
8. For a differently slanted analysis of the play's hidden spaces, which sees them in terms of the classic and grotesque bodies rather than gendered bodies, see Michael Neill, *Issues of Death: Mortality and Identity in English Renaissance Tragedy* (Oxford: Clarendon Press, 1997), pp. 176–97.
9. Caroline di Miceli, 'Sickness and Physic in Some Plays by Middleton and Webster', *Cahiers Elisabéthains* 26 (1984), pp. 41–78, p. 47. Di Miceli makes

a thorough job of rounding up references to medicines in this and other plays. However, her article concentrates primarily on illness and cures, and suffers from being seriously underhistoricised, with remarks such as 'Purgation as a means of relieving sickness has been used since the origins of man' (p. 45) and 'Since Chaucer's day, their associated in crime had not changed' (p. 55, *sic*).

10. Dympna Callaghan argues that the postcoital change in her is confirmed by her growing affection for De Flores (*Woman and Gender in Renaissance Tragedy* [Hemel Hempstead: Harvester Wheatsheaf, 1989], p. 62).
11. Randall, 'Some New Perspectives', p. 196.
12. Sara Eaton, 'Beatrice-Joanna and the Rhetoric of Love in *The Changeling*', *Theatre Journal* 36:3 (1984), pp. 371–82, p. 372.
13. For comment on this passage, see for instance Kay Stockholder, 'The Aristocratic Woman as Scapegoat: Romantic Love and Class Antagonism in *The Spanish Tragedy, The Duchess of Malfi* and *The Changeling*', *The Elizabethan Theatre XIV*, edited by A.L. Magnusson and C.E. McGee (Toronto: P.D. Meany, 1996), pp. 127–51, pp. 145–7.
14. Thomas Middleton and William Rowley, *The Changeling*, edited by Joost Daalder (London: A. & C. Black, 1990), IV.i.35–8. All further quotations from the text will be taken from this edition.
15. Compare for instance Susan J. Wiseman, '*'Tis Pity She's a Whore*: Representing the Incestuous Body', in *Renaissance Bodies*, edited by Lucy Gent and Nigel Llewellyn (London: Reaktion Books, 1990), pp. 180–97. For a powerfully developed argument that we should take the virginity test in *The Changeling* seriously, see Dale J.B. Randall, 'Some Observations on the Theme of Chastity in *The Changeling*', *English Literary Renaissance* 14 (1984), pp. 357–66, pp. 355–60.
16. Cristina Malcolmson, '"As Tame as the Ladies": Politics and Gender in *The Changeling*', *English Literary Renaissance* 20 (1990), pp. 320–39, pp. 326–7.
17. For a rather different reading of the use of the closet here as a site of scientific exploration, see Molly Smith, *Breaking Boundaries: Politics and Play in the Drama of Shakespeare and his Contemporaries* (Aldershot: Ashgate, 1998), p. 92.
18. Malcolmson, '"As Tame as the Ladies"', p. 334, note 37.
19. On the significance of Antoine Mizauld, see Randall, 'Some Observations on the Theme of Chastity in *The Changeling*', pp. 358–9.
20. See Margot Heinemann, *Puritanism and Theatre: Thomas Middleton and Opposition Drama Under the Early Stuarts* (Cambridge: Cambridge University Press, 1980), pp. 178–9; Malcolmson, '"As Tame as the Ladies"', pp. 325–6 and pp. 333–9; Thomas Middleton, *The Witch*, edited by Elizabeth Schafer (London: A. & C. Black, 1994), pp. xv–xix, xxii; J.L. Simmons, 'Diabolical Realism in Middleton and Rowley's *The Changeling*', *Renaissance Drama* 11 (1980), pp. 135–70, pp. 155–65; David Lindley, *The Trials of Frances Howard* (London: Routledge, 1993), pp. 67, 78–9, 114–15 and 120–1; Anne Lancashire, '*The Witch*: Stage Flop or Political Mistake?', in *'Accompaninge the players': Essays Celebrating Thomas Middleton, 1580–1980*, edited by Kenneth Friedenreich (New York: AMS Press, 1983), pp. 161–81, pp. 163–9; and A.A. Bromham and Zara Bruzzi, *The Changeling and the Years of Crisis, 1619–24* (London: Pinter, 1990). Douglas Duncan, in 'Virginity in

196   *The Female Hero in English Renaissance Tragedy*

The Changeling', *English Studies in Canada* 9 (1983), pp. 25–35, p. 28, argues that Beatrice-Joanna's fetishisation of her virginity aligns her very closely with the values attributed to Catholicism, which would work as a further connection between her and the world of the Howards.

21. Beatrice White, *Cast of Ravens: The Strange Case of Sir Thomas Overbury* (London: John Murray, 1965), pp. 63–6.
22. Lindley, *The Trials of Frances Howard*, p. 81.
23. D.J.H. Clifford, ed., *The Diaries of Lady Anne Clifford* (Stroud: Alan Sutton, 1990), p. 35.
24. See Christopher Ricks, 'The Moral and Poetic Structure of *The Changeling*', *Essays in Criticism* 10 (1960), pp. 290–306, p. 301, for both the originality of the episode and comment on some of its possible significances.
25. Quoted in Lindley, *The Trials of Frances Howard*, p. 65. I am grateful to Zara Bruzzi for an illuminating conversation about the episode of the glove.
26. Quoted in Lindley, *The Trials of Frances Howard*, p. 22. Malcolmson comments that the image is reused in *Women Beware Women* ('"As Tame as the Ladies"', p. 337). On connections between Frances Howard, *Hymenaei* and *Women Beware Women*, see also Zara Bruzzi and A.A. Bromham, '"The soil alters; Y'are in another country": Multiple Perspectives and Political Resonances in Middleton's *Women Beware Women*', in *Shakespeare's Italy: Functions of Italian Locations in Renaissance Drama*, edited by Michele Marrapodi, A.J. Hoenselaars, Marcello Cappuzzo and L. Falzon Santucci (Manchester: Manchester University Press, 1993), pp. 251–71, pp. 258–9.
27. Lindley, *The Trials of Frances Howard*, p. 126. Anne Lancashire interestingly suggests that one explanation for the failure of *The Witch* may have been that it worked, through the use of masque technique, to whitewash the Howards ('*The Witch*: Stage Flop or Political Mistake', pp. 171–2).
28. Lindley, *The Trials of Frances Howard*, p. 128.
29. For comment on this, see Martin White, *Middleton and Tourneur* (Basingstoke: Macmillan – now Palgrave Macmillan, 1992), p. 98.
30. William Shakespeare, *Othello*, edited by Kenneth Muir (Harmondsworth: Penguin Books, 1968), V.2.300–1.
31. Malcolmson, '"As Tame as the Ladies"', p. 338.
32. *The Changeling*, ed. Daalder, note on V.iii.164.
33. See Thomas Middleton, *Hengist, King of Kent; or the Mayor of Queenborough*, edited by R.C. Bald (New York: Charles Scribner's Sons, 1938), p. xiii, for the dating of the play. All quotations from *Hengist* will be taken from this edition.
34. Grace Ioppolo, 'Sexual Treason, Treasonous Sexuality, and the Eventful Politics of James I in Middleton's *Hengist, King of Kent*', *Ben Jonson Journal* 3 (1996), pp. 87–107, pp. 96–7.
35. William Barksted and Lewis Machin from a draft by John Marston, *The Insatiate Countess*, in *Four Jacobean Sex Tragedies*, edited by Martin Wiggins (Oxford: Oxford University Press, 1998), V.ii.47–8 and V.ii.78–80. All further quotations from the play will be taken from this edition and reference will be given in the text.
36. For comment on Isabella's use of classical mythology, see for instance Richard Scarr, 'Insatiate Punning in Marston's Courtesan Plays', in *The*

Drama of John Marston: Critical Re-Visions, edited by T.F. Wharton (Cambridge: Cambridge University Press, 2000), pp. 82–99, p. 93.

37. Duncan ('Virginity in *The Changeling*', p. 28) compares Beatrice's attitude to her virginity with that of Isabella in *Measure for Measure*.

38. For a very different view of the form of *The Changeling* which sees it as deliberately unsatisfactory and 'freakish', see Peter Morrison, 'A Cangoun in Zombieland: Middleton's Teratological *Changeling*', in *'Accompaninge the players'*, pp. 219–41, p. 236; for an argument that its form is in fact mannerist, see Raymond J. Pentzell, '*The Changeling*: Notes on Mannerism in Dramatic Form', *Comparative Drama* 9 (1975), pp. 3–28.

39. In the course of an argument developed along different lines, Diane Purkiss also hints at the idea of literary revenge, though this time in *The Witch*, when she observes that 'Frances Howard got off lightly in comparison with what Middleton's text does with ... Anne Turner' (*The Witch in History* [London: Routledge, 1996], p. 216).

40. Thomas Middleton, *Women Beware Women*, edited by Roma Gill (London: Ernest Benn, 1968), p. 3. All further quotations from the play will be from this edition and reference will be given in the text.

41. Though for rather different readings of Livia, see for instance J.P. Batchelor, 'The Pattern of *Women Beware Women*', reprinted in *Three Jacobean Revenge Tragedies: A Casebook*, edited by R.V. Holdsworth (Basingstoke: Macmillan – now Palgrave Macmillan, 1990), D. Dodson, 'Middleton's Livia', *Philological Quarterly* 27 (1948), pp. 376–81; and Ania Loomba, *Gender, Race, Renaissance Drama* (Oxford: Oxford University Press, 1992), p. 46. For comment on the ways in which each of the female characters is depicted in ways that '[depend] on her being a female in a plot that fosters an audience's sense of her as a woman', see for instance Leslie Thomson, 'Making a Woman of the Boy: The Characterization of Women in Middleton's Plays', *The Elizabethan Theatre XIV*, edited by A.L. Magnusson and C.E. McGee (Toronto: P.D. Meany, 1996), pp. 153–74, p. 170. Richard Levin ('If Women Should Beware Women, Bianca Should Beware Mother', *Studies in English Literature* 37 [1997], pp. 371–89) regards the Mother herself as implicated, but I find his argument entirely unconvincing.

42. Inga-Stina Ewbank, 'Realism and Morality in *Women Beware Women*', *Essays and Studies* 22 (1969): 57–70, p. 62.

43. Una Ellis-Fermor, 'Middleton's Tragedies', reprinted in *Three Jacobean Revenge Tragedies*, p. 143.

44. Bruce Thomas Boehrer, *Monarchy and Incest in Renaissance England: Literature, Culture, Kinship, and Kingship* (Philadelphia: University of Pennsylvania Press, 1992), p. 109.

45. Though see Verna Ann Foster, 'The Deed's Creature: The Tragedy of Bianca in *Women Beware Women*', *Journal of English and Germanic Philology* 78 (1979), pp. 508–21, and Stephen Wigler, 'Parent and Child: The Pattern of Love in *Women Beware Women*', in *'Accompaninge the players': Essays Celebrating Thomas Middleton, 1580–1980*, edited by Kenneth Friedenreich (New York, AMS Press, 1983), pp. 183–201.

46. Ann C. Christensen, 'Settling House in Middleton's *Women Beware Women*, *Comparative Drama* 29 (1995), pp. 493–518, p. 499.

47. Ewbank, 'Realism and Morality', p. 58.

48. George R. Hibbard, 'The Tragedies of Thomas Middleton and the Decadence of the Drama', *Renaissance and Modern Studies*, 1 (1957), pp. 35–64, p. 54.
49. Nicholas Brooke, *Horrid Laughter in Jacobean Tragedy* (New York: Harper & Row, 1979), p. 90.
50. Wigler, 'Parent and Child', p. 199. See also Duncan, 'Virginity in *The Changeling*', p. 25, for the view that Middleton's work is characterised by 'often conflicting interests in natural portraiture and schematic morality'.
51. Dorothy M. Farr, *Thomas Middleton and the Drama of Realism* (Edinburgh: Oliver & Boyd, 1973), p. 72.
52. Thomas Middleton, *Women Beware Women*, edited by Roma Gill (London: Ernest Benn, 1968), introduction, p. xxv.
53. Ibid., p. xxvi.
54. For instance, Suzanne Gossett ('"Best Men are Molded out of Faults": Marrying the Rapist in Jacobean Drama', in *Renaissance Historicism: Selections from English Literary Renaissance*, edited by Arthur F. Kinney and Dan S. Collins [Amherst: University of Massachusetts Press, 1987], pp. 168–90, p. 183), points out that 'Middleton's plot can be seen as a response to *The Queen of Corinth*'.
55. For other views of the significant relatiosnhip between medium and message in Middleton's plays, see for instance Peter Morrison, 'A Cangoun in Zombieland: Middleton's Teratological *Changeling*', in *'Accompaninge the players'*, pp. 214–41, p. 236, and Anne Lancashire, '*The Witch*: Stage Flop or Political Mistake?', in *'Accompaninge the players'*, pp. 161–81, p. 171.
56. On the importance of art and sights in the play in general, see Molly Smith, *Breaking Boundaries: Politics and Play in the Drama of Shakespeare and his Contemporaries* (Aldershot: Ashgate, 1998), pp. 94–5. For the argument that this is a rape, see Celia R. Daileader, *Eroticism on the Renaissance Stage: Transcendence, Desire, and the Limits of the Visible* (Cambridge: Cambridge University Press, 1998), p. 25; and Swapan Chakravorty, *Society and Politics in the Plays of Thomas Middleton* (Oxford: Clarendon Press, 1996), pp. 136–7. Caroline Lockett Cherry, who sees Middleton as essentially a feminist dramatist, nevertheless argues that Bianca is by no means merely a victim: 'Although it is uncertain whether she yields to these arguments or simply to the irresistible power of the Duke, it is certain that she accepts and flaunts his bounty after the fall, and is thus guilty of selling herself' (*The Most Unvaluedst Purchase: Women in the Plays of Thomas Middleton* [Salzburg: Universität Salzburg, 1973], p. 191).
57. Ewbank, 'Realism and Morality', p. 201.
58. Tim Benton, Catherine King and Di Norman, *Venice, Rome and Late Fifteenth-Century Florence* (Open University Press, 1986), p. 27. On the difference between Florentine and Venetian accounts of the story of Bianca Cappello, see Zara Bruzzi and A.A. Bromham, '"The soil alters; Y'are in another country": Multiple Perspectives and Political Resonances in Middleton's *Women Beware Women*', in *Shakespeare's Italy: Functions of Italian Locations in Renaissance Drama*, edited by Michele Marrapodi, A.J. Hoenselaars, Marcello Cappuzzo and L. Falzon Santucci (Manchester: Manchester University Press, 1993), pp. 251–71, p. 252.
59. Sawday, *Body Emblazoned*, p. 85.

60. J. B. Batchelor, 'The Pattern of *Women Beware Women*' [1972], reprinted in *Three Jacobean Revenge Tragedies*, pp. 207–21, pp. 209 and 210.
61. J.R. Mulryne, 'Middleton's Italy: The Transformation of the Italian Setting in Middleton's *Women Beware Women*', in *The Italian World of English Renaissance Drama*, edited by Michele Marrapodi (Newark: University of Delaware Press, 1998), pp. 141–64. I am very grateful to Ronnie Mulryne for allowing me to see this paper before its publication.
62. Benton, King and Norman, *Venice, Rome* ..., p. 26. The tradition of *intemedii* would have been peculiarly apposite to this play because, as Louise Olga Fradenburg notes, events connected with precisely the historical events it dramatises had proved influential on English drama: '*The Masque of Blackness* ... was apparently inspired in part by an Italian tournament held at Florence in 1579 for the wedding of Francesco de' Medici and Bianca Capello' (*City, Marriage, Tournament: Arts of Rule in Late Medieval Scotland* [Madison: University of Wisconsin Press, 1991], p. 263).
63. On the effect of this framing, see also Daileader, *Eroticism*, p. 30.
64. Verna Ann Foster, 'The Deed's Creature: The Tragedy of Bianca in *Women Beware Women*', *Journal of English and Germanic Philology* 78 (1979), pp. 508–21.
65. On the importance of the Florentine *intermedii* tradition for the play, see Mulryne, 'Middleton's Italy', and A.A. Bromham and Zara Bruzzi, *The Changeling and the Years of Crisis* (London: Pinter, 1990).
66. Michael McCanles, 'The Moral Dialectic of Middleton's *Women Beware Women*', in '*Accompaninge the players*', pp. 203–18, p. 211.

Chapter 2

1. See, for instance, Allison Heisch, 'Elizabeth I and the Reinforcement of Patriarchy', *Feminist Review* 4 (1980), pp. 45–56.
2. Laura Levine, *Men in Women's Clothing: Antitheatricality and effeminization 1579–1642* (Cambridge: Cambridge University Press, 1994).
3. See Roy Strong, *Gloriana: The Portraits of Queen Elizabeth I* (London: Thames and Hudson, 1987), pp. 163 and 165.
4. Mark Breitenberg, *Anxious Masculinity in Early Modern England* (Cambridge: Cambridge University Press, 1996), p. 1.
5. On the question of homoerotic and heteroerotic bonding in Fletcher in general, see for instance Mario DiGangi, *The Homoerotics of Early Modern Drama* (Cambridge: Cambridge University Press, 1997), p. 145.
6. Lawrence B. Wallis, *Fletcher, Beaumont and Company: Entertainers to the Jacobean Gentry* (New York, 1947), preface, p. ix.
7. Robert Ornstein, *The Moral Vision of Jacobean Tragedy* (Wisconsin: University of Wisconsin Press, 1960), pp. 163 and 152.
8. Philip Edwards, 'The danger not the Death: The Art of John Fletcher', in *Jacobean Theatre*, edited by John Russell Brown and Bernard Harris (London: Edward Arnold, 1960), p. 160.
9. M.C. Bradbrook, *Themes and Conventions of Elizabethan Tragedy* (Cambridge: Cambridge University Press, 1935), p. 68.
10. U.M. Ellis-Fermor, *The Jacobean Drama* (London: Methuen, 1958), p. 202.

11. John F. Danby, 'Beaumont and Fletcher: Jacobean Absolutists', in *Elizabethan Drama: Modern Essays in Criticism*, edited by R.J. Kaufmann (Oxford: Oxford University Press, 1961), p. 280.

12. Arthur Mizener, 'The High Design of *A King and No King*', *Modern Philology* 38 (1940–1), p. 137, note 9.

13. See for instance Francis Beaumont and John Fletcher, *Philaster*, edited by Andrew Gurr (Manchester: Manchester University Press, 1969), introduction, p. xxx, for the comment that the play offers 'a carefully designed story which will operate as a vast and complex metaphor or moral paradigm'. Arthur Mizener finds 'emotional . . . form' in their plays ('The High Design', p. 135). For similarly evaluative rather than judgemental comment see James E. Savage, 'Beaumont and Fletcher's *Philaster* and Sidney's *Arcadia*', *Journal of English History* 14 (1947), pp. 194–207, and most particularly, Sarah P. Sutherland's perception of the relationship between form and meaning in *The Maid's Tragedy* in her book *Masques in Jacobean Tragedy* (New York: AMS Press, 1983).

14. See 'The danger not the Death', p. 171.

15. Francis Beaumont and John Fletcher, *The Maid's Tragedy*, edited by T.W. Craik (Manchester: Manchester University Press, 1988), IV.i.93–5. All further quotations from the play will be taken from this edition and reference will be given in the text.

16. For comment on the question of Aspatia and her brother, see Molly Smith, *Breaking Boundaries: Politics and Plays in the Drama of Shakespeare and his Contemporaries* (Aldershot: Ashgate, 1998), p. 81.

17. Sarah P. Sutherland, *Masques in Jacobean Tragedy* (New York, 1983), p. 9. For comment on the disruptions of the masque, see also Lee Bliss, *Francis Beaumont* (Boston: Twayne, 1987), pp. 92–3.

18. On Amintor as a clear reworking of the composite shepherd/knight hero of romance, see Eugene Waith, *The Pattern of Tragicomedy in Beaumont and Fletcher* (New Haven: Archon, 1952), p. 75.

19. Robert Y. Turner, 'Responses to Tyranny in John Fletcher's Plays', *Medieval and Renaissance Drama in England* 4 (1989), pp. 123–41, p. 128.

20. On the emotional dynamic of this, see for instance Jonathan Dollimore, 'Subjectivity, Sexuality, and Transgression: The Jacobean Connection', *Renaissance Drama* 17 (1986), pp. 53–81, p. 76, and Cristina León Alfar, 'Staging the Feminine Performance of Desire: Masochism in *The Maid's Tragedy*', *Papers on Language and Literature* 31:3 (Summer 1995), pp. 313–33. The *locus classicus* for the use of heterosexual relations to triangulate homosocial ones is Eve Kosofsky Sedgwick, *Between Men: English Literature and Male Homosocial Desire* (New York: Columbia University Press, 1985), p. 3.

21. See for instance Luke Gernon, quoted in Andrew Hadfield and Willy Maley, 'Introduction: Irish Representations and English Alternatives', in Brendan Bradshaw, Andrew Hadfield and Willy Maley, eds, *Representing Ireland: Literature and the Origins of Conflict, 1534–1660* (Cambridge: Cambridge University Press, 1993), pp. 1–23, p. 4.

22. Lynda E. Boose, '*The Taming of the Shrew*, Good Husbandry, and Enclosure', in *Shakespeare Reread: The Texts in New Contexts*, edited by Russ McDonald (Ithaca: Cornell University Press, 1994), pp. 193–225, p. 203. On the

woman-land metaphor, see also Virginia Mason Vaughan, 'Preface: The Mental Maps of English Renaissance Drama', in *Playing the Globe: Genre and Geography in English Renaissance Drama*, edited by John Gillies and Virginia Mason Vaughan (London: Associated University Presses, 1998), pp. 7–16, p. 12; and Louis Montrose, 'The Work of Gender in the Discourse of Discovery', *Representations* 33 (winter 1991), pp. 1–41.

23. On the effeminisation of the King in particular, but also on that of Melantius and Amintor, see Smith, *Breaking Boundaries*, pp. 82–3.

24. For an interesting discussion of the King's personal and political positions, see Rebecca Bushnell, *Tragedies of Tyrants: Political Thought and Theater in the English Renaissance* (Ithaca: Cornell University Press, 1990), pp. 166–7.

25. See Sutherland, *Masques*, pp. 68–9.

26. Michael Neill, '"The Simetry, Which Gives a Poem Grace": Masque, Imagery, and the Fancy of *The Maid's Tragedy*', *Renaissance Drama* 3 (1970), pp. 111–35, p. 120. He notes further examples of gender reversal in the exchanges between Evadne, Amintor, Melantius and the King (pp. 124–5).

27. See for instance Philip J. Finkelpearl, *Court and Country Politics in the Plays of Beaumont and Fletcher* (Princeton: Princeton University Press, 1990), pp. 184 and 194–5.

28. Kathleen McLuskie comments, 'In this speech Amintor quite clearly acknowledges the political connection between the sexual control of women and the maintenance of social order. Amintor is evidently appalled at the prospect of such anarchy but the connection itself can be (and has been) seen as evidence of a subversive and radical sexual politics in these plays' (*Renaissance Dramatists* [Atlantic Highlands, N.J.: Humanities Press International,1989], p. 194).

29. William Shullenberger, '"This For the Most Wrong'd of Women": A Reappraisal of *The Maid's Tragedy*', *Renaissance Drama* 13 (1982), pp. 131–56, p. 146.

30. This version of events is recounted by Leonora in Webster's *The Devil's Law Case* (in John Webster, *The Duchess of Malfi and Other Plays*, edited by René Weis [Oxford: Oxford University Press, 1996], 3.3.270–5).

31. *Four Jacobean Sex Tragedies*, edited by Martin Wiggins (Oxford: Oxford University Press, 1998), introduction, pp. xxx–xxxi.

32. For discussion of both the name of the play and the issue of whether the Lady is a maiden, see Celia R. Daileader, *Eroticism on the Renaissance Stage: Transcendence, Desire, and the Limits of the Visible* (Cambridge: Cambridge University Press, 1998), pp. 93–4.

33. On the abstraction and emblematisation of the Lady in particular, see for instance Sara Eaton, '"Content with art"?: Seeing the Emblematic Woman in *The Second Maiden's Tragedy* and *The Winter's Tale*', in *Shakespearean Power and Punishment: A Volume of Essays*, edited by Gillian Murray Kendall (Cranbury: Associated University Presses, 1998), pp. 59–86, pp. 68–9. Eaton also sees the Lady as obliquely imaging Elizabeth (pp. 80–1).

34. Steven Mullaney, 'Mourning and Misogyny: *Hamlet*, *The Revenger's Tragedy*, and the Final Progress of Elizabeth I, 1600–1607', *Shakespeare Quarterly* 45 (1994), pp. 139–62. See also Louis Montrose, '*A Midsummer Night's Dream* and the Shaping Fantasies of Elizabethan Culture: Gender, Power, Form', *Representations* 2 (1983), pp. 65–87; and *Dissing Elizabeth: Negative*

Representations of Gloriana, edited by Julia M. Walker (London: Duke University Press, 1998).

35. For comment on the presence of the feminine in this passage, see Eileen Allman, *Jacobean Revenge Tragedy and the Politics of Virtue* (Newark: University of Delaware Press, 1999), p. 112.

36. John Marston, *Sophonisba*, in *Three Jacobean Witchcraft Plays*, edited by Peter Corbin and Douglas Sedge (Manchester: Manchester University Press, 1986), III.i.15 and IV.i.58–62. All further quotations from the play will be taken from this edition and reference will be given in the text.

37. Sukanya B. Senapati, '"Two parts in one": Marston and Masculinity', in *The Drama of John Marston: Critical Re-Visions*, edited by T. F. Wharton (Cambridge: Cambridge University Press, 2000), pp. 124–44, p. 134.

Chapter 3

1. Amy Louise Erickson, *Women and Property in Early Modern England* (London: Routledge, 1993), p. 204.

2. Philip Massinger, *A New Way To Pay Old Debts* V.v.54–7.

3. T[homas] E[dgar ed.], *The Lawes Resolution of Womens Rights* [1632], reprinted in N. H. Keeble, ed., *The Cultural Identity of Seventeenth-Century Woman* (London: Routledge, 1994), p. 254.

4. Quoted in Mihoko Suzuki, 'Gender, Class, and the Ideology of Comic Form: *Much Ado About Nothing* and *Twelfth Night*', in *A Feminist Companion to Shakespeare*, edited by Dympna Callaghan (Oxford: Blackwell, 2000), pp. 121–43, p. 123.

5. For comment on this, see Ann Rosalind Jones, '"Italians and Others": *The White Devil* (1612)', in David Scott Kastan and Peter Stallybrass, eds, *Staging the Renaissance: Reinterpretations of Elizabethan and Jacobean Drama* (New York: Routledge, 1991), pp. 251–62.

6. Thomas Dekker, John Ford and William Rowley, *The Witch of Edmonton*, edited by Simon Trussler and Jacqui Russell (London: Methuen, 1983), I.ii.17–18, II.i.47–8 and III.i.40–1. All further quotations will be taken from this edition and reference will be given in the text.

7. See Alison Findlay, 'Heavenly Matters of Theology', in *A Feminist Perspective on Renaissance Drama* (Oxford: Blackwell, 1999).

8. James VI and I, *Daemonologie* (Edinburgh, 1597), Book Three, pp. 69 and 77.

9. Thomas Middleton, *The Witch*, edited by Elizabeth Schafer (London: A. & C. Black, 1994), II.i.169–70 and 173. All subsequent quotations from the play will be taken from this edition and reference will be given in the text.

10. John Webster, *The White Devil*, edited by John Russell Brown (Manchester: Manchester University Press, 1996), I.i.4–9. All my quotations are taken from this edition and reference will be given in the text.

11. See Lisa Hopkins, '"That's wormwood": Hamlet Plays his Mother', *Hamlet Studies* 16:1–2 (1994), 83–5.

12. William Shakespeare and John Fletcher, *Henry VIII*, edited by A.R. Humphreys (Harmondsworth: Penguin Books, 1971), III.i.40 and II.iv.75–8.

13. See Bertram Lloyd, 'An Unprinted Poem by John Ford?', *The Review of*

English Studies 1 (1925), pp. 217–19, and M. Joan Sargeaunt, *John Ford* (Oxford: Blackwell, 1935).

14. See L.E. Stock, Gilles D. Monsarrat, Judith M. Kennedy and Dennis Danielson, eds. *The Nondramatic Works of John Ford* (Binghampton, N.Y.: Medieval & Renaissance Texts & Studies, 1991), p. 284.
15. Glanmor Williams, 'Sir John Stradling of St Donat's (1563–1637)', *Glamorgan Historian* 9 (1973), pp. 11–28, p. 15.
16. Martin Butler is an honourable exception to this. See his *'Love's Sacrifice*: Ford's Metatheatrical Tragedy', in *John Ford: Critical Re-Visions*, edited by Michael Neill (Cambridge: Cambridge University Press, 1988), pp. 201–31.
17. Viviana Comensoli, *Household Business: Domestic Plays of Early Modern England* (Toronto: University of Toronto Press, 1996), p. 121.
18. See Comensoli, *Household Business*, pp. 126–7.
19. William Shakespeare, *Hamlet*, edited by Harold Jenkins (London: Methuen, 1980), III.ii.132–3 and note.
20. Michael Hattaway, 'Women and Witchcraft: The Case of *The Witch of Edmonton'*, *Trivium* 20 (1985), pp. 49–68, p. 59.
21. For discussion of this, see Diane Purkiss, *The Witch in History* (London: Routledge, 1996), pp. 189, 246 and 249 note 41).
22. Elizabeth Schafer, though, in her edition of Middleton's *The Witch*, sees *The Witch of Edmonton* as playing into these stereotypes rather than working to deconstruct them (xx). Diane Purkiss points out the extent to which witchcraft was inherently constructed as theatrical (181, 188) and also interestingly discusses the different ways in which law and literature could work towards the uncovering of the 'truth' of witchcraft (231–3).

Chapter 4

1. The influence of Burton on Ford was comprehensively traced by S. Blaine Ewing, *Burtonian Melancholy in the Plays of John Ford* (Princeton: Princeton University Press, 1940).
2. John Ford, *The Lover's Melancholy*, edited by R.F. Hill (Manchester: Manchester University Press, 1985) (III.iii.108–17).
3. Francis Bacon, *The Advancement of Learning* and *The New Atlantis*, edited by Arthur Johnston (Oxford: The Clarendon Press, 1974), p. 104.
4. The *locus classicus* of this view is G.F. Sensabaugh, *The Tragic Muse of John Ford* (Stanford: Stanford University Press, 1944), but see also F.S. Boas, *An Introduction to Stuart Drama* (Oxford: The Clarendon Press, 1946), especially p. 341; Karl J. Holzknecht, *Outlines of Tudor and Stuart Plays 1497–1642* (London: n.p., 1947), p. 390; Wallace A. Bacon, 'The Literary Reputation of John Ford', *Huntington Library Quarterly* 11 (1947–8), pp. 181–99, p. 183; Juliet Sutton, 'Platonic Love in Ford's *The Fancies, Chaste and Noble'*, *Studies in English Literature 1500–1900* 7 (1967), pp. 299–309; and Peter Ure, 'Cult and Initiates in Ford's *Love's Sacrifice'*, *Modern Language Quarterly* 2 (1950), pp. 298–306.
5. Lisa Hopkins, *John Ford's Political Theatre* (Manchester: Manchester University Press, 1994).

6. On Ford's debt to Webster in *The Lover's Melancholy*, see for instance Kathleen McLuskie, '"Language and Matter with a Fit of Mirth": Dramatic Construction in the Plays of John Ford', in *John Ford: Critical Re-Visions*, edited by Michael Neill (Cambridge: Cambridge University Press, 1988), pp. 97–127, p. 115.

7. John Webster, *The White Devil*, edited by John Russell Brown (Manchester: Manchester University Press, 1996), V.vi.259–60. All further quotations from the play will be taken from this edition and reference will be given in the text.

8. Maurice Hunt, 'Webster and Jacobean Medicine: The Case of *The Duchess of Malfi*', *Essays in Literature* 16:1 (1989), pp. 33–49, pp. 35 and 40.

9. William Kerwin, '"Physicians are like Kings": Medical Politics and *The Duchess of Malfi*', *English Literary Renaissance* 28:1 (Winter, 1998), pp. 95–117, p. 96.

10. John Webster, *The Duchess of Malfi*, edited by John Russell Brown (Manchester: Manchester University Press, 1976), I.i.76–82. All further quotations from the play will be taken from this edition and reference will be given in the text.

11. On the importance of bodies and mirrors in the play, see also Martha Ronk, 'Embodied Morality', in *Sexuality and Politics in Renaissance Drama*, edited by Carole Levin and Karen Robertson (Lewiston: The Edwin Mellen Press, 1991), pp. 237–54, p. 240. Michael Neill calls it a play 'haunted by images of grotesque anatomical disclosure' (*Issues of Death: Mortality and Identity in English Renaissance Tragedy* [Oxford: Oxford University Press, 1997], p. 137), and Sheryl Craig points to how Ferdinand 'is fascinated by severed body parts throughout the play; he gives his sister a detached human hand ... and carries a cadaver's leg about the graveyard' ('"She and I were twins": Double Identity in *The Duchess of Malfi*', *Publications of the Missouri Philological Association* 19 [1994], pp. 21–7, p. 23).

12. Celia R. Daileader, *Eroticism on the Renaissance Stage: Transcendence, Desire, and the Limits of the Visible* (Cambridge: Cambridge University Press, 1998), p. 8. See also pp. 84–5.

13. Karin S. Coddon argues that madness, which Ferdinand chooses as an important feature of his persecution of his sister, is in this play 'emphatically identified with outwardness' ('*The Duchess of Malfi*: Tyranny and Spectacle in Jacobean Drama', in *Madness in Drama*, edited by James Redmond [Cambridge: Cambridge University Press, 1993], pp. 1–18], p. 1), and Kay Stockholder observes that '[t]he utter secrecy of the Duchess' marriage renders its intimate domesticity the polar opposite of the corrupt public world of her brothers' ('The Aristocratic Woman as Scapegoat: Romantic Love and Class Antagonism in *The Spanish Tragedy*, *The Duchess of Malfi* and *The Changeling*', *The Elizabethan Theatre XIV*, edited by A.L. Magnusson and C.E. McGee [Toronto: P.D. Meany, 1996], pp. 127–51, p. 141). Mariangela Tempera comments on 'Ferdinand's "scientific" approach' to issues of interiority ('The Rhetoric of Poison in John Webster's Italianate Plays', in *Shakespeare's Italy: Functions of Italian Locations in Renaissance Drama*, edited by Michele Marrapodi, A.J. Hoenselaars, Marcello Cappuzzo and L. Falzon Santucci (Manchester: Manchester University Press, 1993), pp. 229–50, p. 239).

14. Robert Rentoul Reed, Jr, *Bedlam on the Jacobean Stage* (New York: Octagon Books, 1970), p. 85.

15. On Ferdinand's illness as symbolically linked with the Duchess's own interiors since it was one which sometimes affected pregnant women, see Molly Smith, *Breaking Boundaries: Politics and Play in the Drama of Shakespeare and His Contemporaries* (Aldershot: Ashgate, 1998), p. 85. (Indeed in its very control by the moon it mimics the menstrual cycle.) For commentary on this passage and on how it may relate to the Galenic theory of men's bodies turned inward as being equivalent to women's, see also Lynn Enterline, *The Tears of Narcissus: Melancholia and Masculinity in Early Modern Writing* (Stanford: Stanford University Press, 1995), pp. 256 and 275.

16. I am indebted for this suggestion to my former student Stephen Collins. Sheryl Craig, however, who sees the twinship of the Duchess and Ferdinand as of paramount importance, suggests that 'perhaps her other self, Ferdinand, keeps her tied to this life' ('"Double Identity"', p. 24).

17. For a full analysis of Ford's use of the words 'heart' and 'blood' in these ways, see my *John Ford's Political Theatre* (Manchester: Manchester University Press, 1994), chapter five.

18. John Ford, *'Tis Pity She's a Whore*, edited by Brian Morris (London: Ernest Benn, 1968), introduction, pp. xxiv. All further quotations will be taken from this edition and reference will be given in the text.

19. See for instance Carol C. Rosen, 'The Language of Cruelty in Ford's *'Tis Pity She's a Whore*', *Comparative Drama* 8, 1974, pp. 356–68; and Terri Clerico, 'The Politics of Blood: John Ford's *'Tis Pity She's a Whore*', *English Literary Renaissance* 22 (1992), pp. 405–324.

20. Cyrus Hoy's '"Ignorance in knowledge": Marlowe's Faustus and Ford's Giovanni', *Modern Philology*, LVII (February 1960), pp. 145–54, is of course a major exception. Dorothy M. Farr, in her chapter on the play in *John Ford and the Caroline Theatre* (London: Macmillan, 1979), p. 36, lists what she sees Giovanni and Annabella as knowing, but does not interrogate the concept of knowledge.

21. John S. Wilks, *The Idea of Conscience in Renaissance Tragedy* (London: Routledge, 1990), p. 170. Stanley Cavell uses similar terms of *Othello*, a play which may be thought to have influenced the depiction of the Soranzo/Annabella relationship (*Disowning Knowledge in Six Plays of Shakespeare* [Cambridge: Cambridge University Press, 1987], pp. 8–9).

22. Bruce Boehrer, '"Nice Philosophy": *'Tis Pity She's a Whore* and The Two Books of God', *Studies in English Literature* 24 (1984), pp. 355–71, p. 362.

23. See for instance H.J. Oliver, *The Problem of John Ford* (Melbourne: Melbourne University Press, 1955), p. 86, and Clifford Leech, *John Ford and the Drama of his Time* (London: Longmans, 1957), p. 56.

24. For the very different epistemological assumptions of Giovanni here, see Claudine Defaye, 'Annabella's Unborn Baby: The Heart in the Womb in *'Tis Pity She's a Whore*', *Cahiers Elisabéthains* 15 (1979), pp. 35–42, p. 36.

25. See Coburn Freer on Ford in *The Poetics of Jacobean Drama* (Baltimore: Johns Hopkins University Press, 1981).

26. For the argument that Giovanni is mad, see for instance Ronald J. Boling, 'Prayer, Mirrors, and Self-Deification in John Ford's *'Tis Pity She's a Whore*',

Publications of the Arkansas Philological Association 17:1 (1991), pp. 1–12, pp. 1 and 5; Mark Stavig, 'Shakespearean and Jacobean Patterns in *'Tis Pity She's a Whore*', in *Concord in Discord: The Plays of John Ford, 1586–1986*, ed. Donald K. Anderson, Jr (New York: AMS Press, 1986), pp. 221–40, p. 236; Richard Madelaine, '"Sensationalism" and "Melodrama" in Ford's Plays', in *John Ford: Critical Re-Visions*, ed. Michael Neill (Cambridge: Cambridge University Press, 1988), pp. 29–54, pp. 33 and 41; Verna Foster, *''Tis Pity She's a Whore* as City Tragedy', in *John Ford: Critical Re-Visions*, pp. 181–200, p. 195; and my own 'John Ford's *'Tis Pity She's a Whore* and early diagnoses of *folie à deux*', *Notes and Queries*, 239 (March 1994), pp. 71–4. Michael Neill, in '"What Strange Riddle's This?": Deciphering *'Tis Pity She's a Whore*', in *John Ford: Critical Re-Visions*, pp. 153–80, also points out Ford's debt to Fletcher's *The Mad Lover* (pp. 158–60); recognition of the allusion would seem to increase the audience's chances of perceiving Giovanni as mad. The act of exploring Annabella's womb might possibly have been read in the light of the early printed accounts of the doings of Vlad Dracul, who would be an equally negative avatar for Giovanni.

27. Luke Wilson, 'William Harvey's *Prelectiones*: The Performance of the Body in the Renaissance Theater of Anatomy', *Representations* 17 (1987), pp. 62–95, p. 62.

28. On the ritualised exclusion of men from the birth chamber, see Diane Purkiss, *The Witch in History* (London: Routledge, 1996), pp. 101–3.

29. The phrase is quoted from Garthine Walker's account of a woman burglar who assaulted a householder's pregnant wife: 'she ript her up the belly, making herself a tragicall midwife' (Garthine Walker, '"Demons in female form": Representations of Women and Gender in Murder Pamphlets of the Late Sixteenth and Early Seventeenth Centuries', in *Writing and the English Renaissance*, ed. William Zunder and Suzanne Trill [Harlow, Essex: Longman, 1996], pp. 129–39, p. 126). I quote it because the assocation with burglary here seems to me an apt correlative for the ways in which Giovanni's action is inflected by imagery of the invasion of forbidden space, as has already been dramatised in the play by the clash at the Cardinal's gate.

30. Nathaniel Strout, 'The Tragedy of Annabella in *'Tis Pity She's a Whore*', in David G. Allen, ed., *Traditions and Innovations* (Newark: University of Delaware Press, 1990), p. 169. I am grateful to Derek Roper for drawing this essay to my attention.

31. William D. Dyer, 'Holding/Withholding Environments: A Psychoanalytic Approach to Ford's *The Broken Heart*', *English Literary Renaissance* 21 (1991), pp. 401–24, p. 422.

32. See my notes, 'A Source for John Ford's *Love's Sacrifice*: The Life of Carlo Gesualdo' (published under my maiden name, Lisa Cronin), *Notes and Queries* 233 (March 1988), pp. 66–7, and '"Elegy by W.S.": A Possible Candidate for Authorship?', forthcoming in *Philological Quarterly* 76.2 (Summer 1997), 159–68.

33. Jeremy Tambling, *Confession: Sexuality, Sin, The Subject* (Manchester: Manchester University Press, 1990), pp. 68–9. I am very grateful to Richard Wilson for alerting me to this passage.

34. Wilks, *Idea of Conscience*, p. 254.

35. Though for a rather different interpretation of these celebrated lines, see Rick Bowers, 'John Ford and the Sleep of Death', *Texas Studies in Language and Literature* 28 (1986), pp. 358–87, p. 357. I am grateful to Derek Roper for drawing this essay to my attention.
36. This is best explored in M. Joan Sargeaunt, *John Ford* (Oxford: Basil Blackwell, 1935), pp. 14–16.
37. See for instance Verna Ann Foster and Stephen Foster, 'Structure and History in *The Broken Heart*: Sparta, England, and the "Truth"', *English Literary Renaissance*, 1988, pp. 305–28, p. 309, on Ford's technical use of the term 'presentment', 'a statement on oath by a jury of a fact within their own knowledge', in the prologue to *The Broken Heart*.
38. Some versions of the trial of Sir Walter Ralegh have Lord Chief Justice Popham, who was Ford's great-uncle, warning the defendant against letting Marlowe show him the way to hell. Accounts vary, however, and the reference may in fact have been to Thomas Harriot, or to a third, unidentified person: see George T. Buckley, *Atheism in the English Renaissance* (Chicago: University of Chicago Press, 1932), p. 144; and Ernest A. Strathmann, *Sir Walter Ralegh: A Study in Elizabethan Skepticism* (New York: Octagon Books, 1973), p. 58. Strathmann argues that Ralegh was not an atheist but was rather displaying a Pyrrhonist scepticism about human knowledge (p. 222). As well as his involuntary connection with Popham on this occasion, Ralegh was also related to the Gamages and Stradlings, connections of Ford on the mother's side. Sir John Stradling's apology for Justus Lipsius is noted by Wilks (*Idea of Conscience*, p. 230) as part of the general Renaissance debate over 'right reason'.
39. Charles Harrison, 'Giotto and the "rise of painting"', in *Siena, Florence and Padua: Art, Society and Religion 1280–1400*, ed. Diana Norman (2 vols) (New Haven and London: Yale University Press, 1995), I, pp. 73–96, p. 88.
40. Pamela Benson, ed., *Italian Tales From the Age of Shakespeare* (London: J.M. Dent, 1996), pp. 255 and 269.
41. Marc Shell, *Elizabeth's Glass* (Lincoln: University of Nebraska Press, 1993), p. 36.
42. Ronald J. Boling argues that their 'disparity in moral knowledge is what produces the moral closure of the play whereby Annabella repents and then is saved, while her brother remains defiantly in his sin and is damned' ('Prayer, Mirrors, and Self-Deification', p. 5).
43. See my 'John Ford's Annabella and the Virgin Mary', *Notes and Queries*, 240: 3 (September 1995), p. 380.
44. On the epistemological issues surrounding the concealment and detection of Annabella's pregnancy, see Susan J. Wiseman, '*'Tis Pity She's a Whore*: Representing the Incestuous Body', in *Renaissance Bodies*, ed. Lucy Gent and Nigel Llewellyn (London: Reaktion Books, 1990), pp. 180–97.
45. William Shakespeare, *The Comedy of Errors*, edited by Stanley Wells (Harmondsworth: Penguin Books, 1972), II.ii.68.
46. For the ambiguity in the referent here, see *'Tis Pity*, ed. Morris, note on V.vi.133.
47. This is comparable with the similar displacement of guilt onto an alleged witch which is dramatised in Ford, Dekker and Rowley's *The Witch of Edmonton*.

48. On the Oedipal resonances of this, see for instance Denis Gauer, 'Nature and Culture in *'Tis Pity She's a Whore'*, *Cahiers Elisabéthains* (1987), pp. 45–57, p. 49.
49. John Ford, *The Broken Heart*, ed. Brian Morris (London: Ernest Benn, 1965), IV.i.140–1.
50. On the implications of our knowledge of other plays for our reading of *'Tis Pity*, see Neill, '"What Strange Riddle's This?"', Richard S. Ide, 'Ford's *'Tis Pity She's a Whore* and the Benefits of Belatedness', in *'Concord in Discord'*, pp. 61–86; and Martin Coyle, 'Hamlet, Gertrude and the Ghost: The Punishment of Women in Renaissance Drama', *Q/W/E/R/T/Y* 6 (October, 1996), pp. 29–38, p. 33. On the question of knowledge in *'Tis Pity*, see also Rowland Wymer, *Webster and Ford* (Basingstoke: Macmillan – now Palgrave Macmillan, 1995), p. 126.

Chapter 5

1. Quoted in *Culture and Belief in Europe 1450–1600*, edited by David Englander, Diana Norman, Rosemary O'Day and W.R. Owens (Oxford: Basil Blackwell, 1990), p. 412.
2. Quoted in Englander et al., *Culture and Belief*, p. 407.
3. See for instance Dennis Moore, 'Dutifully Defending Elizabeth: Lord Henry Howard and the Question of Queenship', in *Political Rhetoric, Power, and Renaissance Women*, edited by Carole Levin and Patricia A. Sullivan (Albany: State University of New York Press, 1995), pp. 113–36, p. 113.
4. For discussion of this see Diane Purkiss, ed., *Renaissance Women: The Plays of Elizabeth Cary, The Poems of Aemilia Lanyer* (London: William Pickering, 1994), introduction, p. xxiv.
5. Though Kim F. Hall has recently argued that in women's texts, in clear opposition to those by men, the darkness of Cleopatra is often stressed, as it is in *Mariam* (Kim F. Hall, in *Things of Darkness: Economies of Race and Gender in Early Modern England* [Ithaca: Cornell University Press, 1995], p. 155; for her discussion of Cleopatra in *Mariam*, see pp. 184–5).
6. William Shakespeare, *Antony and Cleopatra*, edited by Emrys Jones (Harmondsworth: Penguin, 1977), IV.14.53–4. All further quotations from the play will be taken from this edition and reference will be given in the text.
7. Robin Moffet, '*Cymbeline* and the Nativity', *Shakespeare Quarterly* 13 (1962), pp. 207–18, p. 215. See also Arthur Kirsch, *Shakespeare and the Experience of Love* (Cambridge: Cambridge University Press, 1981), p. 163, Hugh M. Richmond, 'Shakespeare's Roman Trilogy: The Climax in *Cymbeline*', *Studies in the Literary Imagination* 5 (1972), pp. 129–39, and Alexander Leggatt, 'The Island of Miracles: An Approach to *Cymbeline*', *Shakespeare Survey* 10 (1977), pp. 191–209, p. 207, who calls the nativity something which the play 'cannot show'.
8. Though for a notable exception see Gilberto Sacerdoti, 'Three Kings, Herod of Jewry, and a Child: Apocalypse and Infinity of the World in *Antony and Cleopatra*', in *Italian Studies in Shakespeare and His Contemporaries*, edited by Michele Marrapodi and Giorgio Melchiori (Newark: University of Delaware Press, 1999), pp. 165–84.

9. For comment on the Messianic resonances of this, see for instance Steve Sohmer, *Shakespeare's Mystery Play: The Opening of the Globe Theatre, 1599* (Manchester: Manchester University Press, 1999), p. 122.

10. Mary Sidney, *The Tragedie of Antonie*, in S.P. Cerasano and Marion Wynne-Davies, eds, *Renaissance Drama by Women: Texts and Documents* (London: Routledge, 1996), IV.82–3.

11. Elizabeth Cary, *The Tragedy of Mariam*, edited by Stephanie Wright (Keele: Keele University Press, 1996), Argument. All future quotations from the play will be taken from this edition and reference will be given in the text.

12. For the argument that Cary is indeed directly critiquing James in the play, see Karen L. Raber, 'Gender and the Political Subject in *The Tragedy of Mariam*', *Studies in English Literature 1500–1900* 35:2 (Spring 1995), pp. 321–43.

13. Keith M. Brown, 'The Vanishing Emperor: British Kingship and its Decline 1603–1707', in *Scots and Britons: Scottish Political Thought and the Union of 1603*, edited by Roger A. Mason (Cambridge: Cambridge University Press, 1994), pp. 58–67, p. 64.

14. See Stephanie Wright's edition, introduction, p. 17.

15. Sandra K. Fischer, 'Elizabeth Cary and Tyranny, Domestic and Religious', in Margaret Patterson Hannay, ed., *Silent But for the Word* (Ohio: Kent State University Press, 1985), pp. 225–37, p. 288, note 12; for the links between the two women, see Fischer, p. 229; Marta Straznicky, '"Profane Stoical Paradoxes": *The Tragedie of Mariam* and Sidnean Closet Drama', *English Literary Renaissance* 24 (1994), pp. 104–34; and Elizabeth Cary, Lady Falkland, *The Tragedy of Mariam*, edited by Barry Weller and Margaret W. Ferguson (Berkeley and Los Angeles: University of California Press, 1994), pp. 28–9.

16. Dympna Callaghan, 'Re-Reading Elizabeth Cary's *The Tragedie of Mariam, Faire Queene of Jewry*', in *Women, 'Race', and Writing in the Early Modern Period*, edited by Margo Hendricks and Patricia Parker (London: Routledge, 1994), pp. 163–77, p. 171. Shakespeare and Fletcher seem also to have thought of a connection between Cleopatra and Anne Boleyn, whom the Old Lady in *Henry VIII* terms 'One that would not be a queen, that would she not, / For all the mud in Egypt' (II.3.91–2). However, *The Tragedy of Mariam* was entered for publication in December 1612, and *Henry VIII* was first acted in 1613, which would make the question of cross-fertilisation purely conjectural (though not necessarily impossible – and the conjunction is, I think, in any case a culturally interesting one purely in terms of synchronicity).

17. William Shakespeare, *A Midsummer Night's Dream*, edited by Stanley Wells (Harmondsworth: Penguin Books, 1967), II.I.231. All further quotations from the play will be taken from this edition and reference will be given in the text.

18. See particularly Peter Erickson, 'Representations of Blacks and Blackness in the Renaissance', *Criticism* 35 (1993), pp. 499–527, p. 518.

19. See William Shakespeare, *A Midsummer Night's Dream*, edited by Harold F. Brooks (London: Methuen, 1979), introduction, p. lvi, and Steven May, '*A Midsummer Night's Dream* and the Carey–Berkeley Wedding', *Renaissance Papers* (1993), pp. 43–52.

20. Quoted from Gerald Bullett, ed., *Silver Poets of the Sixteenth Century* (London: J.M. Dent, 1947), p. 118.
21. W.A. Sessions, *Henry Howard, The Poet Earl of Surrey: A Life* (Oxford: Oxford University Press, 1999), p. 264.
22. *Sir Thomas Wyatt: The Complete Poems*, edited by R.A. Rebholz (Harmondsworth: Penguin Books, 1978), p. 77. All further quotations from Wyatt's poems will be taken from this edition and reference will be given in the text.
23. Straznicky, '"Profane Stoical Paradoxes"', p. 125.
24. Hall, *Things of Darkness*, p. 100.
25. See for instance Erickson, 'Representations', pp. 506–15. Erickson also points to the importance of this paradigm in Webster's *The White Devil* (p. 516), a play performed in 1612, the year before *Mariam* was published. For further comment on the use of this schema in *The White Devil*, see Rowland Wymer, *Webster and Ford* (Basingstoke: Macmillan – now Palgrave Macmillan, 1995), pp. 35–7, and Dympna Callaghan, *Woman and Gender in Renaissance Tragedy* (Hemel Hempstead: Harvester Wheatsheaf, 1989), p. 142.
26. Weller and Ferguson, pp. 30–5. Betty Travitsky implicitly refers all Renaissance constructions of the disloyal wife, or petty traitor, back to Anne Boleyn and her cousin and successor Katherine Howard (Betty S. Travitsky, 'Husband-Murder and Petty Treason in English Renaissance Tragedy', *Renaissance Drama* 21 (1991), pp. 171–98, p. 173. Jeanne Addison Roberts, however, suggests that the divorce petition of Frances Howard as a stimulus for both this play and *The Insatiate Countess* ('Marriage and Divorce in 1613: Elizabeth Cary, Frances Howard, and Others', in *Textual Formations and Reformations*, edited by Laurie E. Maguire and Thomas L. Berger (Newark: University of Delaware Press, 1998), pp. 161–78, p. 162. Danielle Clarke relates the play more to Princess Elizabeth and the Countess of Essex, however ('"This domestic kingdome or Monarchy": Cary's *The Tragedy of Mariam* and the Resistance to Patriarchal Government', *Mediaeval and Renaissance Drama in England* 10 [1998], pp. 179–200, p. 180).
27. Elizabeth Cary, *The Tragedy of Mariam*, edited by Stephanie Wright (Keele: Keele University Press, 1996), I.ii.62–3. All future quotations from the play will be taken from this edition and reference will be given in the text. Suggestively, 'King Salomon' is specified by John Pikeryng as the tune sung by Clytemnestra and Egistus in his *Horestes* (see *Horestes*, in *Three Tudor Classical Interludes*, edited by Marie Axton [Cambridge: D.S. Brewer, 1982], l.537 s.d.), and Betty Travitsky discusses *Horestes* as a husband-murdering play in the same mould as *Mariam* ('Husband-Murder', p. 180).
28. John N. King, 'Henry VIII as David: The King's Image and Reformation Politics', in *Rethinking the Henrician Era*, edited by Peter C. Herman (Urbana: University of Illinois Press, 1994), pp. 78–92, pp. 87 and 88. On James as Solomon, see also John N. King, 'The Royal Image, 1535–1603', in *Tudor Political Culture*, edited by Dale Hoak (Cambridge: Cambridge University Press, 1995), pp. 104–32, p. 106, and Arthur F. Kinney, 'Shakespeare's *Macbeth* and the Question of Nationalism', in *Literature and Nationalism*, edited by Vincent Newey and Ann Thompson (Liverpool: Liverpool University Press, 1991), p. 62.

29. Jasper Ridley, ed., *The Love Letters of Henry VIII* (London: Cassell, 1988), introduction, p. 13.

30. Retha M. Warnicke, *The Rise and Fall of Anne Boleyn* (Cambridge: Cambridge University Press, 1989), p. 37; for other such masques see also Marie Louise Bruce, *Anne Boleyn* [1972] (London: Pan, 1975), pp. 12 and 39. Anne herself is also reputed to have written a masque (Warnicke, p. 59), while Henry VIII is alleged to have 'displayed to the bishop of Carlisle a tragedy about her death that he had allegedly written prior to her arrest' (Warnicke, p. 235).

31. See Perez Zagorin, 'Sir Thomas Wyatt and the Court of Henry VIII: The Courtier's Ambivalence', *Journal of Medieval and Renaissance Science* 23:1 (1993), pp. 113–41, p. 129.

32. William Shakespeare and John Fletcher, *Henry VIII*, edited by A.R. Humphreys (Harmondsworth: Penguin Books, 1971), IV.i.46–7). All further quotations from the play will be taken from this edition and reference will be given in the text.

33. See for instance Bruce, *Anne Boleyn*, p. 13.

34. Hall, *Things of Darkness*, p. 109, note 39, offers a list of discussions of the question of Sheba's blackness.

35. Weller and Ferguson, p. 32. They argue, surely rightly, that Cary's decision to align both Mariam and Salome with Anne is a profoundly resonant one (pp. 32–3).

36. Michael Drayton, *Poly-Olbion*, in *The Complete Works of Michael Drayton*, edited by J. W. Hebel, 5 vols (Oxford: Basil Blackwell, 1933), vol. 4, p. 7.

37. See Bruce Thomas Boehrer, *Monarchy and Incest in Renaissance England: Literature, Culture, Kinship, and Kingship* (Philadelphia: University of Pennsylvania Press, 1992), p. 55.

38. Drayton, *Poly-Olbion*, pp. 25 and 44.

39. John Ford, *The Broken Heart*, in *John Ford: Three Plays*, edited by Keith Sturgess (Harmondsworth: Penguin Books, 1970), I.i.12–13.

40. Robyn Bolam has recently argued for Wroth's *Pamphilia to Amphilanthus* as an influence on *'Tis Pity She's a Whore* ('Ford, Mary Wroth, and the Final Scene of *'Tis Pity She's a Whore*', in *A Companion to English Renaissance Literature*, edited by Michael Hattaway [Oxford: Blackwell, 2000], pp. 276–83).

41. Sir Philip Sidney, *The Countess of Pembroke's Arcadia*, ed. Maurice Evans (Harmondsworth: Penguin, 1977), introduction, p. 19.

42. John Ford, *The Broken Heart*, edited by Brian Morris (London: Ernest Benn, 1965), Prologue, ll.14–15. All further quotations from the play will be taken from this edition.

43. See for instance S.P. Sherman, 'Stella and *The Broken Heart*', *PMLA*, XXIV (1909), pp. 274–85, and, more recently, Verna Ann Foster and Stephen Foster, 'Structure and History in *The Broken Heart*: Sparta, England, and the "Truth"', *English Literary Renaissance*, 1988, pp. 305–28.

44. Vivian Nutton, 'The rise of medical humanism: Ferrara, 1464–1555', *Renaissance Studies* 11:1 (1997), pp. 2–19, p. 10.

45. For full discussion of this, see my 'John Ford's *'Tis Pity She's a Whore* and Early Diagnoses of *folie à deux*', *Notes and Queries* 41:3 (March 1994), 71–4.

46. See Oliver Lawson Dick, ed., *Aubrey's Brief Lives* [1949] (Harmondsworth: Peregrine, 1962), pp. 188–9.

47. James Shirley, *The Lady of Pleasure*, edited by Ronald Huebert (Manchester: Manchester University Press, 1986), V.ii.179 and V.iii.191–4.

48. Though Jane Stevenson and Peter Davidson remark that in her poem to her grandmother Lady Jane makes no mention of Arbella or of her mother, Bess's daughter, concentrating only on Bess's sons (*Early Modern Women Poets (1520–1700): An Anthology*, edited by Jane Stevenson and Peter Davidson [Oxford: Oxford University Press, 2001], p. 290).

49. For Newcastle's close relations with his cousins, see Margaret Cavendish, *The Lives of William Cavendish, Duke of Newcastle, and of his wife . . .*, edited by M.A. Lower (London, 1872): 204, and Neil Cuddy, 'The Revival of the Entourage: The Bedchamber of James I, 1603–1625', in *The English Court: from the Wars of the Roses to the Civil War*, edited by David Starkey (Harlow: Longman, 1987), p. 195.

50. For comment on the place of their writing within this group, see Margaret J.M. Ezell, '"To Be Your Daughter in Your Pen": The Social Functions of Literature in the Writings of Lady Elizabeth Brackley and Lady Jane Cavendish', *Huntington Libary Quarterly* 51 (1988), pp. 281–96.

51. For comment on the political significance of Newcastle's play *The Variety*, see Martin Butler, *Theatre and Crisis 1632–42* (Cambridge: Cambridge University Press, 1984), pp. 25 and 195.

52. For the date of the marriage, see Starr, p. 803. Cerasano and Wynne-Davies give it as 1636, but there is something amiss here, for they also assert that Elizabeth was born in 1616 and married at the age of 15, which would make the date 1631.

53. Lucy Worsley, *Bolsover Castle* (London: English Heritage, 2000), p. 22. She also points to the way in which the ascent through the house emblematises the neoplatonic model of ascent from the physical to the spiritual (p. 26). I am grateful to Lucy Worsley for kindly sending me a copy of this.

54. Alison Findlay, '"She gave you the civility of the house: Household Performance in *The Concealed Fancies*', in *Readings in Renaissance Women's Drama*, edited by S.P. Cerasano and Marion Wynne-Davies (London: Routledge, 1998). I am very grateful to Alison Findlay for the opportunity to see this paper before publication.

55. See Nathan Comfort Starr, '*The Concealed Fansyes*: A Play by Lady Jane Cavendish and Lady Elizabeth Brackley', *PMLA* 46 (1931), pp. 802–38.

56. Lady Jane Cavendish and Lady Elizabeth Brackley, *The Concealed Fancies*, in *Renaissance Drama By Women: Texts and Documents*, edited by S.P. Cerasano and Marion Wynne-Davies (London: Routledge, 1996), p. 143. All further quotations from the play will be taken from this edition and reference will be given in the text. On the Civil War setting of the play, see for instance Susan Wiseman, 'Gender and Status in Dramatic Discourse: Margaret Cavendish, Duchess of Newcastle', in *Women, Writing, History 1640–1740*, edited by Isobel Grundy and Susan Wiseman (Athens: University of Georgia Press, 1992), pp. 159–77, especially p. 162.

57. For comment on this, see Findlay, 'Civility'.

58. I am deeply grateful to Mr William Parente for drawing my attention to the existence of this ceiling, to Mr Keith Crossland, assistant bursar of Welbeck

College, for giving up a considerable amount of time to showing me round the Abbey, to the bursar, Mr Gordon Payne, for arranging the visit, and to Lucy Worsley of English Heritage for pointing out the date.

59. *Dramatic Works of William Cavendish*, p. 120.
60. S.P. Cerasano and Marion Wynne-Davies, *Renaissance Drama by Women: Texts and Documents* (London: Routledge, 1992), III.iv.4–18.
61. Sophie Tomlinson, '"My Brain the Stage": Margaret Cavendish and the Fantasy of Female Performance', *Women, Texts and Histories 1570–1670*, Clare Brant and Diane Purkiss, eds, (London: Routledge, 1992): 134–63, 138.
62. William Shakespeare, *As You Like It*, edited by Agnes Latham [1975] (London: Routledge, 1989), V.iv.198–209.
63. John Webster, *The Duchess of Malfi*, edited by John Russell Brown [1964] (Manchester: Manchester University Press, 1976), IV.i.100–1.
64. See Sara Jayne Steen, 'The Crime of Marriage: Arbella Stuart and *The Duchess of Malfi*', *Sixteenth Century Journal* 22 (1991), pp. 61–76; and *The Letters of Lady Arbella Stuart* (Oxford: Oxford University Press, 1994), introduction, pp. 94–5.
65. See Cerasano and Wynne-Davies, pp. 129 and 211.
66. Quoted in John Ford, *The Broken Heart*, edited by Brian Morris (London: Ernest Benn, 1965), introduction, p. ix.

Bibliography

Primary

Aubrey, John. *Aubrey's Brief Lives*, edited by Oliver Lawson Dick [1949] (Harmondsworth: Peregrine, 1962).

Bacon, Francis. *The Advancement of Learning* and *The New Atlantis*, edited by Arthur Johnston (Oxford: The Clarendon Press, 1974).

Beaumont, Francis, and John Fletcher. *The Maid's Tragedy*, edited by T.W. Craik (Manchester: Manchester University Press, 1988).

——. *Philaster*, edited by Andrew Gurr (Manchester: Manchester University Press, 1969).

Benson, Pamela, ed. *Italian Tales From the Age of Shakespeare* (London: J.M. Dent, 1996).

Cary, Elizabeth. *The Tragedy of Mariam*, edited by Barry Weller and Margaret W. Ferguson (Berkeley and Los Angeles: University of California Press, 1994).

——. *The Tragedy of Mariam*, edited by Stephanie Wright (Keele: Keele University Press, 1996).

Cavendish, Lady Jane, and Lady Elizabeth Brackley. *The Concealed Fancies*, in *Renaissance Drama By Women: Texts and Documents*, edited by S.P. Cerasano and Marion Wynne-Davies (London: Routledge, 1996).

Cavendish, Margaret. *Bell in Campo* (1662).

——. *The Lives of William Cavendish, Duke of Newcastle, and of his wife ...*, edited by M.A. Lower (London, 1872).

Clifford, D.J.H., ed. *The Diaries of Lady Anne Clifford* (Stroud: Alan Sutton, 1990).

Dekker, Thomas, John Ford and William Rowley. *The Witch of Edmonton*, edited by Simon Trussler and Jacqui Russell (London: Methuen, 1983).

E[dgar], T[homas]. *The Lawes Resolution of Womens Rights* [1632].

Ford, John. *The Lover's Melancholy*, edited by R.F. Hill (Manchester: Manchester University Press, 1985).

——. *The Broken Heart*, ed. Brian Morris (London: Ernest Benn, 1965).

——. *'Tis Pity She's a Whore*, edited by Brian Morris (London: Ernest Benn, 1968).

James VI and I, *Daemonologie* (Edinburgh, 1597).

Keeble, N.H., ed. *The Cultural Identity of Seventeenth-Century Woman* (London: Routledge, 1994).

Marston, John. *Sophonisba*, in *Three Jacobean Witchcraft Plays*, edited by Peter Corbin and Douglas Sedge (Manchester: Manchester University Press, 1986).

Martin, Randall, ed. *Women Writers in Renaissance England* (Harlow, Essex: Longman, 1997).

Massinger, Philip. *A New Way To Pay Old Debts*, edited by T.W. Craik (London: Ernest Benn, 1964).

Middleton, Thomas. *The Witch*, edited by Elizabeth Schafer (London: A. & C. Black, 1994).

Middleton, Thomas. *Hengist, King of Kent; or the Mayor of Queenborough*, edited by R.C. Bald (New York: Charles Scribner's Sons, 1938).

——. *Women Beware Women*, edited by Roma Gill (London: Ernest Benn, 1968).

——. and William Rowley. *The Changeling*, edited by Joost Daalder (London: A. & C. Black, 1990).

Pikeryng, John. *Horestes*, in *Three Tudor Classical Interludes*, edited by Marie Axton (Cambridge: D.S. Brewer, 1982).

Purkiss, Diane, ed. *Renaissance Women: The Plays of Elizabeth Cary, The Poems of Aemilia Lanyer* (London: William Pickering, 1994).

Ridley, Jasper, ed. *The Love Letters of Henry VIII* (London: Cassell, 1988).

Shakespeare, William. *Hamlet*, edited by Harold Jenkins (London: Methuen, 1980).

——. *Othello*, edited by Kenneth Muir (Harmondsworth: Penguin Books, 1968).

——. *Antony and Cleopatra*, edited by Emrys Jones (Harmondsworth: Penguin, 1977).

——. *As You Like It*, edited by Agnes Latham [1975] (London: Routledge, 1989).

——. *The Comedy of Errors*, edited by Stanley Wells (Harmondsworth: Penguin Books, 1972).

——. *A Midsummer Night's Dream*, edited by Stanley Wells (Harmondsworth: Penguin Books, 1967).

——. and John Fletcher. *Henry VIII*, edited by A.R. Humphreys (Harmondsworth: Penguin Books, 1971).

Sharp, Jane. *The Midwives Book, Or the Whole Art of Midwifery Discovered*, edited by Elaine Hobby (Oxford: Oxford University Press, 1999).

Sidney, Mary. *The Tragedie of Antonie*, in S.P. Cerasano and Marion Wynne-Davies, eds, *Renaissance Drama by Women: Texts and Documents* (London: Routledge, 1996).

Sidney, Philip. *The Countess of Pembroke's Arcadia*, ed. Maurice Evans (Harmondsworth: Penguin Books, 1977).

Starr, Nathan Comfort, ed. '*The Concealed Fansyes*: A Play by Lady Jane Cavendish and Lady Elizabeth Brackley', *PMLA* 46 (1931), pp. 802–38.

Stevenson, Jane, and Peter Davidson, eds. *Early Modern Women Poets (1520–1700): An Anthology* (Oxford: Oxford University Press, 2001).

Stock, L.E., Gilles D. Monsarrat, Judith M. Kennedy and Dennis Danielson, eds. *The Nondramatic Works of John Ford* (Binghampton, N.Y.: Medieval & Renaissance Texts & Studies, 1991).

Webster, John. *The Duchess of Malfi and Other Plays*, edited by René Weis (Oxford: Oxford University Press, 1996).

——. *The White Devil*, edited by John Russell Brown (Manchester: Manchester University Press, 1996).

——. *The Duchess of Malfi*, edited by John Russell Brown (Manchester: Manchester University Press, 1976).

Wiggins, Martin, ed. *Four Jacobean Sex Tragedies* Oxford: Oxford University Press, 1998).

Wyatt, Sir Thomas. *Sir Thomas Wyatt: The Complete Poems*, edited by R.A. Rebholz (Harmondsworth: Penguin Books, 1978).

Secondary

Alfar, Cristina León. 'Staging the Feminine Performance of Desire: Masochism in *The Maid's Tragedy*', *Papers on Language and Literature* 31:3 (summer 1995), pp. 313–33.

Allman, Eileen. *Jacobean Revenge Tragedy and the Politics of Virtue* (Newark: University of Delaware Press, 1999).

Aughterson, Kate. *Renaissance Woman: A Sourcebook* (London: Routledge, 1995).

Bacon, Wallace A. 'The Literary Reputation of John Ford', *Huntington Library Quarterly* 11 (1947–8), pp. 181–99.

Batchelor, J. P. 'The Pattern of *Women Beware Women*', reprinted in *Three Jacobean Revenge Tragedies: A Casebook*, edited by R.V. Holdsworth (Basingstoke: Macmillan – now Palgrave Macmillan, 1990).

Benton, Tim, Catherine King and Di Norman, *Venice, Rome and Late Fifteenth-Century Florence* (Open University Press, 1986).

Bliss, Lee. *Francis Beaumont* (Boston: Twayne, 1987).

Boas, F.S. *An Introduction to Stuart Drama* (Oxford: The Clarendon Press, 1946).

Boehrer, Bruce Thomas. *Monarchy and Incest in Renaissance England: Literature, Culture, Kinship, and Kingship* (Philadelphia: University of Pennsylvania Press, 1992).

——. '"Nice Philosophy": *'Tis Pity She's a Whore* and The Two Books of God', *Studies in English Literature* 24 (1984), pp. 355–71.

Bolam, Robyn. 'Ford, Mary Wroth, and the Final Scene of *'Tis Pity She's a Whore*', in *A Companion to English Renaissance Literature*, edited by Michael Hattaway (Oxford: Blackwell, 2000), pp. 276–83.

Boling, Ronald J. 'Prayer, Mirrors, and Self-Deification in John Ford's *'Tis Pity She's a Whore*', *Publications of the Arkansas Philological Association* 17:1 (1991), pp. 1–12.

Boose, Lynda E. '*The Taming of the Shrew*, Good Husbandry, and Enclosure', in *Shakespeare Reread: The Texts in New Contexts*, edited by Russ McDonald (Ithaca: Cornell University Press, 1994), pp.193–225.

Bowen, Barbara. 'Aemilia Lanyer and the Invention of White Womanhood', in *Maids and Mistresses, Cousins and Queens*, edited by Susan Frye and Karen Robertson (Oxford: Oxford University Press, 1999), pp. 274–303.

Bowers, Rick. 'John Ford and the Sleep of Death', *Texas Studies in Language and Literature* 28 (1986), pp. 358–87.

Bradbrook, M.C. *Themes and Conventions of Elizabethan Tragedy* (Cambridge: Cambridge University Press, 1935).

Breitenberg, Mark. *Anxious Masculinity in Early Modern England* (Cambridge: Cambridge University Press, 1996).

Bromham, A. A., and Zara Bruzzi. *The Changeling and the Years of Crisis, 1619–24* (London: Pinter, 1990).

——. '"The soil alters; Y'are in another country": Multiple Perspectives and Political Resonances in Middleton's *Women Beware Women*', in *Shakespeare's Italy: Functions of Italian Locations in Renaissance Drama*, edited by Michele Marrapodi, A.J. Hoenselaars, Marcello Cappuzzo and L. Falzon Santucci (Manchester: Manchester University Press, 1993), pp. 251–71.

Brooke, Nicholas. *Horrid Laughter in Jacobean Tragedy* (New York: Harper & Row, 1979).

Brown, Keith M. 'The Vanishing Emperor: British Kingship and its Decline 1603–1707', in *Scots and Britons: Scottish Political Thought and the Union of 1603*, edited by Roger A. Mason (Cambridge: Cambridge University Press, 1994), pp. 58–67.

Bruce, Marie Louise. *Anne Boleyn* [1972] (London: Pan, 1975).

Buckley, George T. *Atheism in the English Renaissance* (Chicago: University of Chicago Press, 1932).

Bushnell, Rebecca. *Tragedies of Tyrants: Political Thought and Theater in the English Renaissance* (Ithaca: Cornell University Press, 1990).

Butler, Judith. *Bodies That Matter: On the Discursive Limits of 'Sex'* (New York and London: Routledge, 1993).

Butler, Martin. *Theatre and Crisis 1632–42* (Cambridge: Cambridge University Press, 1984).

——.'*Love's Sacrifice*: Ford's Metatheatrical Tragedy', in *John Ford: Critical Re-Visions*, edited by Michael Neill (Cambridge: Cambridge University Press, 1988), pp. 201–31.

Callaghan, Dympna. *Woman and Gender in Renaissance Tragedy* (Hemel Hempstead: Harvester Wheatsheaf, 1989).

——. 'Re-Reading Elizabeth Cary's *The Tragedie of Mariam, Faire Queene of Jewry*', in *Women, 'Race', and Writing in the Early Modern Period*, edited by Margo Hendricks and Patricia Parker (London: Routledge, 1994), pp. 163–77.

Cavell, Stanley. *Disowning Knowledge in Six Plays of Shakespeare* (Cambridge: Cambridge University Press, 1987).

Cherry, Caroline Lockett. *The Most Unvaluedst Purchase: Women in the Plays of Thomas Middleton* (Salzburg: Universität Salzburg, 1973).

Christensen, Ann C. 'Settling House in Middleton's *Women Beware Women*', *Comparative Drama* 29 (1995), pp. 493–518.

Clarke, Danielle. '"This domestic kingdome or Monarchy": Cary's *The Tragedy of Mariam* and the Resistance to Patriarchal Government', *Mediaeval and Renaissance Drama in England* 10 (1998), pp. 179–200.

Clerico, Terri. 'The Politics of Blood: John Ford's *'Tis Pity She's a Whore*', *English Literary Renaissance* 22 (1992), pp. 405–34.

Coddon, Karin S. '*The Duchess of Malfi*: Tyranny and Spectacle in Jacobean Drama', in *Madness in Drama*, edited by James Redmond (Cambridge: Cambridge University Press, 1993), pp. 1–18.

Comensoli, Viviana. *Household Business: Domestic Plays of Early Modern England* (Toronto: University of Toronto Press, 1996).

Coyle, Martin. 'Hamlet, Gertrude and the Ghost: The Punishment of Women in Renaissance Drama', *Q/W/E/R/T/Y* 6 (October 1996), pp. 29–38.

Craig, Sheryl. '"She and I were twins": Double Identity in *The Duchess of Malfi*', *Publications of the Missouri Philological Association* 19 (1994), pp. 21–7.

Cronin, Lisa. 'A Source for John Ford's *Love's Sacrifice*: The Life of Carlo Gesualdo', *Notes and Queries* 233 (March 1988), pp. 66–7.

Cuddy, Neil. 'The Revival of the Entourage: The Bedchamber of James I, 1603–1625', in *The English Court: From the Wars of the Roses to the Civil War*, edited by David Starkey (Harlow: Longman, 1987).

Daileader, Celia R. *Eroticism on the Renaissance Stage: Transcendence, Desire, and the Limits of the Visible* (Cambridge: Cambridge University Press, 1998).

Danby, John F. 'Beaumont and Fletcher: Jacobean Absolutists', in *Elizabethan*

Drama: Modern Essays in Criticism, edited by R.J. Kaufmann (Oxford: Oxford University Press, 1961).

Defaye, Claudine. 'Annabella's Unborn Baby: The Heart in the Womb in *'Tis Pity She's a Whore'*, *Cahiers Elisabéthains* 15 (1979), pp. 35–42.

DiGangi, Mario. *The Homoerotics of Early Modern Drama* (Cambridge: Cambridge University Press, 1997).

Di Miceli, Caroline. 'Sickness and Physic in Some Plays by Middleton and Webster', *Cahiers Elisabéthains* 26 (1984), pp. 41–78.

Dodson, David. 'Middleton's Livia', *Philological Quarterly* 27 (1948): 376–81.

Dollimore, Jonathan. 'Subjectivity, Sexuality, and Transgression: The Jacobean Connection', *Renaissance Drama* 17 (1986), pp. 53–81.

Duncan, Douglas. 'Virginity in *The Changeling'*, *English Studies in Canada* 9 (1983): 25–35.

Dyer, William D. 'Holding/Withholding Environments: A Psychoanalytic Approach to Ford's *The Broken Heart'*, *English Literary Renaissance* 21 (1991), pp. 401–24.

Eaton, Sara. '"Content with art"?: Seeing the Emblematic Woman in *The Second Maiden's Tragedy* and *The Winter's Tale'*, in *Shakespearean Power and Punishment: A Volume of Essays*, edited by Gillian Murray Kendall (Cranbury: Associated University Presses, 1998), pp. 59–86.

——. 'Beatrice-Joanna and the Rhetoric of Love in *The Changeling'*, *Theatre Journal* 36.3 (1984), pp. 371–82.

Edwards, Philip. 'The danger not the Death: The Art of John Fletcher', in *Jacobean Theatre*, edited by John Russell Brown and Bernard Harris (London: Edward Arnold, 1960).

Ellis-Fermor, Una. 'Middleton's Tragedies', reprinted in *Three Jacobean Revenge Tragedies: A Collection of Critical Essays*, edited by R.V. Holdsworth (Basingstoke: Macmillan – Palgrave Macmillan, 1990).

—. *The Jacobean Drama* (London: Methuen, 1958).

Englander, David, and Diana Norman, Rosemary O'Day and W.R. Owens, eds. *Culture and Belief in Europe 1450–1600* (Oxford: Basil Blackwell, 1990).

Enterline, Lynn. *The Tears of Narcissus: Melancholia and Masculinity in Early Modern Writing* (Stanford: Stanford University Press, 1995).

Erickson, Amy Louise. *Women and Property in Early Modern England* (London: Routledge, 1993).

Erickson, Peter. 'Representations of Blacks and Blackness in the Renaissance', *Criticism* 35 (1993), pp. 499–527.

Ewbank, Inga-Stina. 'Realism and Morality in *Women Beware Women'*, *Essays and Studies* 22 (1969), pp. 57–70.

Ewing, S. Blaine. *Burtonian Melancholy in the Plays of John Ford* (Princeton: Princeton University Press, 1940).

Ezell, Margaret J.M. '"To Be Your Daughter in Your Pen": The Social Functions of Literature in the Writings of Lady Elizabeth Brackley and Lady Jane Cavendish', *Huntington Libary Quarterly* 51 (1988), pp. 281–96.

Farr, Dorothy M. *Thomas Middleton and the Drama of Realism* (Edinburgh: Oliver & Boyd, 1973).

——. *John Ford and the Caroline Theatre* (London: Macmillan, 1979).

Findlay, Alison. *A Feminist Perspective on Renaissance Drama* (Oxford: Blackwell, 1999).

Findlay, Alison. '"She gave you the civility of the house": Household Performance in *The Concealed Fancies*', in *Readings in Renaissance Women's Drama*, edited by S.P. Cerasano and Marion Wynne-Davies (London: Routledge, 1998), pp. 259–71.

Finkelpearl, Philip J. *Court and Country Politics in the Plays of Beaumont and Fletcher* (Princeton: Princeton University Press, 1990).

Fischer, Sandra K. 'Elizabeth Cary and Tyranny, Domestic and Religious', in Margaret Patterson Hannay, ed., *Silent But for the Word* (Ohio: Kent State University Press, 1985), pp. 225–37.

Foster, Verna Ann. 'The Deed's Creature: The Tragedy of Bianca in *Women Beware Women*', *Journal of English and Germanic Philology* 78 (1979): 508–21.

——. "*Tis Pity She's a Whore* as City Tragedy', in *John Ford: Critical Re-Visions*, edited by Michael Neill (Cambridge: Cambridge University Press, 1988), pp. 181–200.

——. Stephen Foster. 'Structure and History in *The Broken Heart*: Sparta, England, and the "Truth"', *English Literary Renaissance* 18 (1988), pp. 305–28.

Fradenburg, Louise Olga. *City, Marriage, Tournament: Arts of Rule in Late Medieval Scotland* (Madison: University of Wisconsin Press, 1991).

Freer, Coburn. *The Poetics of Jacobean Drama* (Baltimore: Johns Hopkins University Press, 1981).

Gauer, Denis. 'Nature and Culture in *'Tis Pity She's a Whore*', *Cahiers Elisabéthains* (1987), pp. 45–57.

Gossett, Susanne. '"Best Men are Molded out of Faults": Marrying the Rapist in Jacobean Drama', in *Renaissance Historicism: Selections from English Literary Renaissance*, edited by Arthur F. Kinney and Dan S. Collins (Amherst: University of Massachusetts Press, 1987), pp. 168–90.

Hadfield, Andrew, and Willy Maley. 'Introduction: Irish Representations and English Alternatives', in Brendan Bradshaw, Andrew Hadfield, and Willy Maley, eds, *Representing Ireland: Literature and the Origins of Conflict, 1534–1660* (Cambridge: Cambridge University Press, 1993), pp. 1–23.

Hall, Kim F. *Things of Darkness: Economies of Race and Gender in Early Modern England* (Ithaca: Cornell University Press, 1995).

Harrison, Charles. 'Giotto and the "rise of painting"', in *Siena, Florence and Padua: Art, Society and Religion 1280–1400*, ed. Diana Norman (2 vols) (New Haven and London: Yale University Press, 1995), I, pp. 73–96.

Hattaway, Michael. 'Women and Witchcraft: The Case of *The Witch of Edmonton*', *Trivium* 20 (1985), pp. 49–68.

Heinemann, Margot. *Puritanism and Theatre: Thomas Middleton and Opposition Drama Under the Early Stuarts* (Cambridge: Cambridge University Press, 1980).

Heisch, Allison. 'Elizabeth I and the Reinforcement of Patriarchy', *Feminist Review* 4 (1980), pp. 45–56.

Hibbard, George R. 'The Tragedies of Thomas Middleton and the Decadence of the Drama', *Renaissance and Modern Studies* 1 (1957), pp. 35–64.

Holzknecht, Karl J. *Outlines of Tudor and Stuart Plays 1497–1642* (London: n.p., 1947).

Hopkins, Lisa. *John Ford's Political Theatre* (Manchester: Manchester University Press, 1994).

——.'"That's wormwood": Hamlet Plays his Mother', *Hamlet Studies* 16.1–2 (1994), pp. 83–5.

Hopkins, Lisa. 'John Ford's *'Tis Pity She's a Whore* and Early Diagnoses of *folie à deux'*, *Notes and Queries* 239 (March 1994), pp. 71–4.

——. '"Elegy by W.S.": A Possible Candidate for Authorship?', *Philological Quarterly* 76.2 (summer 1997), pp. 159–68.

——. 'John Ford's Annabella and the Virgin Mary', *Notes and Queries* 240 (September 1995), p. 380.

——. 'Renaissance Queens and Foucauldian Carcerality', *Renaissance and Reformation* 20:2 (spring 1996), pp. 17–32.

Hoy, Cyrus. '"Ignorance in knowledge": Marlowe's Faustus and Ford's Giovanni', *Modern Philology* 57 (1960), pp. 145–54.

Hunt, Maurice. 'Webster and Jacobean Medicine: The Case of *The Duchess of Malfi'*, *Essays in Literature* 16:1 (1989), pp. 33–49.

Ide, Richard S. 'Ford's *'Tis Pity She's a Whore* and the Benefits of Belatedness', in *'Concord in Discord': The Plays of John Ford, 1586–1986*, edited by Donald K. Anderson, Jr. (New York: AMS Press, 1986), pp. 61–86.

Jardine, Lisa. *Still Harping on Daughters* (Brighton: Harvester Press, 1983).

Jones, Ann Rosalind. '"Italians and Others": *The White Devil* (1612)', in David Scott Kastan and Peter Stallybrass, eds, *Staging the Renaissance: Reinterpretations of Elizabethan and Jacobean Drama* (New York: Routledge, 1991), pp. 251–62.

Kerwin, William. '"Physicians are like Kings": Medical Politics and *The Duchess of Malfi'*, *English Literary Renaissance* 28:1 (winter 1998), pp. 95–117.

King, John N. 'Henry VIII as David: The King's Image and Reformation Politics', in *Rethinking the Henrician Era*, edited by Peter C. Herman (Urbana: University of Illinois Press, 1994), pp. 78–92.

——. 'The royal image, 1535–1603', in *Tudor Political Culture*, edited by Dale Hoak (Cambridge: Cambridge University Press, 1995), pp. 104–32.

Kinney, Arthur F. 'Shakespeare's *Macbeth* and the Question of Nationalism', in *Literature and Nationalism*, edited by Vincent Newey and Ann Thompson (Liverpool: Liverpool University Press, 1991), pp. 56–75.

Kirsch, Arthur. *Shakespeare and the Experience of Love* (Cambridge: Cambridge University Press, 1981).

Lancashire, Anne. '*The Witch*: Stage Flop or Political Mistake?', in *'Accompaninge the players': Essays Celebrating Thomas Middleton, 1580–1980*, edited by Kenneth Friendenreich (New York: AMS Press, 1983), pp. 161–81.

Laqueur, Thomas. *Making Sex: Body and Gender from the Greeks to Freud* (Cambridge, Mass.: Harvard University Press, 1990).

Leech, Clifford. *John Ford and the Drama of his Time* (London: Longman, 1957).

Leggatt, Alexander. 'The Island of Miracles: An Approach to *Cymbeline'*, *Shakespeare Survey 10* (1977), pp. 191–209.

Levin, Richard. 'If Women Should Beware Women, Bianca Should Beware Mother', *Studies in English Literature* 37 (1997), pp. 371–89.

Levine, Laura. *Men in Women's Clothing: Antitheatricality and Effeminization 1579–1642* (Cambridge: Cambridge University Press, 1994).

Lindley, David. *The Trials of Frances Howard* (London: Routledge, 1993).

Little, Arthur. *Shakespeare Jungle Fever: National-Imperial Re-Visions of Race, Rape, and Sacrifice* (Stanford: Stanford University Press, 2000).

Lloyd, Bertram. 'An Unprinted Poem by John Ford?', *The Review of English Studies* 1 (1925), pp. 217–19.

Loomba, Ania. *Gender, Race, Renaissance Drama* (Oxford: Oxford University Press, 1992).

McCanles, Michael. 'The Moral Dialectic of Middleton's *Women Beware Women*', in *'Accompaninge the players': Essays Celebrating Thomas Middleton, 1580–1980*, edited by Kenneth Friedenreich (New York, AMS Press, 1983), pp. 203–18.

McLuskie, Kathleen. *Renaissance Dramatists* (Atlantic Highlands, N.J.: Humanities Press International,1989).

——. '"Language and Matter with a Fit of Mirth": Dramatic Construction in the Plays of John Ford', in *John Ford: Critical Re-Visions*, edited by Michael Neill (Cambridge: Cambridge University Press, 1988), pp. 97–127.

Madelaine, Richard. '"Sensationalism" and "Melodrama" in Ford's Plays', in *John Ford: Critical Re-Visions*, ed. Michael Neill (Cambridge: Cambridge University Press, 1988), pp. 29–54.

Mahler, Andreas. 'Italian Vices: Cross-cultural Constructions of Temptation and Desire in English Renaissance Drama', in *Shakespeare's Italy: Functions of Italian Locations in Renaissance Drama*, edited by Michele Marrapodi, A.J. Hoenselaars, Marcello Cappuzzo and L. Falzon Santucci (Manchester: Manchester University Press, 1993).

Malcolmson, Cristina. '"As Tame as the Ladies": Politics and Gender in *The Changeling*', *English Literary Renaissance* 20 (1990), pp. 320–39.

May, Steven. '*A Midsummer Night's Dream* and the Carey–Berkeley Wedding', *Renaissance Papers* (1993), pp. 43–52.

Mizener, Arthur. 'The High Design of *A King and No King*', *Modern Philology* 38 (1940–1).

Moffet, Robin. '*Cymbeline* and the Nativity', *Shakespeare Quarterly* 13 (1962), pp. 207–18.

Montrose, Louis. '*A Midsummer Night's Dream* and the Shaping Fantasies of Elizabethan Culture: Gender, Power, Form', *Representations* 2 (1983), pp. 65–87.

——. 'The Work of Gender in the Discourse of Discovery', *Representations* 33 (1991): 1–41.

Moore, Dennis. 'Dutifully Defending Elizabeth: Lord Henry Howard and the Question of Queenship', in *Political Rhetoric, Power, and Renaissance Women*, edited by Carole Levin and Patricia A. Sullivan (Albany: State University of New York Press, 1995), pp. 113–36.

Morrison, Peter. 'A Cangoun in Zombieland: Middleton's Teratological *Changeling*', in *'Accompaninge the players': Essays Celebrating Thomas Middleton, 1580–1980*, edited by Kenneth Friedenreich (New York, AMS Press, 1983), pp. 219–41.

Mullaney, Steven. 'Mourning and Misogyny: *Hamlet*, *The Revenger's Tragedy*, and the Final Progress of Elizabeth I, 1600–1607', *Shakespeare Quarterly* 45 (1994), pp. 139–62.

Mulryne, J.R. 'Middleton's Italy: The Transformation of the Italian Setting in Middleton's *Women Beware Women*', in *The Italian World of English Renaissance Drama*, edited by Michele Marrapodi (Newark: University of Delaware Press, 1998), pp. 141–64.

Neill, Michael. '"The Simetry, Which Gives a Poem Grace": Masque, Imagery, and the Fancy of *The Maid's Tragedy*', *Renaissance Drama* 3 (1970), pp. 111–35.

Neill, Michael. *Issues of Death: Mortality and Identity in English Renaissance Tragedy* (Oxford: The Clarendon Press, 1997).

——. '"What Strange Riddle's This?": Deciphering *'Tis Pity She's a Whore'*, in *John Ford: Critical Re-Visions*, edited by Michael Neill (Cambridge: Cambridge University Press, 1988), pp. 153–80.

Nutton, Vivian. 'The Rise of Medical Humanism: Ferrara, 1464–1555', *Renaissance Studies* 11.1 (1997), pp. 2–19.

Oliver, H.J. *The Problem of John Ford* (Melbourne: Melbourne University Press, 1955).

Ornstein, Robert B. *The Moral Vision of Jacobean Tragedy* (Wisconsin: University of Wisconsin Press, 1960).

Park, Katharine, and Robert A. Nye. Review of Thomas Laqueur, *Making Sex: Body and Gender from the Greeks to Freud*, *New Republic* 18:2 (1991), pp. 53–5.

Pentzell, Raymond J. '*The Changeling*: Notes on Mannerism in Dramatic Form', *Comparative Drama* 9 (1975), pp. 3–28.

Purkiss, Diane. *The Witch in History* (London: Routledge, 1996).

Raber, Karen L. 'Gender and the Political Subject in *The Tragedy of Mariam*', *Studies in English Literature 1500–1900* 35:2 (spring 1995), pp. 321–43.

Randall, Dale J.B. 'Some New Perspectives on the Spanish Setting of *The Changeling* and its Source', *Medieval and Renaissance Drama in England* 3 (1986), pp. 189–216.

——. 'Some Observations on the Theme of Chastity in *The Changeling*', *English Literary Renaissance* 14 (1984), pp. 357–66.

Reed, Robert Rentoul, Jr. *Bedlam on the Jacobean Stage* (New York: Octagon Books, 1970).

Richmond, Hugh M. 'Shakespeare's Roman Trilogy: The Climax in *Cymbeline*', *Studies in the Literary Imagination* 5 (1972), pp. 129–39.

Ricks, Christopher. 'The Moral and Poetic Structure of *The Changeling*', *Essays in Criticism* 10 (1960), pp. 290–306.

Roberts, Jeanne Addison. 'Marriage and Divorce in 1613: Elizabeth Cary, Frances Howard, and Others', in *Textual Formations and Reformations*, edited by Laurie E. Maguire and Thomas L. Berger (Newark: University of Delaware Press, 1998), pp. 161–78.

Ronk, Martha. 'Embodied Morality', in *Sexuality and Politics in Renaissance Drama*, edited by Carole Levin and Karen Robertson (Lewiston: The Edwin Mellen Press, 1991), pp. 237–54.

Rosen, Carol C. 'The Language of Cruelty in Ford's *'Tis Pity She's a Whore*', *Comparative Drama* 8 (1974), pp. 356–68.

Sacerdoti, Gilberti. 'Three Kings, Herod of Jewry, and a Child: Apocalypse and Infinity of the World in *Antony and Cleopatra*', in *Italian Studies in Shakespeare and His Contemporaries*, edited by Michele Marrapodi and Giorgio Melchiori (Newark: University of Delaware Press, 1999), pp. 165–84.

Sargeaunt, M. Joan. *John Ford* (Oxford: Basil Blackwell, 1935).

Savage, James E. 'Beaumont and Fletcher's *Philaster* and Sidney's *Arcadia*', *Journal of English History* 14 (1947), pp. 194–207.

Sawday, Jonathan. *The Body Emblazoned* (London: Routledge, 1995).

Scarr, Richard. 'Insatiate Punning in Marston's Courtesan Plays', in *The Drama of John Marston: Critical Re-Visions*, edited by T.F. Wharton (Cambridge: Cambridge University Press, 2000), pp. 82–99.

Schleiner, Winifred. 'Early Modern Controversies about the One-Sex Model', *Renaissance Quarterly* 53:1 (spring, 2000), pp. 180–91.

Sedgwick, Eve Kosofsky. *Between Men: English Literature and Male Homosocial Desire* (New York: Columbia University Press, 1985).

Senapati, Sukanya B. '"Two parts in one": Marston and Masculinity', in *The Drama of John Marston: Critical Re-Visions*, edited by T. F. Wharton (Cambridge: Cambridge University Press, 2000), pp. 124–44.

Sensabaugh, G. F. *The Tragic Muse of John Ford* (Stanford: Stanford University Press, 1944).

Shell, Marc. *Elizabeth's Glass* (Lincoln: University of Nebraska Press, 1993).

Sherman, Stuart P. 'Stella and *The Broken Heart*', *PMLA* 24 (1909), pp. 274–85.

Shullenberger, William. '"This For the Most Wrong'd of Women": A Reappraisal of *The Maid's Tragedy*', *Renaissance Drama* 13 (1982), pp. 131–56.

Simmons, J. L. 'Diabolical Realism in Middleton and Rowley's *The Changeling*', *Renaissance Drama* 11 (1980), pp. 135–70.

Smith, Molly. *Breaking Boundaries: Politics and Plays in the Drama of Shakespeare and his Contemporaries* (Aldershot: Ashgate, 1998).

Sohmer, Steve. *Shakespeare's Mystery Play: The Opening of the Globe theatre, 1599* (Manchester: Manchester University Press, 1999).

Stavig, Mark. 'Shakespearean and Jacobean Patterns in *'Tis Pity She's a Whore*', in *Concord in Discord: The Plays of John Ford, 1586–1986*, ed. Donald K. Anderson, jr. (New York: AMS Press, 1986), pp. 221–240.

Steen, Sara Jayne. *The Letters of Lady Arbella Stuart* (Oxford: Oxford University Press, 1994).

——.'The Crime of Marriage: Arbella Stuart and *The Duchess of Malfi*', *Sixteenth Century Journal* 22 (1991), pp. 61–76.

Stockholder, Kay. 'The Aristocratic Woman as Scapegoat: Romantic Love and Class Antagonism in *The Spanish Tragedy*, *The Duchess of Malfi* and *The Changeling*', *The Elizabethan Theatre XIV*, edited by A.L. Magnusson and C.E. McGee (Toronto: P.D. Meany, 1996), pp. 127–51.

Strathmann, Ernest A. *Sir Walter Ralegh: A Study in Elizabethan Skepticism* (New York: Octagon Books, 1973).

Straznicky, Marta. '"Profane Stoical Paradoxes": *The Tragedie of Mariam* and Sidnean Closet Drama', *English Literary Renaissance* 24 (1994), pp. 104–34.

Strong, Roy. *Gloriana: The Portraits of Queen Elizabeth I* (London: Thames and Hudson, 1987).

Strout, Nathaniel. 'The Tragedy of Annabella in *'Tis Pity She's a Whore*', in David G. Allen, ed., *Traditions and Innovations* (Newark: University of Delaware Press, 1990), pp. 163–76.

Sutherland, Sarah P. *Masques in Jacobean Tragedy* (New York: AMS, 1983).

Sutton, Juliet. 'Platonic Love in Ford's *The Fancies, Chaste and Noble*', *Studies in English Literature 1500–1900* 7 (1967), pp. 299–309.

Suzuki, Mihoko. 'Gender, Class, and the Ideology of Comic Form: *Much Ado About Nothing* and *Twelfth Night*', in *A Feminist Companion to Shakespeare*, edited by Dympna Callaghan (Oxford: Basil Blackwell, 2000), pp. 121–43.

Tambling, Jeremy. *Confession: Sexuality, Sin, The Subject* (Manchester: Manchester University Press, 1990).

Tempera, Mariangela. 'The Rhetoric of Poison in John Webster's Italianate Plays', in *Shakespeare's Italy: Functions of Italian Locations in Renaissance*

Drama, edited by Michele Marrapodi, A.J. Hoenselaars, Marcello Cappuzzo and L. Falzon Santucci (Manchester: Manchester University Press, 1993), pp. 229–50.

Thomson, Leslie. 'Making a Woman of the Boy: The Characterization of Women in Middleton's Plays', *The Elizabethan Theatre XIV*, edited by A.L. Magnusson and C.E. McGee (Toronto: P.D. Meany, 1996), pp. 153–74.

Tomlinson, Sophie. '"My Brain the Stage": Margaret Cavendish and the Fantasy of Female Performance', *Women, Texts and Histories 1570–1670*, edited by Clare Brant and Diane Purkiss (London: Routledge, 1992), pp. 134–63.

Travitsky, Betty S. 'Husband-Murder and Petty Treason in English Renaissance Tragedy', *Renaissance Drama* 21 (1991), pp. 171–98.

Turner, Robert Y. 'Responses to Tyranny in John Fletcher's Plays', *Medieval and Renaissance Drama in England* 4 (1989), pp. 123–41.

Ure, Peter. 'Cult and Initiates in Ford's *Love's Sacrifice*', *Modern Language Quarterly* 2 (1950), pp. 298–306.

Vaughan, Virginia Mason. 'Preface: The Mental Maps of English Renaissance Drama', in *Playing the Globe: Genre and Geography in English Renaissance Drama*, edited by John Gillies and Virginia Mason Vaughan (London: Associated University Presses, 1998), pp. 7–16.

Waith, Eugene. *The Pattern of Tragicomedy in Beaumont and Fletcher* (New Haven: Yale University Press, 1952).

Walker, Garthine. '"Demons in female form": Representations of Women and Gender in Murder Pamphlets of the Late Sixteenth and Early Seventeenth Centuries', in *Writing and the English Renaissance*, edited by William Zunder and Suzanne Trill (Harlow, Essex: Longman, 1996), pp. 129–39.

Walker, Julia M., ed. *Dissing Elizabeth: Negative Representations of Gloriana* (London: Duke University Press, 1998).

Wall, Wendy. 'Reading for the Blot: Textual Desire in Early Modern English Literature', in *Reading and Writing in Shakespeare*, edited by David M. Bergeron (Newark and London: University of Delaware Press, 1996), pp. 131–59.

Wallis, Lawrence B. *Fletcher, Beaumont and Company: Entertainers to the Jacobean Gentry* (New York: Archon, 1947).

Warnicke, Retha M. *The Rise and Fall of Anne Boleyn* (Cambridge: Cambridge University Press, 1989).

White, Beatrice. *Cast of Ravens: The Strange Case of Sir Thomas Overbury* (London: John Murray, 1965).

White, Martin. *Middleton and Tourneur* (Basingstoke: Macmillan – now Palgrave Macmillan, 1992).

Wigler, Stephen. 'Parent and Child: The Pattern of Love in *Women Beware Women*', in *'Accompaninge the players': Essays Celebrating Thomas Middleton, 1580–1980*, edited by Kenneth Friedenreich (New York, AMS Press, 1983), pp. 183–201.

Wilks, John S. *The Idea of Conscience in Renaissance Tragedy* (London: Routledge, 1990).

Williams, Glanmor. 'Sir John Stradling of St Donat's (1563–1637)', *Glamorgan Historian* 9 (1973), pp. 11–28.

Wilson, Luke. 'William Harvey's *Prelectiones*: The Performance of the Body in the Renaissance Theater of Anatomy', *Representations* 17 (1987), pp. 62–95.

Wiseman, Susan J. *''Tis Pity She's a Whore*: Representing the Incestuous Body', in *Renaissance Bodies*, edited by Lucy Gent and Nigel Llewellyn (London: Reaktion Books, 1990), pp. 180–97.

——. 'Gender and Status in Dramatic Discourse: Margaret Cavendish, Duchess of Newcastle', in *Women, Writing, History 1640–1740*, edited by Isobel Grundy and Susan Wiseman (Athens: University of Georgia Press, 1992), pp. 159–77.

Woodbridge, Linda. 'Black and White and Red All Over: The Sonnet Mistress amongst the Ndembu', *Renaissance Quarterly* 40.2 (summer 1987), pp. 247–97.

Worsley, Lucy. *Bolsover Castle* (London: English Heritage, 2000).

Wymer, Rowland. *Webster and Ford* (Basingstoke: Macmillan – now Palgrave Macmillan, 1995).

Index